LIFE AT FOUR CORNERS

Rural America

Hal S. Barron
David L. Brown
Kathleen Neils Conzen
Cornelia Butler Flora
Donald Worster

Series Editors

LIFE AT FOUR CORNERS

*Religion, Gender, and Education
in a German-Lutheran
Community, 1868–1945*

CAROL K. COBURN

UNIVERSITY PRESS OF KANSAS

Published by the University Press of Kansas (Lawrence, Kansas 66049),
which was organized by the Kansas Board of Regents and is operated and
funded by Emporia State University, Fort Hays State University, Kansas
State University, Pittsburg State University, the University of Kansas, and
Wichita State University

Library of Congress Cataloging-in-Publication Data

Coburn, Carol.
    Life at four corners : religion, gender, and education in a German-
Lutheran community, 1868–1945 / Carol K. Coburn.
        p.   cm. — (Rural America)
    Includes bibliographical references and index.
    ISBN 0-7006-0557-6 (hardcover)   ISBN 0-7006-0682-3 (pbk.)
    1. Block (Kan.) — Social life and customs. 2. German Americans —
Kansas — Block — Social life and customs. 3. German Americans —
Kansas — Block — Ethnic identity. 4. Lutherans — Kansas — Block —
History — 19th century. 5. Lutherans — Kansas — Block — History — 20th
century. 6. Sex role — Kansas — Block — History — 19th century. 7. Sex
role — Kansas — Block — History — 20th century. 8. Education — Kansas —
Block — History — 19th century. 9. Education — Kansas — Block —
History — 20th century. I. Title. II. Series: Rural America
(Lawrence, Kan.)
F689.B54C63   1992
978.1'68 — dc20   92-11905

British Library Cataloguing in Publication Data is available.

Printed in the United States of America
10 9 8 7 6 5 4 3 2

For my grandmother
Lydia Prothe Schultz

CONTENTS

List of Maps and Illustrations   ix

Acknowledgments   xi

Introduction   1

1   Community Overview   9

2   Church   31

3   School   60

4   Family   81

5   The Outside World   112

6   At War with Germany   136

Conclusion   152

Note on Sources   163

Notes   165

Bibliography   203

Index   219

MAPS AND ILLUSTRATIONS

Maps

Block (Miami County), Kansas, circa 1920s   17

Block, Kansas, circa 1910   21

Illustrations

Early Block settlers   19

Dietrich and Gesche Mahnken Block   20

Reifel General Store   22

Trinity Lutheran Church, circa 1890   33

Trinity Lutheran Church, circa 1910   38

Altar and pulpit of Trinity Lutheran Church   42

Ladies Aid gathering   49

Ladies Aid members with founder, Pastor Droegemueller   52

Jugendverein "youth group"   56

Trinity Lutheran School, 1905   63

Trinity Lutheran School exterior, 1930s   66

School chums   70

Students with male and female teachers, 1940   74

Classmates at the end of formal schooling, 1925   75

Confirmation class with minister and teacher   78

Elsie Gerken on confirmation day   79

Henry Prothe family, 1911   82

Lydia Prothe Schultz   84

Boy caring for younger siblings   86

Girls helping with the fieldwork   87

Preparing to milk the cows, 1918   90

August Prothe family, 1936   95

Threshing crew at work   98

Using horses to clear land   99

Two generations   101

Baptism, 1914   105

Wedding party, 1914   108

Young men's social gathering   119

Hired girls in Paola, 1918   123

Irene Minden Prothe and friends   125

Free afternoon in Kansas City for hired girls   126

School picnic, 1920s   132

Block baseball team   134

Block soldier Martin Prothe, 1918   138

Block soldier George Dageforde, 1918   138

Camp Funston   142

Alien registration photo, 1918   144

Block soldier serving in New Guinea, WWII   149

Block ambulance driver in England, WWII   150

ACKNOWLEDGMENTS

The publication of this book would not have been possible without the help and support of many individuals. I wish to thank the congregation of Trinity Lutheran Church (Block, Kansas) and the Reverend Lane A. Burgland for access to the rich archival materials that detail the history of the congregation. Specific individuals gave me their time, cooperation, and expertise, and I would particularly like to thank Myrtle Neu Thoden, local historian, and Irene Minden Prothe. Both provided contacts and vast amounts of information; their continuous support and interest cannot be overemphasized. Additionally, I would like to thank the current and former residents of Block who took time to share their childhood and adult memories with me: Frieda Timken Baumgardt, Mildred Block, Clarence Clausen, Elsie Prothe Dageforde, Alma Clausen Debrick, Minnie Cahman Debrick, Esther Prothe Maisch, Louise Timken Mammen, Marie Dageforde Monthey, Ida Minden Peckman, Nora Ohlmeier Prothe, Elmer Prothe, Josephine Overbeck Prothe, and Marie Peckman Wendte.

This work could not have been completed without the excellent work of Ursula Huelsbergen, whose skill as a translator of German church records and documents is unparalleled. This book would be far less complete, if not unfinished, without the benefit of her time and skill in translating a large body of church documents.

There are many people who have helped and supported me over the years as I worked toward completion of this book. I would like to thank N. Ray Hiner and Ann Schofield who gave me helpful advice and encouragement with earlier versions of the manuscript; the staff of the University Press of Kansas who provided valuable support and expertise throughout the final stages of preparing the manuscript for publication; and Daniel Keegan who drew the maps. I would also like to thank friends and family who took time away from their own lives to provide support and assistance when it was most needed: Sharon England, Bill and Ada Ruth Coburn, Elaine Coburn Watskey, and Martha Smith, CSJ. Lastly, I owe my initial interest and information about the Block community to my grandmother Lydia Prothe Schultz, who filled my childhood and adulthood with stories, anecdotes, and laughter.

INTRODUCTION

In south-central Miami County, Kansas, where county road 343 and Block Road intersect, a large metal sign marks the location of this rural crossroad for the passing motorist; it is a blue sign with bold white letters that says simply, "Block Corners." To an uninformed traveler the name means nothing, but one hundred years ago these four corners clamored with horses, wagons, and people. Block Corners served as a gathering place and commercial hub for the German-Lutheran community that had grown around the spot. Today, asphalt roads, houses, and trailers have replaced the dirt roads, small businesses, and post office, and the traveler no longer needs to speak German to buy, sell, or converse with the residents.

One-half mile south of Block Corners, a two-story parsonage comes into view, and soon one sees the church grounds spreading along the west side of the road. A modern-looking church faces east, and its glassed-in sign reads

Trinity Lutheran Church
Faith, Grace, Scripture
Rt. 2
Paola, Kansas

The cemetery south of the church reveals the history of the congregation, and over four hundred tombstones attest to those who died in "faith." A few hundred yards away school children play outside their rural schoolhouse amid an array of buildings, playgrounds, and open pasture. The two-room Lutheran schoolhouse and the wood-framed house for the teacher complete the church grounds.

This type of rural scene is not uncommon in Kansas or elsewhere in the Midwest. Many rural churches still have Sunday services and some rural schools have survived even in the face of extensive bus service and school consolidation. The religious and ethnic character of the Block Corners' community is representative of the many nineteenth-century rural-ethnic communities scattered throughout the Midwest.

These communities, many no longer visible on the rural landscape, provide lasting legacies for the generations of women and men who came from their midst—a legacy that began, and sometimes ended, at "four corners" on the midwestern landscape.

Religion, ethnicity, and gender mark and shape our past, providing richness and texture to individual and group experience. It is this combination of factors that creates identities and communities, which, in turn, educate the young and ensure the transmission of values, beliefs, and culture across generations. In 1868 the community of Block, Kansas, was the starting place for such an endeavor. Most of the original settlers were farmers from northern Germany who came to Kansas after brief stopovers in other midwestern states. The German Lutherans at Block used their ethnic heritage in combination with their religious doctrines to create an ethnic enclave, continue their agrarian lifestyle, and perpetuate family and farm life on American soil. Trinity Lutheran Church (Missouri Synod) and its school served as focal points in the development of Block's people and community.

It is important to note that although the community was incorporated and had a post office for twenty-one years, Block was a village community in every sense. Its location and size make the discussion of demographics and population somewhat problematic. The commercial hub at Block Corners developed in conjunction with the ethnic and religious aspects of the church and school; these buildings and Block Corners were located in the southeast corner of East Valley Township, but many church members and store patrons lived in three other adjoining townships. German-Lutheran homesteads fanned out in all directions around Block Corners and the church grounds.

Since state and federal census data were organized around township demographics, there was no official census for the Block community; church membership data provided the best opportunity to assess population numbers. In 1884 Trinity Lutheran Church boasted 278 members; membership in the congregation peaked in 1920 with 485 members, and the church population never dipped below the 400 mark through 1945.[1] Plat and land-ownership maps matched with church membership data provided the best information on the size and range of the Block community, but the cohesiveness and identity of the community were defined and maintained more by religious and ethnic identity than by geographic boundaries.

Moreover, problems arise when demographics alone are used to portray a community since most public documents reflect and record white male activity. Although such records tell part of the story, the viewpoints and perspectives of ethnic groups, women, children, and people who were not landowners receive little elaboration except as seen through the eyes of the male officials or the clergy who created the documents.

Nineteenth-century rural communities prevalent throughout the Midwest and the western United States provide another challenge: Much research has centered on medium-sized towns and the "urban frontier," but only a few studies have attempted to re-create life and community in nineteenth-century rural America.[2] Studying the Block community reinforces the importance of using a variety of sources, but more important, it adds a new dimension to the existing historiography of village communities. Like the historians of colonial communities, I have focused on one community and have attempted to study it in depth; however, since demographics alone do not tell the complete story, I have also incorporated qualitative research methods, including newspaper accounts, church records, reminiscences, and oral histories of persons who grew up in the community.

Within this village community setting, I chose to focus on the transmission of education and culture across four generations. I use the term "education" in its broadest sense to include the acquisition of cultural knowledge, socialization, and the transmission of beliefs and values. This broad view of education enables me to see the Block community as a whole and not in isolated fragments. The interdependence of men, women, and children, as well as the institutions they created to perpetuate ideals, values, and beliefs, comes to the fore. By using and integrating research methodology and ideas from an interdisciplinary perspective, women, families, communities, networks of kinship and association, and all aspects of culture as potential educators become a part of history.[3]

By asking questions about rural ethnicity, religion, and gender, I intend for this study of a community to serve as a nexus for interdisciplinary research. Specifically, how did the Block community transmit its culture? How did the content and process of education for females differ from the experience of males? How did the religious institutions of church and parochial school serve as transmitters of education and culture? How did the ethnic family function as educator? What were the effects of the rural topography and of American culture on education in Block?

METHODOLOGY

The German-Lutheran community of Block, Kansas, provides a provocative setting for asking questions about education and culture. Yet to comprehend the lives that the people of Block created for themselves it is necessary to develop a new theoretical framework, which, unlike those used by many historians, does not assume a dichotomy between public (male) and private (female) spheres. This public/private construct is not always helpful in describing rural or ethnic peoples' experiences, because for many women and men a clear separation of worlds does not exist and never has. For historians to operate solely within such a polarized construct may render many individual contributions and experiences invisible or insignificant.

With most dichotomies, one side tends to be viewed as more "valuable," depending upon cultural beliefs and the interpretation of their sources by historians. Separating female and male behavior into competing and opposing spheres does little to enhance understanding of the reciprocity needed to maintain any community. To reject the notion of a dichotomy is not to ignore gender differences or to assume that reciprocal interactions ensure equality of opportunity or experience. Certainly, in theological terms, the Block community was a patriarchal environment.[4] Still, under this patriarchal umbrella, individual women and men developed their own consciousness and behaved in specific ways that the historian may understand better if preconceived notions about dichotomies and polarities are set aside before interpretations are made.

To avoid entering the Block community from the front door of male domination/female victimization or from the back door of female superiority/male indifference, I have attempted to construct a side door into the intricacies of the community. I used a theoretical framework designed to examine "networks of association" and to explore the ways these networks transmitted education and culture across four generations in Block.[5] In other words, networks of association are the arenas in which to discover how gender, ethnicity, class, region, and religion educate and affect both group and individual behavior.[6] This approach permits me to analyze the interactions between the people and their institutions within the context of a specific setting; moreover, the reciprocity and interdependence of women, men, and children can be noted and explored.

I have chosen to examine four educational networks for the Block community: church, school, family, and the outside world. Analyzing these networks gave me the opportunity to discuss the formal as well as the informal ways that individuals functioned within this rural-ethnic community. Within each of these networks, life-course differences, gender differences, and continuity/change across generations were assessed. Such an analysis also facilitated examining the influence of American technology and culture within the community.

A close look at gender, ethnicity, and religion within each network provided insights into four generations of struggle, change, and assimilation in the community. For example, although all the networks of association played a role in the transmission of beliefs, values, and culture, the church and the school functioned as the hub around which the entire community lived and worked. This powerful combination of ethnic-religious institutions effectively resisted linguistic change (German to English), succumbing only after much internal controversy and two world wars with Germany. The third generation in Block, who came of age just before World War I, provided the pivotal point for change. The availability of birth control, increased economic options, military service, advances in transportation, and outside secular contacts served to change this generation's perceptions of themselves and their community.

Even in this highly patriarchal, authoritarian community, men, women, and children adapted and transformed their own educational networks and activities. By the 1930s the youth group and the Ladies Aid Society had expanded self-governance, increased autonomy, and learned to parlay organizational activities into money-making endeavors that increased their prestige and assured their existence. Clearly, the role of these informal educational (nonschool) settings cannot be ignored or understated as part of the impetus for change. Finally, the educational networks of association demonstrated the important role that rural topography and advanced technology played in this four-generational portrait. The availability of cars, trains, modern conveniences, and radio changed forever the dynamics of religious and geographic isolation that had solidified nineteenth- and early twentieth-century life in Block.

CRITICAL COMPONENTS FOR LONGEVITY

Through examining and analyzing formal and informal educational experiences, I explore the transmission of education across four generations in the Block community. Focusing specifically on education, I examine continuity and change over time, comparing and contrasting Block's development to that of other German and immigrant communities, urban and rural, that developed during the nineteenth century. Further, I argue that the education of four generations in Block was more total, ongoing, and pervasive than that in most nineteenth-century immigrant communities. Three critical factors combined to create a community that actively resisted assimilation and encouraged community cohesiveness, achieving longevity well into the twentieth century. First, the German Lutherans in Block belonged to a religious group of Lutherans (Missouri Synod) that tightly bonded ethnicity to religious beliefs. Missouri Synod Lutheranism emphasized the interdependence between German language and culture and *reine Lehre* ("pure doctrine"), requiring members to shun Americanism and promoting isolation and a defensive posture toward any religious group, including other Germans or Lutherans, who differed on theological or social issues. Exposure to "outsiders" was strongly discouraged, and the authority and doctrine of Missouri Synod Lutheranism insulated members by stressing their Germanness and their religious purity. In fact, the clergy often told members of the community that associating with "outsiders" was a sin and a threat to their salvation. In the synod's view, religion and ethnicity were inseparable—they were explicitly bound together, so both must be protected.

> With its theological-linguistic stance, its rural immigrant character and its thorough educational system, the Missouri Synod was considered "the most compact German culture group in the United States . . . perhaps the only separate culture-group which has a perfect organism for self-perpetuation on such a high and well-rationalized plane."[7]

The church and parochial schools instilled the necessary education in four generations in Block, reinforcing this ethnic and religious identity through the use of a national publishing house and all levels of educational institutions to educate children, teachers, and clergy.

Second, the Block community had a high level of homogeneity in its population throughout the seventy-seven years covered in this generational study. The largest group of people who settled the community at Block came from northern Germany (Hannover Province). They had similar rural backgrounds, spoke a Hannoverian dialect, and had come to the United States to own land and to continue their farm and family patterns. Generational land inheritance patterns and endogamy helped perpetuate the patterns of homogeneity; also, until 1924 slow but continuous migration from Germany encouraged the continued use of the German language and maintained constant interaction with the mother culture.[8] Throughout its seventy-seven-year history, Block maintained the educational institutions of church and school, and this triad of church, school, and family successfully indoctrinated four generations. Only the economic and political exigencies of World War I and its aftermath began to wear away some of the deepest layers of homogeneity.[9]

Third, Block's midwestern location and rural isolation created an environment that severely limited contacts during the first fifty years of the community's existence. Kansas, and most of the states west of the Mississippi River, offered land and opportunity to build communities and ways of life to land-hungry immigrants in the nineteenth century. Unlike the densely populated eastern states, western expansion provided white European immigrants with an opportunity to re-create communities patterned on Old World customs. Compounding regional isolation, early roads in and around Block were often impassable and rivers uncrossable until the county began improving roads and building bridges in the late nineteenth century. Until the advent of the automobile and World War I, the people traveled by foot or by horse and buggy. Although many passenger trains ran through the county, seven miles stood between most residents of Block and the train depot in nearby Paola. The rural community maintained its own commercial center, post office, telephone service, school, and church until well into the twentieth century. The first and second generation purchased most of the supplies they needed at Block Corners and thus avoided trips to larger nearby towns. Students in Block went to the parochial school, attending high school in large numbers only when rural bus service began in the late 1930s.

How representative was the Block community in comparison to other ethnic settlements or other rural-ethnic enclaves? Nineteenth-century Kansas was replete with small, rural-ethnic settlements, and in many ways Block was no different from other midwestern rural-ethnic communities, many of which developed around an ethnic church and espoused traditional, conservative values. Yet rarely do these immigrant settlements contain the three critical components of longevity: a religious-ethnic bond (that discouraged outside contacts), homogeneity of population, and regional isolation. For example, Scandinavian-Lutheran settlements in the Midwest often included a homogeneous group living in rural isolation, but their ethnic identity was not as closely tied with their religious identity, nor were their religious practices as restrictive.[10] German Catholics created rural villages, had homogeneous populations, and had a parish church and school, but their ethnic identity was not directly reinforced by their religious allegiance to the Vatican. The ethnic diversity of the Roman Catholic church forces it to accommodate a more pluralistic ethnic identity.[11] For Roman Catholics, remaining true to their religious prerogatives did not depend on their ethnic culture, or vice versa. Urban immigrants, although they created strong ethnic enclaves within large cities, lost any initial homogeneity sooner because the outside world surrounded their subcommunity and could hardly be ignored for many generations.[12] Certainly the Block community serves as a model for religious-ethnic communities in rural areas; furthermore, it also represents an example of a community that effectively encapsulated itself in the nineteenth and early twentieth centuries. In many ways, it falls on the accommodation-assimilation continuum between religiously conservative, rural communities and the religious exclusivity typical of Amish, Mennonite, and Mormon rural communities.

1
COMMUNITY OVERVIEW

They were rather, I think, people who traveled thousands of grim miles in
order to keep their roots, their habits, their united families and the kind
of future they wanted for their families.[1]

Although not written specifically about any one German community or group, Mack Walker's analysis of nineteenth-century German
emigration fits the people and families of the Block community in
Miami County, Kansas. Most of the people who emigrated there left
Germany during the middle to the latter part of the nineteenth century,
and they typically emigrated as families from small, rural villages in
northern Germany.[2] For most of the families, a long history of seden-
tary, agrarian living preceded their radical and dramatic move "across
the water."

Most scholars agree that the German farmers who came to the Midwest sought to establish if not to re-create, much of the rural village life
they had left behind. With a tradition of locational stability in German
rural areas and a long-range investment in the family farm, most of
these emigrants intended to settle permanently, and their desire to re-
gain and conserve the "old" was strong, partly because they felt their
way of life was being destroyed in Germany.[3]

EMIGRANTS

In the 1830s and 1840s many religious and political refugees came
to the United States, partly because of a combination of social and economic problems brought on by early nineteenth-century industriali-
zation, agricultural reform, and overpopulation that affected farmers,
small shopkeepers, and craftspeople.[4] Post–Civil War emigration,

which included many families who settled in Block, was reported to be "very strong in northern and northeastern areas of Germany, where Protestantism dominated," and in the 1880s, many young men fled to avoid Bismarck's military conscription laws.[5]

Other important factors lured Germans to America, including the well-publicized work of Gottfried Duden, *Report on a Journey to the Western States of North America* (1829), which provided lyrical, vivid descriptions, particularly of the state of Missouri.[6] This book, one of the most popular and influential nineteenth-century descriptions of the United States ever published in Germany, and the cheap transportation fares in the 1830s and 1840s combined to lure many Germans to America. And by the 1850s the majority of the transatlantic crossings were made by steam-powered ships, which were safer and faster than sailing vessels.[7]

Another popular incentive to emigrate came from letters and descriptions from family members who had already traveled to the United States. Like most emigrants, Germans wanted their families to see their move as a successful journey to a new country; consequently, most of them wrote to relatives in glowing if not exaggerated terms about life in America. Clarence Clausen related one story that was passed down in the Block community:

> Like old man Rodewald wrote Fred Wilkins, . . . they never hauled manure here. They moved the barn instead. And he came over here and Rodewald got him a job, as a carpenter at New Lancaster. And he couldn't understand the language. [His boss] handed him a pitchfork and then he made a motion toward the manure, and [Wilkins] said, "Here I was my first day, my first job, here I was hauling manure."[8]

Although the vast majority of the Germans who settled in Block came to the United States between 1850 and 1900, emigration from Germany continued until 1924. This small, twentieth-century group provided an important infusion of ethnicity and German traditions that slowed the assimilation process linguistically and culturally. Clannish and segregated from non-German Lutherans, the community continued to absorb new German immigrants for almost sixty years, and the small but steady flow of immigrants helped linguistically conservative members of the community retain the German language and culture longer than in many other rural settings.[9]

For many residents in Block, the reasons why their families emigrated have been lost. In interviewing third-generation families, I was often told their grandparents never talked about why they had come. Either no one asked, or the members of the first generation simply did not feel a need to discuss their dramatic and permanent departures from Germany. When reasons for emigrating were passed down to children and grandchildren, the first-generation emigrants typically stated that economic problems, lack of land, and military conscription had led to their move to the United States. In 1887, for instance, the brothers Dietrich and Johann Ohlmeier came to Block as young men, hoping to "have an easier life" and before "they had to go into the service."[10]

Whatever the reasons for leaving Germany, the ocean crossing and initial experiences in America often proved to be arduous and difficult for both individuals and families. Although most trips were uneventful, some of the emigrants to Block experienced difficulties during the voyage or right after landing in the United States. Gesche Schnakenberg Block witnessed her sister's illness and death during the long sea voyage and later told a granddaughter that "they put the body on a board and just buried it at sea. It took so long they couldn't keep her."[11] In 1866, August Prothe, as an infant, was seriously ill on the crossing to New York with his family; the story came down to his grandchildren that the crew threatened to throw him overboard to avoid the possibility of a contagious disease.[12] Eidena Johnson Cahman spent six weeks on a sailing ship with her five children in order to join her husband in the United States. Often she and her children did not have enough to eat and drink, but she described how the ship's crew often had fun with the children: The crew members "placed a pan of molasses with plums in it for the children to fish out with their mouths. . . . The mothers had a hard time getting the children cleaned up."[13]

After landing in an American port, problems continued for many unsuspecting emigrants. Difficulties in communication were paramount, and often the trusting emigrant would be duped by German-American con men. In 1851, F. W. Bogen published a book of advice and instruction for German emigrants, telling his fellow emigrants to pay after, never before completion of the trip; to go to the Midwest by way of New Orleans (New York City was too corrupt); to stay on board ship with baggage for forty-eight hours (to avoid con men at the dock); and never to listen to urban German Americans because they tended to lie about the "horrors" of the West.[14]

Whether the emigrants in Block had read Bogen or had taken his advice is impossible to determine, but some Germans who eventually settled there did experience problems soon after arriving in port. After landing in New York in 1887, Dietrich Ohlmeier had immediate language difficulties and kept receiving pie when he attempted to purchase pancakes.[15] August Monthey had much more serious difficulties to surmount; after disembarking from his seven-week ocean voyage, he realized during his check-in process that he had been robbed the night before he left the ship. He was in New York with only twenty-five cents in his pocket.[16]

The first German-Lutheran emigrants arrived in Miami County, Kansas, around 1860, and after 1900 few new emigrants were added to the church membership in Block. The most extensive migration to Block took place in the late 1860s, 1870s, and 1880s, as those emigrating in the mid-nineteenth century established initial residence in a midwestern state, typically Missouri, Indiana, Illinois, or Iowa, before coming to Kansas.

There were several reasons for the migrations to Kansas from other midwestern states. The Homestead Act of 1862, advertisements by railroad companies, and extravagant claims of the state board of immigration attracted many emigrants to Kansas. In 1871 the Kansas Immigration Society published an eight-page pamphlet claiming the state had "the choicest lands of the earth, only waiting the skilled hand of the cultivator."[17] For European peasants, land ownership had great symbolic value, and the 160 acres offered to homesteaders attracted many landless farmers to Kansas. Coming from a European society that paid respect and honor to landowners, immigrants wanted immediate land ownership, which compensated for the "confusion, anxiety, and rootlessness that afflicted many immigrants as they adjusted to life in a strange and alien environment."[18]

Two main German-Lutheran groups came to south-central Miami County and had a significant impact on the growth of the church and community in Block. The larger group was composed of northern Germans, predominantly from the Hannover region, who migrated in family groups after residing approximately a decade in Benton and Morgan counties in Missouri. These families had clustered in the Cole Camp, Missouri, region where three rural Missouri Synod Lutheran churches were already in existence.[19] Either because of their number and influence or because of their prior affiliations in Missouri Synod churches, males from the Missouri group and their descendants held many of the church offices in Block well into the twentieth century. The main exceptions to the dominance of the Missouri contingent were John and Fred Prothe. Although the Prothe brothers came from Illinois, they established and maintained extensive influence in church decision making, which their eight sons continued to exercise through their church activities. The Prothes fit in well and were included in the powerful "Missouri group" because they originated from northern Germany and spoke the prevalent Hannoverian dialect.

This Missouri group and most of the first-generation immigrants spoke low German with a Hannoverian dialect that became the main informal language of discourse within the Block community. In the church and the schoolhouse, standard (high) German was taught, read, and written by adults and children; this was the language of Martin Luther and the Lutheran confessions and therefore was deemed necessary to preserve the Lutheran faith and "pure doctrine."

The second and much smaller group of immigrants living in Block consisted of families from eastern Germany, predominantly the Posen region, who migrated first to LaPorte, Indiana, moving to the Block area in the late 1860s and settling west of the Marais des Cygnes River. In the early days of the community, crossing this river posed problems that often hindered regular church and school attendance. This environmental obstacle caused initial isolation for these families—effectively separating them from the main settlement area. One story describes the difficulties that George Reifel encountered while trying to cross the river to visit his grandparents:

> He and his brother would throw rocks in the water while their father chained the wagon wheels together. This was necessary or the wagon would run into the horses going down the bank. Then the boys would ride across the river in the bed. Often the water would run clear up into the wagon bed.[20]

The minutes from the voters' meetings often referred to these families as the group "across the river." As bridges were built in the county this geographic separation diminished, but a language difference remained. Their East Prussian dialect was significantly different from the Hannoverian dialect of the main settlement, and misunderstandings in informal communication always remained a problem for some individuals. The Hannoverian dialect was the dominant playground speech of the parochial school, so some children from East Prussian families learned to adapt linguistically through their school experience. Few residents were totally comfortable communicating in both dialects, however. In the 1920s, when Marie Dageforde began dating her future husband, Ed Monthey, they finally agreed to speak English to each other since she could not always understand his East Prussian dialect.[21]

Although these two groups represented the largest number of families to "chain migrate," other emigrants came individually or in single families from Iowa, Illinois, and from other communities in Missouri.[22] Chain migration refers to the migration of families and neighbors who leave one area to join neighbors, friends, and family in a specific place. Many scholars have documented the importance of chain migration, and arguably the influx of friends and relatives from northern Germany, specifically from Hannover Province, to the Midwest and eventually to Kansas helped define the Block community and add to its homogeneity. Chain migration from Indiana and Missouri to Block provided the second link in the transatlantic connections.

Travel to Block varied widely, but transportation by wagon, railroad, riverboat, or some combination of the three served to bring the emigrants west. In describing his family's move to Block from Indiana in 1868, Michael Schultz reported:

> We rode on the train to Kansas City. The people sat in the caboose. The wagons and household goods were loaded on the train with us. We had to unload the goods on the Missouri side and ferry across the river. We stayed four days in Kansas City with a German cobbler and then we started for Block. Paola was a small town of frame buildings and that is where we bought our supplies.[23]

After residing in Illinois, Nebraska, and western Missouri, the Cahman family traveled to Block in 1900. Minnie Cahman Debrick described the journey of her parents and older siblings:

> And they came in the nighttime, course them days they didn't have no cars or nothing, they just had big old lumber wagons, and it was dark and they had one lantern, and I know my brother said when they got there it was dark. On roads that you don't know

nothing about you know, to a strange place it was quite a job to find a little house.[24]

Most of the emigration to Block was complete by 1900, but the community flourished and expanded for two more decades. The immigrants farmed, reared children, and settled into a secure atmosphere where German and American traditions blended easily with little cultural conflict. By 1918 that secure existence would be shattered when the labels "German" and "American" could no longer be comfortably joined.

PHYSICAL AND CULTURAL ENVIRONMENT

Despite their difficulties in coming to the United States and eventually to Block, the German Lutherans began to buy land and to populate south-central Miami County, Kansas, located in the eastern strip of Kansas counties that border Missouri. In geography and climate, these counties resemble the prairies, hills, and timbers of western Missouri much more than the plains of central and western Kansas. Miami County is located in the center of these eastern border counties.

The village of Block was located in the south-central part of the county, seven miles southeast of Paola, the county seat. The Marais des Cygnes River curled around the southern portion of the county, one mile from the area that was to become the village. Bull Creek was the main north-south creek running to the Marais des Cygnes; small tributaries feeding the river included Elm Branch, Willow Creek, Middle Creek, and Walnut Creek. Oak, hickory, walnut, elm, and maple trees lined the creek and river beds. Although prairie grasses predominated, the abundance of timber and water provided wood for buildings and well water for most homesteads. Sand and limestone for barns and fences could be found in streams, and concrete sandstone was found in the high bluffs of streams. Clay provided the material for brick foundries and served as another useful building material.[25]

An 1868 sectional map marked the earliest known mineral deposits in this area. Shallow coal reserves were located in the southeastern section of the county, near Lancaster, and rich coal mining areas were abundant south of Block in Linn County and throughout southeastern

Kansas. The Sugar Creek mining area on the Linn County border became an important coal resource for the Block community. Farmers from Block drove wagons to the mines to collect coal for their families, church, school, parsonage, and teacher's residence. Oil and natural gas reserves were located throughout Miami County.[26]

The farmers grew a variety of crops, including wheat, corn, oats, sorghum, hay, and potatoes, and vegetable gardens and orchards dotted the landscape. The climate was also hospitable for raising dairy cows, cattle, chickens, and pigs. Although the physical terrain was isolating and rigorous, the environment provided ample resources to allow for semisubsistence farming as well as cash crops.[27]

In interviewing third- and fourth-generation community members, I was told repeatedly that no matter how difficult times were, even during the depression, families almost always had enough to eat; they might lack cash, clothing, and conveniences but they rarely went hungry. Vegetable gardens and small animals, typically the domain of farmwomen, kept the family fed and provided a consistent, stable income during the worst economic and farm crises of the nineteenth and early twentieth centuries.

In Miami County and most of eastern Kansas, the choicest acres of land were acquired soon after the Kansas-Nebraska Act of 1854. The public sale of Indian Trust Lands in June 1857 brought thousands of people into Paola to buy "the finest land in the county."[28] By 1861, eastern land speculators, railroads, and government agencies owned much of the fertile sections of eastern Kansas.[29] The 1865 state census contains six names that formed the core of the early community, church, and school of Block: The Bergman, Beckman, Mahnken, Miller, Gerken, and Windler families resided on land close to the area that later became Block village.[30] By 1863 there were enough German-Lutheran families in Block that a Missouri Synod mission station was established by Pastor F. W. Lange, and the Trinity Lutheran Church of Block, Kansas, was formally organized in 1868 and a permanent pastor called.

The 1878 county plat map shows the extent to which the German Lutherans acquired land after the initial efforts of this first group of families. The area typified the predominant method of rural expansion for Germans in the Midwest; they would come into an area and buy out non-Germans, expanding land-holdings and obtaining higher quality land. The Germans sometimes were willing to pay higher than mar-

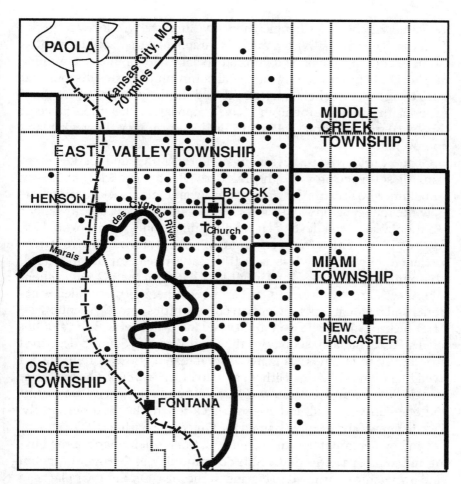

PAOLA

Kansas City, MO
70 miles

MIDDLE
CREEK
TOWNSHIP

EAST VALLEY TOWNSHIP

HENSON

BLOCK

des Cygnes River

† Church

Marais

MIAMI
TOWNSHIP

NEW
LANCASTER

OSAGE
TOWNSHIP

FONTANA

Block (Miami County), Kansas
Circa 1920s

Dot ● indicates land ownership by
German-Lutheran families

N

W ——|—— E

S

KANSAS

Kansas City, MO

Topeka

Lawrence

MISSOURI

Block

ket value, and non-German neighbors willingly moved away from the "clannish" Germans. With a nucleus established that could support a German church, school, and familiar social patterns, the community lured other Germans to buy land, and community norms discouraged sales to outsiders. Scholars have analyzed similar patterns of German-American rural settlement and have emphasized the importance of this pattern to ethnic, religious, and community longevity and homogeneity.[31]

Of the early arrivals, Beckman, Windler, Miller, and Gerken were from Missouri and provided the link to the Benton and Morgan county emigrants who became the largest contingent in the Block community. How the Indiana group and others heard about Block is unknown, but often railroads, land developers, and immigration societies would advertise the existence of various ethnic-religious communities to attract settlers to buy land. As late as 1910 a real estate company in Drexel, Missouri, asked to have farms near Block listed for their German clientele in western Missouri.[32] German newspapers also provided a national and regional link for German communities across the country.[33] After hearing about the availability of land, Michael Schultz's father left La Porte, Indiana, soon after the Civil War, and Schultz described how family and friends emigrated from Indiana: "I was born in 1861. I lived in Indiana six years. Father came to Block in 1866. The next year two uncles and an aunt followed him. Then in '68, when I was seven and one-half years old, father came back for mother and our family. Two nephews and a fellow named Joe Guy came with us."[34]

Land-ownership maps and official plat maps demonstrate the buying and selling patterns of the Block community, as German-Lutheran land ownership continued to expand in the area. On the 1901 plat map a significant cluster of German names surrounds Block and overlaps into four different townships in the county. East Valley Township contained the largest German-Lutheran contingent and included the village of Block, the church, school, parsonage, teacher's residence, and cemetery; Miami and Osage townships, and to a lesser extent Middle Creek Township, had significant numbers of German Lutherans. If one German Lutheran sold out, another would typically buy the land. Only in the 1930s did this trend begin to change, and English names once again began appearing on sections previously owned by German Lutherans.[35]

These buying patterns reveal a critical factor that created and main-

Early Block settlers, Johann and Magdelena Rehr Prothe, circa 1890.

tained the necessary homogeneity prevalent in the community. German Lutherans retained important links to ethnicity, religion, and community mores that influenced the institutions as well as individual family members. Although the German-Lutheran community expanded into four different townships, the economic, religious, and cultural institutions at Block Corners anchored and maintained the cohesiveness necessary to educate and indoctrinate all ages within the community.

By the 1880s the population had grown to the extent that local trading became possible, and residents could avoid the long trek into Paola for

Dietrich and Gesche Mahnken Block sold land to the church, and the community was named for them. Gesche Block, better known as "Grandma" Block, served as the community's midwife until the early twentieth century.

supplies. In 1882 Frank Yorky, from Atchison, opened a general store at "Four Corners"; this crossroads soon developed into the small village of Block. In 1884, when Yorky wanted to house a post office, a name for the village had to be created, and the community was subsequently named for Dietrich Block, Sr., who owned land west of Four Corners. Highly respected members of the church, he and his wife, Gesche Mahnken Block, sold part of their land, 13.5 acres, to the congregation as a permanent location for the church, school, and cemetery. The Blocks had come to the United States around 1850, living over a decade in the Benton-Morgan, Missouri, region before coming to Miami County.

By the turn of the century, the village of Block included two general stores, a creamery, a blacksmith shop, and a post office; a dance hall, ice house, barbershop, and drugstore survived for short periods. Yorky did not last as the proprietor of the first general store, and he was soon bought out by a German Lutheran, Jacob Neu. Another general store also opened and passed through the hands of German Lutherans — Henry Bergman, Dietrich Miller, and Fred Prothe. For a short period, Neu and Prothe combined forces but separated after a few years. In 1901

N

Tinken
Blacksmith
Shop

Reifel
General
Store

Ohlmeier
Creamery

Neu General
Store

Block Grove

Baseball
Diamond

1/2 mile

Parsonage

Church

Cemetery

School

Teacherage

Block, Kansas
Circa 1910

S

The Reifel General Store at Block Corners around 1940.

George Reifel bought Prothe's store and kept it in the family until it closed in 1942. A description of the Reifel store illustrates the thriving commerce and social life that linked the community. As Herman Clausen recalled:

> There was little need for residents to travel anywhere because the store provided everything that most households would need. . . . It was so busy most of the time that there were two storekeepers on hand. Merchandise was hauled in from Paola since there was no train in that area and flour was brought in from Pleasanton. The store also was a gathering place at night for [men] where they gathered to exchange the latest news.[36]

Besides the general stores, other businesses grew around Block Corners. Fritz Alpert opened the first blacksmith shop in the 1880s, but the Tinken family acquired the shop, which was passed down from father to son until 1946. Dick Ohlmeier operated a creamery in the late 1890s and early 1900s; in 1897, his operation handled twelve thousand to fifteen thousand pounds of cream a week. During this same year the Debrick-Schultz cane mill was in operation, a short-lived enterprise, but like Dick Block's mill in the 1880s, it served local needs.[37]

The importance of the village of Block to the community cannot be overstated: it functioned as a hub for social, economic, and political activities. Robert Slayton points out the importance of the re-created "Old World" village as a bond for immigrant communities in the United States.

> The perfect social bond was the Old-World Village. It was small enough to guarantee face to face recognition but large enough to provide a full range of services. . . . The village became, therefore, the basis of the first major form of community organization, the segmented group. This system worked because most peasants were already accustomed to identifying themselves as members of a specific village.[38]

Slayton's study further illustrates the applicability of his analysis to Block: The social bond of the Old World village ensured closeness, made behavior predictable, and provided stability and reassurance. This group effort and communal support provided important social and psychological advantages, particularly when that group spoke a common language or dialect.[39]

The commerce associated with the village changed in conjunction with the transportation available to community members. Early roads were used only when weather permitted; mud, snow, and other road conditions determined the time and length of travel, particularly when drivers negotiated heavy lumber wagons loaded with supplies. Until automobiles became readily available, walking was the most common form of travel except when heavy loads or supplies had to be transported. The lack of bridges across the Marais des Cygnes and its tributaries caused special problems for families who lived close to the river or who needed to cross the river to gather supplies, go to church, or send children to school. The need for county bridges and improved roads was a constant topic of conversation in the Block community and certainly remained one issue that community members took very seriously when electing county commissioners and road overseers.[40] In the early days of the community the rural topography played a critical role in perpetuating Block's physical isolation from other nearby towns or urban centers.

From Block's first days the railroad maintained a strong and growing presence in the county. By the 1860s, the Missouri River, Ft. Scott, and

Gulf Railroad had track running north and south through the county, passing through Paola, Henson, and Fontana. Henson, or Pendleton as it was called until the late nineteenth century, was located three miles west of Block and served as an early railhead; farmers drove cattle the three miles of dirt roads to reach it.[41] Until a bridge was built over Bull Creek, however, getting supplies to and from Henson was determined by the rise and fall of the creek. George Reifel, reminiscing about his many attempts to haul barrel salt from Henson to Block without a bridge, recalled that on one trip, driving his team of sorrel mules through mud, the end gate on his wagon came out when he was halfway up the creek bank, letting barrels of salt roll down into the stream. This, he said, caused "plenty of excitement."[42]

The railroads grew rapidly in the county but never included Block on their lines, so the seven-mile trip to Paola remained necessary in order to catch a passenger train. In 1892 the Missouri Pacific advertised that one hundred trains (freight and passenger) were leaving Paola for Kansas City every day. The trip took ninety minutes for passengers, and all stock could be sent in half a day.[43] At the peak of railroad activity in 1918, three lines out of Paola—the St. Louis & San Francisco (the Frisco), the Missouri Pacific, and the Missouri, Kansas & Texas—took passengers and freight any direction they needed to go.[44]

In 1910 the first car dealership in Paola opened its doors and offered Studebakers with a top for $1,300 and without a top for $800, but it was not until prices dropped during World War I that automobiles became a fact of life in the Block community. Car travel greatly diminished the need for a local marketplace as road improvements made the seven-mile trip to Paola far more desirable and comfortable; less time and energy were spent in travel than ever before. By the late 1920s, when car travel became common in the community, the only shops left in Block were the Reifel general store and the Tinken blacksmith shop. Both disappeared in the 1940s, and Block Corners became only a symbol of community life.

Along with transportation, communication links created connections to the outside world; by 1884, with a brand new post office and name, Block and its community had a communication center linking the village to this larger world. The post office was operated by Jacob Neu from inside his general store, where local, regional, and sometimes international mail moved through the small office. Letters to and from Germany were not uncommon until World War I, when correspondence with German friends and relatives became difficult if not impossible for the residents of Block. This wartime crisis effectively severed the main connection of Block's Germans to the old country. Most interviewees said that after the war, families stopped most communication with German relatives and friends.

The Block Post Office was served by the Star Route, which circulated letters from Rockville, New Lancaster, Block, and Paola. The round trip could be made in one day with a buggy, with a change of horses every other day if the roads were bad.[45] In 1905, Rural Route 9, which covered most of East Valley Township, was created, and Block lost its post office.[46] Still in that same year another form of communication came to the Block community: Block Mutual Telephone Company. The list of twenty-four patrons included only one English surname; the rest were German-Lutheran farmers organizing their own communication system. The telephone switchboard was set up in the general store, and George Reifel took care of it without charge for the first few years; later, he hired operators and moved the switchboard upstairs. Throughout its existence, the switchboard was moved to and operated by various households close to Block Corners; the list of operators included single women or married couples from the Block community. The switchboard maintained four lines, matching the crossroads, and served approximately thirty-five phones scattered around the perimeter of the community.[47] With four party lines, at any given time a listener might hear Hannoverian dialect, East Prussian dialect, or English being spoken. This diversity of speech caused acute anxiety for some English-only speakers, especially during World War I and World War II.[48]

RELIGION/ETHNICITY

Although the interaction of people and their environment is critical to historical inquiry, the study of Block can be accomplished most effectively when individual and group behaviors are examined within the context of the community's particular belief system and worldview. To understand the Block community fully, it is necessary to comprehend the powerful combination of religion and ethnicity that influenced, maintained, and reinforced this rural midwestern community and its people, or in other words, to understand the background and beliefs of the Lutheran Church–Missouri Synod. Trinity Lutheran Church and school were a product of these beliefs, and four generations in the community were inculcated with a Missouri Synod worldview.

From its founding in 1847, the Lutheran Church–Missouri Synod charted its own course, often independent from and at odds with American Protestantism. As an immigrant church it had long insulated itself through the use of the German language and its claim to *reine Lehre* ("pure doctrine") based on divinely inspired, inerrant Scripture.[49] The synod fathers perceived the enemy as American liberalism and a secularism that destroyed God's natural order and threatened the very core of Lutheran doctrine and beliefs. Historian Alan Graebner writes, "Synod leaders attempted to maintain a social structure defined by ethnic and religious boundaries that was, save for politics and economics, as self-contained as possible."[50] Rural congregations such as Trinity Lutheran in Block personified this closed, hierarchical system that was content to maintain and insulate itself from outside influence and potential threats to its unity.

The original nucleus for the Missouri Synod included a group of Saxon immigrants under the leadership of Pastor Martin Stephan.[51] In 1839 five ships carrying Stephan and his followers sailed from Bremen, Germany, to America, hoping to establish a religious colony based on conservative, "confessional" Lutheranism. The "Old Lutherans," as they were sometimes called, abhorred both the rationalism and the pietism gaining power and influence in nineteenth-century Germany.[52]

Soon after arriving in St. Louis and purchasing land in Perry County, Missouri, a scandal arose and Martin Stephan fell into disfavor. After many accusations and denials of fiscal and sexual misconduct, Stephan was banished from the community. A period of disillusionment and uncertainty followed. Then, C. F. W. Walther assumed leadership and played a dominant role in the synod throughout the nineteenth century, his writings, orations, and debates leaving a permanent mark. His 1844 publication of *Der Lutheraner* served as "a catalyst for unaffiliated Lutherans to rally behind a conservative, common cause."[53]

The synod was formally organized in 1847 and included German-Lutheran groups throughout the Midwest. Because of the Stephan fiasco, the synod adopted a "non-binding clause" to ensure local congregations power over synodical resolutions, stating that local congregations had the right to decide themselves whether to adopt the recommendations presented by the synod. Although each congregation had the power to accept or reject synod resolutions, rejection rarely occurred at Block or anywhere else in the synod. Clergy and seminary faculty retained tremendous influence over individual congregations; the nonbinding clause was more rhetoric than reality. The Missouri Synod's structure bound the highly educated clergy to uneducated German immigrants, who revered the sacred calling of the ministry and respected their pastor's educational background.[54] Conservative doctrine and the strong bond of language and culture further cemented clergy and laity.[55] The educational gap between seminary-educated clergy and the laity in Block who, at best, had an eighth-grade education, reinforced the religious hierarchy within the synod and, coupled with the presence of German-born pastors until 1926, helped ensure the religious and ethnic conservatism, as well as the linguistic and cultural conservatism, of the Block community.

By the mid-nineteenth century, the Missouri Synod had created a unique educational system, including two seminaries, elementary schools supported by individual congregations, preparatory schools, and junior colleges.[56] In fact, until World War I, the synod supported the largest educational system in American Protestantism. This well-organized system guaranteed a well-educated clergy and a lay membership with common loyalties and beliefs. Should congregations or members be confused on synodical attitudes or doctrine, the continued growth of the synod's own publishing firm, Concordia Publishing House, ensured a steady flow of literature expressing the synod's viewpoint.

From its founding in 1869, the publishing company functioned as a powerful educator for nineteenth- and twentieth-century Lutherans. Nearly all the Lutherans in Block read the monthly lay magazines *Der Lutheraner* and later the *Lutheran Witness*. Written and controlled by clergy, the publications taught the laity what to believe and how to live a Christian life. The magazines espoused the importance of family life and obedience to a higher authority and told parishioners what to avoid, i.e., "outsiders," women's suffrage, birth control, and other American vices. Children learned to read using synod books and as adolescents received a barrage of prescriptive literature on appropriate behavior.

From its initial inception, the Missouri Synod sought to be an immigrant church and took immediate measures to move west, to the frontier, looking for German immigrants isolated and unaffiliated with existing churches. The *Reiseprediger* ("traveling preacher") journeyed throughout the Midwest and West and was highly successful in finding unaffiliated Germans. As German family groups were located, a pastor would serve three or four congregations within a given area, usually on a once-a-month basis. Graebner writes:

> A Pastor was sent into an area to look for German-Lutherans. . . . As more German settlers moved into areas and preaching stations grew congregations organized and called their own Pastor. German language schools began as soon as possible, strengthening church ties and attracting more German immigrants to congregations.[57]

The immigrant character of the synod significantly affected its approach to the indoctrination of its followers and its relationship to the outside world. Synod founders saw the preservation of the faith as a paramount concern. After being attacked for their confessionalism in Germany they now had to preserve the "true Lutheran faith" in a foreign milieu replete with Calvinists, Roman Catholics, evangelical Protestants, and secular American liberals. Religious isolation was deemed imperative, and synod clergy felt this could be assured only by the perpetuation of the German language and culture. In discussing the synod's conservatism, Frederick Luebke writes that "the German culture with all of its trappings was used to perpetuate the religious conservatism which had become their hallmark."[58]

Religious compromise was not viewed as conciliatory but as heresy. "No Union without Unity" was strictly adhered to, making interaction even with other Lutheran groups a threat to *reine Lehre*, which demanded the acceptance of the literal interpretation of the Bible and of the Lutheran confessions as contained in the sixteenth-century Book of Concord.[59] As articulated by Martin Luther, a sinner gains salvation not through good works or individual merit but through faith alone. Through a sinner's faith in his or her redemption by Christ, "God is moved to justify us by His grace."[60]

The synod viewed family life as primary and as the main center for the education of children. Although elementary schools were at first deemed mandatory for admission to the synod, the home was never to be usurped as the primary realm of education and religious activity. Children must be taught to respect and submit to parents, elders, and those in authority over them. Unlike other Protestant denominations, the Missouri Synod viewed Sunday school as a poor substitute for a Christian day school; in fact, many Missouri Synod congregations did not have Sunday school until the mid-twentieth century.[61] Centered within the parameters of home and family, women played a specific role in the Missouri Synod belief system. Although women as mothers were seen as central to the family and home, they were always to be in submission to their husbands and other males in authority. The position of women in the synod has been consistently based on 1 Corinthians 14:34–35: "Let your women keep silence in the churches, for it is not permitted unto them to speak; but they are commanded to be under obedience, as also saith the Law. And if they will learn anything let them ask their husbands at home; for it is a shame for women to speak in the church."

Although all Christian denominations are basically patriarchal, there are some marked differences. Unlike their sisters in Catholicism who had a representative in the Virgin Mary or who could enter religious communities and unlike their Protestant sisters who could participate in revivals and evangelical practices of preaching and teaching, Missouri Synod women operated from within a traditional, patriarchal male worldview. Synod theology made clear the complementary but different calling of males and females. For women to challenge their maternal and domestic role was to question God's order and their "natural" subordination brought about by the sins of Eve.[62] Husbands and fathers, on the other hand, were to rule a patriarchal household and to hold all decision-making positions in the church. This theology effectively kept females from any source of power within the church and focused their behavior narrowly within the family setting. As females in Block slowly entered into formal church work and the public economic sphere, this theological tenet stood as an unyielding barrier to change.

To protect the church, school, and family from outside influences, the Missouri Synod banned or discouraged any contact with non-Lutherans. Although the arenas of economics and politics were somewhat exempt, the synod attempted to forbid its members from interacting with any secular or church groups and was particularly virulent in attacking memberships in secret societies. Missouri Synod Lutherans were not allowed to attend other religious services or to have nonsynod pastors preach, even if they were Lutheran. Many pastors interpreted strictly this ban on outside socializing and encouraged members to avoid friendships with non-Lutherans, believing that any type of contact could allow an alien culture or idea to take hold. In discussing this attitude, Luebke writes, "Thus, no matter which way he turned the German Lutheran immigrant leader saw hostility and harassment, real or imaginary. . . . Every possible social, cultural, and theological weapon was to be wielded in this battle for survival in a hostile environment."[63] This insulation would be broken only in order to join forces with Catholics to protect the "sacred" separation of church and state in defense of its schools and language.[64] Not until after World War II did the synod slowly begin to change its attitude and become more actively involved in outside endeavors. The church in Block experienced many transitional difficulties similar to those of the national synod; however, in some specific ways Trinity Lutheran at Block charted its own course, particularly in the twentieth century.

Ethnic homogeneity in the community, the natural and man-made environment, and religious imperatives combined to create and maintain the core of Block's values and belief systems. The educational networks of church, school, and family provided a pervasive control and an exclusive system. The avoidance of outsiders ensured the insulation of members and kept them effectively isolated from most outside influences, including the assimilation of and the accommodation to American culture. The community remained self-contained and self-sufficient until changes in transportation and communication began to erode the rural isolation. By World War I the social, economic, and political influences of the outside world began to intrude, forcing cracks in the community's institutions and belief systems.

2

CHURCH

It appears that the German church, of whatever denomination, occupies a more central role in the life of the community than does the non-German church. German churches . . . have a substantial degree of continuity, in terms of both time and membership. The church, typically, has been in the community in nearly its present form since early settlement, and its membership traces through at least several generations.[1]

To understand fully the importance of the local church to the Block community, it is necessary to trace the development of Trinity Lutheran Church from its earliest beginnings. The Missouri Synod mission station established in 1863 at Block had developed into a formal church body by 1868; Trinity Lutheran Church was organized and a constitution written and signed by the adult males in the congregation. Leaders in Block called Pastor W. Zschoche to serve the community, and church services were initially held in the homes of members.[2]

The first church/school building, which included a two-room apartment for the pastor, was erected in 1870 after the congregation purchased thirteen acres south of Block Corners. A separate parsonage was later added in 1875, and in 1884 a larger frame church was erected. The old church had been moved south on the site and served as the school. The church grounds also included a cemetery and a parsonage complete with smokehouse, chicken house, and other outbuildings. This assemblage of church, school, and cemetery on church grounds changed only when a teacher's residence was added in 1892.[3]

By 1872, when the congregation applied for admittance into the Missouri Synod, the membership had grown rapidly, with the addition of nine families from Indiana and the large contingent from Benton and Morgan counties in Missouri who continued to migrate to the Block community. By 1884, when the new four-hundred-seat church was built, Pastor J. Matthias reported a membership of 278 to the synod office in St. Louis; by 1895 the congregation had had four pastors, and membership stood at 330. Children accounted for one-third of the congregation, and approximately seventy were voters (adult males). The congregation continued to grow, with membership peaking in 1920 at 485 members, including 99 voters, approximately 160 children, and a school population of 72 students. Through 1945 membership never dipped below the level of 400.[4]

There were three types of membership in the congregation: baptized members (usually children under fourteen years; communicant members (fourteen and older, which included all baptized and confirmed women and men; and voting members (males twenty-one years and older). Children were baptized usually within a few weeks of their birth. Communion membership was granted after successful completion of a two-year instruction class provided for seventh and eighth graders. The voters' assembly elected its own officers and had supreme power to administer and manage all external and internal church affairs, from the mundane matters of church upkeep to disciplinary actions against individuals.

The formal constitution of Trinity Lutheran made clear the structure of hierarchy and governance and prescribed the duties and responsibilities of clergy and laity; thus it played a prominent role in church affairs.[5] Before an adult male joined the voters' assembly, the document was read aloud for each new member before he was asked to sign it. Except for the articles concerning Lutheran doctrine and confessions, the constitution could be altered by the voters' assembly, which often led to spirited exchanges between members and groups with differing ideas. Besides financial concerns, the voters struggled constantly with the issue of which language to use in the services — German or English or both. During World War I and for the next three decades, this issue always resulted in differing opinions and strife.

Although controversies filled the early church records at Block, some of the difficulties may have occurred because members were adapting to democratic principles in church governance. In Germany, the Lutheran Church was sponsored, financed, and supported by individual German states; congregations and individual members had little control over pastors or local congregational affairs.[6] After coming to America, first-generation males found themselves involved in all aspects of church activities, including decision making and financing.

The earliest known photograph of Trinity Lutheran Church and congregation, circa 1890. (Reproduced by permission of the University of Kansas Libraries, Kansas Collection)

This new-found autonomy may have accentuated the difficulties for voting men unaccustomed to directing and controlling the destiny of the congregation.

Although controversies forced these voters in Block into struggles involving both social and theological questions, the men had the opportunity to develop skills in theology, persuasion, and at times compromise. Voters debated the importance of education and the methods of disciplining members, and early in the 1870s and 1880s they struggled with theological questions involving engagement, marriage, divorce, and excommunication. Jon Gjerde describes similar types of controversies (theological and nontheological) that encumbered Norwegian Lutherans in nineteenth-century Crow River, Minnesota, stating that conflict was a central component of "social, religious, and theological development among immigrant settlements which helped redefine social relationships and reorient central beliefs."[7]

Paramount among other controversies was the continued struggle for financing. Early economic difficulties overwhelmed most of the first-generation males, who were attempting to establish ecomomic stability on their farms. Besides their farm expenses, male heads of households and single men had to pay the pastor and finance every item purchased for the church and school. For men unaccustomed to church financing, the need to open their pockets for the church was often viewed with reluctance, skepticism, and resentment.[8]

The voting group was also allowed to question or challenge their pastor's behavior and decisions. If a disagreement between pastor and voters' assembly occurred that could not be resolved, a representative of the district synod came to mediate and then to decide the issue in question. Disagreements happened often in the early decades of the church at Block. In the 1870s Pastor J. M. Maisch and later Pastor J. Matthias came under heated attack from some of the men in the voters' assembly. Decriptions of these controversies are somewhat difficult to interpret because the meetings' minutes seem to leave out important information. In both cases the congregation appeared to be satisfied with the pastors' personal behavior but felt each pastor had made serious errors in handling his duties, particularly in conducting the school. Church members constantly discussed the school and never hesitated to admonish the pastor if they found him lacking in his teaching duties.[9] During both controversies district President Buenger finally came to Block, resolved the issue, and reproved both parties for the continued strife.[10]

The relationship between clergy and laity was an uneven one throughout the history of the church and community at Block. The early pastors there were German-born but received their education at Concordia Seminary in St. Louis. The German immigrants brought with them a respect for the formal education of clergy and their authority as representatives of God. Interactions between laity and clergy were based on this respect for authority and the institutions created to support it.[11]

The continued use of the German language well into the twentieth century bolstered the local pastor's control and power in two important ways. First, the language of the church and school was standard German, not the low German spoken by the congregation in their daily activities. Standard German served as a symbol of education and authority and was viewed as culturally superior to the low-German dialects used by German peasants in northern rural Germany.[12] Second, the pastor's use of German helped establish and preserve German culture and practices in America, solidifying and maintaining the immigrants' ties to the mother country. Although discussing urban Catholic immigrants, Robert Slayton in *Back of the Yards* clearly saw the parish church as providing stability and the priest as serving a special function. Slayton viewed the priest as a connection to the old country and the most important person in making the church "seem like home."[13]

In discussing rural immigrant communities, Frederick Luebke and Kathleen Neils Conzen confirm the importance of the pastor's role in effectively slowing down the assimilation process or at least in making it less traumatic.[14] Alan Graebner describes the importance of the pastor to German-Lutheran immigrants:

Unable to bring with him all that marked the cycle of life in his homeland, [the immigrant] attached more importance to the basic ceremonies of life, baptism, marriage and burial. Correspondingly, the officiant at these acts — the officiant who performed them as was done in the old country — became more valued and esteemed.[15]

When older residents of Block discuss their memories of early pastors they tend to describe them as "serious" and "strict." The pastor and his wife were expected to set the standards of Christian behavior for men and women in the congregation. Esther Prothe Maisch related a story I heard many times when conducting oral interviews: "At a wedding I know one time, they [the men] were playing cards, and the pastor drove in. They all jumped and ran . . . it was a sin." Such was the power of the pastors that they could make grown men scurry to hide their "sinful" activities.[16]

Although pastors in Block, as well as other Missouri Synod clergy, would cringe at the mere mention of piety and Calvinistic beliefs concerning appropriate behavior, the early pastors at Trinity Lutheran set puritanical standards for behavior. The German American's love of music, food, drink, and entertainment is well documented, and the German Lutherans of Block were no exception; they saw baptisms, confirmations, and particularly weddings as events that required music and other forms of entertainment. Interestingly, the laity seemed privately to ignore bans or limitations on drinking, card playing, and dancing, and the third generation, who came of age around World War I, clearly ignored many earlier taboos. A young man who had been seen in a dancing establishment was seriously reprimanded by the pastor in an 1878 voters' meeting and was required to ask publicly for forgiveness. Although angry, he submitted to the authority of the pastor and the congregation. Forty years later, another young man was more willing to defy the pastor's authority publicly. Louis Schultz loved to play the fiddle for a local dance band but was told directly by the pastor to stop this "sinful" behavior. When he ignored the pastor's warning he was publicly excluded from communion, and the pastor threatened excommunication. Schultz again ignored the pastor, and although nothing was discussed publicly, the pastor overlooked the behavior and eventually reinstated Schultz.[17]

In a small, insulated community like Block, the pastors rarely received such open challenges to their authority. Their education, status, and power prevailed over a community that revered and respected them but did not always agree with their dictates. The laity publicly accommodated their bidding but often privately behaved as they pleased. Almost as a child operates with a parent, the laity of Block at times quietly defied the pastor's orders concerning their personal behavior, but always the idea was not to get caught. American-born pastors, who had grown up in communities similar to Block, were seen by parishioners as more assimilated to American customs and mores. Although the pastors remained highly conservative, the interviewees said that these American-born pastors acted more "American" than German and appeared to be much less rigid in their thinking.

The pastor's wife served as a feminine role model for the community; she was expected to be an exemplary wife and mother and also the local representative of German-Lutheran womanhood. Along with her husband and children, she had to meet higher standards of behavior than the laity. Her duties were often compounded when invited speakers, seminary students, and teachers were housed in the parsonage for temporary or long-term visits. In a church where the position of women was subservient to men, she had to remain silent to avoid reflecting adversely on her husband's authority, either as a male or as the pastor; however, "pastor's wife" received additional respect from other women and men because of her husband's ordained authority. Nora Ohlmeier Prothe compared contemporary wives of ministers to the ones of her youth and young adulthood. The early pastor's wife "was supposed to keep still and take things. They're so different now. You call them by their first names, and they do what other people do. They should too."[18]

Like many other ministers, Block's pastors were paid a small salary but lived in the parsonage and received ample amounts of wood and coal for the winter months; the congregation provided free services and commodities for the pastor's family. Periodically, the parsonage would be repaired and additional buildings constructed since most pastors and their wives also did limited farming and food producing to support their families. Men hauled coal and wood to the parsonage on a quarterly basis, and women in the congregation and later the Ladies Aid gave gifts to the pastor and his family. Quilts, fresh vegetables, and canned goods made their way to the parsonage, sent by the women's group or by individual families. Birthdays, anniversaries, and holidays at the parsonage were often remembered by members of the congregation. Such gift-giving and celebrating were predominantly initiated by the women since the gifts were typically the result of women's domestic production and the activities organized by the women's group. On the rare occasions when the voters' assembly gave a gift to the pastor it would be money, fuel, or travel time.

In contrast to the pastor's well-defined position, lay activity at Trinity Lutheran reflected the Missouri Synod's ambivalent attitudes toward appropriate lay endeavors. With the exception of the voters' assembly, Missouri Synod lay groups of any gender or age did not become prevalent until the first and second decades of the twentieth century. Unlike other nineteenth-century Protestant denominations, the Lutheran Church–Missouri Synod seemed immune to the social egalitarianism of most Protestant groups that sponsored all manner of lay activities, from public ministry to charitable societies.

Trinity Lutheran Church on Easter Sunday, circa 1910. The separation of men and women reflects the practice of their sitting on opposite sides of the aisle during services. (Kansas Collection, University of Kansas Libraries)

In discussing this phenomenon historians have postulated two possible reasons for the synod's unwillingness to encourage lay activity. First, the sacramental duties of the ordained clergy kept pastors firmly separated from the "priesthood of all believers" since active lay participation could be perceived as a usurpation of clerical authority. And for some synod leaders, creating organizations for fellowship and recreation appeared as a "pious bribe" to encourage membership.[19] Second, the synod's immigrant history and origin discouraged assimilation of American ideas. "American volunteerism" and the prevalence of secular groups with religious purposes were seen as a threat to the separation of church and state and as an interference with the patriarchal family and its responsibilities.[20]

Protokoll clearly demonstrates that for the church at Block the male voters' meeting was the extent of nineteenth-century lay activity. Although less theoretical than the synod's explanation, two practical considerations may have had more to do with the laity's lack of activity. First, Block was a rural church, and most early lay activity, including church philanthropy, typically began in urban churches. The "evils" associated with the big city (prostitution, saloons, crime) probably seemed less threatening and more remote to a rural dweller in the Midwest, particularly in an isolated and insulated community like Block.[21]

Second, in the Block community, the laity may have been reluctant or simply unable to view any lay activity, particularly philanthropy, as a necessary duty of the congregation. The immediate economic and social concerns of family and farm kept men and women busy with the welfare of their own families and neighbors. Helping someone may have been viewed as an informal, individual activity, not necessarily as a formal group endeavor. Kinship ties created the necessary support system when individuals or a family needed assistance. Surviving in a new milieu took tremendous energy and perseverance on the part of the first and second generations in Block. "Taking care of your own" may have taken everyone's time and energy so that looking beyond the community may have been impossible or impractical. In the early twentieth century when the church began to engage in charitable activities consistently, money was sent only to synod-affiliated schools, churches, or institutions.[22]

The Gilderhaus sisters, however, provide an interesting exception to this lack of formal philanthropy toward those outside the networks of family and church. Mina and Mary Gilderhaus lived within a mile of Block Corners; their origins are unknown and if they had family in the area, they received little if any assistance. In an unusual entry, *Protokoll* in July 1895 recorded that the voters' assembly paid Mina ten dollars for "caring for the Louis Timken family during their sickness." Families in the Block community also helped the sisters during difficult times, and although the sisters were not members of the church, they seem to have been accepted and cared for during their elderly years. Little else is remembered about these two unmarried sisters, but *Protokoll* of May 1932 recorded a remarkable and highly unusual decision: The men voted permission for the "Gilderhaus girls" to be buried in the east row of the cemetery "in case they want to."[23]

For the first forty years of the church at Block, lay activities remained minimal, and until 1912, when the Ladies Aid was formed, only the male voters' assembly offered the chance for direct interaction of the laity in church affairs. The male voters' assembly served as a primary place for important decision making, however, functioning as the main adult male educational network of the church. The group met quarterly with the pastor and the teacher to conduct the ongoing business of the church and school. The leadership consisted of an assembly chairman to conduct meetings and a secretary to record all minutes. Each January these officers, including elders and trustees, were elected to serve for the coming year. As the church grew, a treasurer and a finance committee were added to the list of elected officers.

The three trustees were to "represent the congregation in all suits of law and transact all business." They also served as the administrators in maintaining all church property. The two elders (also called deacons) were "to be an example of Christian conduct and conversation." Their duties were to "assist the pastor in all matters pertaining to the spiritual welfare of the congregation." These men were typically sent to talk with members who had committed "gross offenses" and to report this behavior to the pastor.[24] In a sense they served as the spiritual supervisors for the congregation, and their duties also included overseeing the parochial school.

Those men chosen for offices in the early decades of the church continued to be reelected, either to the same office or in a different capacity. Once having acquired the power of an office, these men were able to maintain that power through most of their lives, an early phenomenon that might be explained in two ways. Initially, the Block community was settled by families of young or middle-aged men and women. In the early decades, older people were present in the community but not in large numbers; typically, they lived in the household of an adult child. Although the older men might own some land or have personal property, they often did not have independent households, and their sons or sons-in-law in effect functioned as head of the house. With few exceptions in the first decade (the 1870s), church leaders were men in their thirties and early forties; having acquired their stature, these men continued to hold office well into their sixties. Younger men were elected along with these older men, but the average age of the church officers increased with each decade. Thus this first generation had immense control over the church for a lengthy period of its development. Combined with the German-born pastors, this control undoubtedly contributed to the church's conservative trends in maintaining the German language and traditions, successfully staving off outside influences and assimilation.

The profile of this first generation of male leadership shows some interesting differences in class, language (dialect), and birthplace. Geography and land ownership affected church leadership positions. German Lutherans who lived east of the Marais des Cygnes River (near the church and school) held slightly larger portions of land (80 to 160 acres) than those men living west of the river, and they spoke a Hannoverian dialect. The "across the river" group arrived in Block five to ten years later than the original settlers, had smaller landholdings, and spoke an East Prussian dialect. The difficulty of fording the river kept them geographically removed from regular interaction with the Hannoverian group. *Protokoll* constantly admonishes these men for not attending meetings and not sending their children to school. This group became clearly frustrated with their second-class status and for four years (1878–1882) attempted to operate a church and school separate from the church in Block. St. Peter's German Evangelical Church ultimately failed to thrive, and eventually this group returned to Trinity Lutheran Church and school.[25]

The Hannoverian group provided the main leadership throughout the nineteenth century. Land ownership was vital to holding church office but, at least initially, large landowners did not clearly dominate. Church leadership therefore seemed to hinge on other factors such as age and literacy (older members had a higher proportion of those who were illiterate), force of personality, and willingness to give to the church both financially and in other ways.

The other important factor in assessing church leadership involves the young men chosen to serve with or to replace the older men. Often, a powerful older male would have sons elected as officers also. John and Fred Prothe each had four sons, and the church continued to elect Prothe descendants through 1945 and beyond; the Gerken, Grother, Koopman, and Block families have had two or three generations of males in elective office. There are other examples of father/son officers, but these particular names are first-generation families who have lived in Block since the 1870s or earlier.

The voters' assembly functioned primarily in two important ways. This group of men administered and maintained the organized church in its physical form and also served as a governing body responsible for controlling, educating, and disciplining members of the congregation. Maintenance included building and repairing the church grounds and all the structures upon it; this task and the financing needed to achieve it took a large amount of time. *Protokoll* is replete with details of the constant mending, building, and buying of materials for one of the structures. These men took their responsibility seriously and meticulously recorded the exact dimensions of the church, school, parsonage, and teacher's residence buildings and the exact cost of materials and labor. The church built in 1884 was to be constructed on the "exact spot" of the first church.

The structure of the church, particularly the interior portion, reflected a strong European tradition. The church altar was extremely

*The altar and pulpit of Trinity Lutheran Church. The
pulpit was elevated, and the minister climbed four
steps (behind the pulpit) in order to preach the
sermon.*

ornate with carved wood (dark walnut) and marble statues; the baptismal font and stained-glass windows added to the Old World ambience.
The pulpit was raised, and the pastor had to ascend four steps to preach
on Sunday, a setting that clearly elevated his authority and power over
his flock. Visitors and later generations often remarked that the church
looked "Catholic," far different from most Protestant churches built
in the late nineteenth century.

Voters took special pride in the construction of their church tower and the large purchases of the tower bell and a new organ. The bell and organ were such a source of pride that only certain men were elected to ring the bell and pump the organ for Sunday services. The bell was a powerful reminder of special moments in the community — Sunday services and deaths of church members. The voters' assembly spent the October 1897 meeting outlining the number of bell rings for special occasions. These decisions are significant because they reflect the members' beliefs and values: Only appointed laymen could ring the bell on Sunday one hour before and at the beginning of the service; only the pastor could ring the bell on Saturday night at sundown or to signify a death in the church; at death a nonconfirmed member received three rings, a young unmarried person received six rings, and an older person received nine rings.[26] Clearly, there was a hierarchy that valued age and confirmed membership in the church.

The church design and the bell tower reminded early generations of the old country and seemed to reinforce religious and communal ties within the new community. Slayton discusses the importance of immigrants creating an "old world village" setting in which specific rules and activities "ensured closeness, made behavior predictable," and assured stability, providing reassurance during times of stress. These recreations of village life provided social and psychological advantages, particularly where the native language continued to unite villagers: "In the peasant farmlands of Europe, the parish and the village were concurrently the major social, economic, and political units: the church district, therefore, was easily perceived as a reasonable, similar basis for organized community life."[27]

Whenever possible the voters' assembly opted to do its own building and repairing. For many years church member William Dageforde did much of the carpentry repairs on the church and other buildings. The church always paid Dageforde for his services, and although group volunteer work was prevalent, many times the trustees would pay individual members to provide needed services. Supplying wood, coal, some donations of grain, and a salary for the pastor and the teacher were seen as obligations, but the men typically expected to be paid for extra duties such as hauling, cleaning, building, and repairing church buildings and grounds. Young boys were also paid to pump the organ on Sundays. The information about who received pay and who volunteered is murky and at times difficult to assess. The usual procedure seemed to be that when groups of men were required to undertake large projects, volunteer work was expected; when individuals performed specific and at times skilled tasks they were typically paid for their services.[28]

The method of church financing changed dramatically from the system used in the mid-nineteenth century to that of the mid-twentieth. Early in the church's history, the congregation borrowed money from a few of their wealthier members. For decades, money was collected by reading the list of names in voters' assembly, and each man was expected to make a verbal pledge to pay the amount he felt he could donate. This was a powerful form of peer pressure since individuals often knew the financial status of others and did not hesitate to tell them if their pledge seemed less than they could afford. If not enough money was pledged initially, the list of names was read again until the needed amount was promised. Church officers were expected to give more, setting a good example for the others. After the pledges, the elders went individually to each man's house and collected the money. Single men often complained about an unfair burden of financial responsibility and typically were expected to pay less than married men.[29] Since the average age of marriage for males was 26.6 years, a young man usually spent about five years in voters' assembly before he married. He might lack funds because he often did not own land until his father died or bequeathed it to him upon marriage or because his income would increase only if he married and combined his resources with his wife's domestic production (throughout the four generations in Block, a woman's domestic production played an important economic role in her family). To avoid financial strain some unmarried men did not join voters' assembly until they married.

Until the 1920s, Trinity Lutheran Church practiced another German tradition to obtain monies from the Sunday collection. Immediately following the pastor's sermon, church officers used a *Klingelbeutel* (a cloth "alms bag" with a bell attached) to collect Sunday donations. The bag was fastened at the end of a long pole and extended down the pews so that members could deposit change and bills directly into the bag as it was placed before them. Even in 1923 when the church began using an envelope system for collection, the *Klingelbeutel* was retained.[30]

Besides the continuous building and financing concerns of the voters' assembly, the group saw to the education and discipline of its members and provided an arena for any controversy within the church.

Although the voters' assembly usually included one-fourth to one-third of the total members of the congregation, in its minutes and transactions this group always called itself "the congregation," with women, children, and other males (nonvoting members) subsumed under its leadership and decision-making power.

Early minutes included detailed theological discussions on Luther's *Small Catechism* and on the issues of engagement, divorce, adultery, and parent-child education.[31] Although the speaker's name was not recorded, the monologue or the dialogue heard by the membership certainly functioned as an educational process designed to further their knowledge of Lutheran doctrine and beliefs. Whether this information was always comprehended or appreciated is impossible to know, but the voters' assembly had the opportunity to hear and discuss all aspects of doctrine, whether it concerned issues of theology or morals. Such theological discussions with the pastor probably elevated the men's sense of importance in the congregation and the community. Early pastors used extensive amounts of time detailing and defining Lutheran doctrine and appropriate behavior for the congregation, an example of adult education in its most formal sense, but only male voters had the opportunity to develop expertise in dealing with theological issues and in group decision making. Just as each man was expected to assert patriarchal power over his family, this group knew it alone had the official power to discuss serious religious issues and to form resolutions that affected the total membership of the congregation.

As members struggled with the democratic processes of majority votes and compromise, early meetings must have been somewhat disorganized and rowdy when controversy forced members into opposing factions. In the first two decades of the voters' assembly, it was not unusual for members to have vehement disagreements and to walk out in the middle of a discussion. The secretary finished the minutes of the June 1878 meeting by writing that "the meeting dissolved in an unorderly and angry way."[32] The controversy revolved around the pastor's handling of a young man who had been seen drunk at a dance hall. One group thought the pastor had "gone too far" when he publicly accused the man of "dishonoring his pious parents in the grave" and "ruining the congregation," but another faction argued that the pastor had been far too lenient with the young man. This example demonstrates the serious approach of the voters' assembly toward its duties, but it also reveals the community's struggle in censoring and disciplining its members. Like Gjerde's Norwegian immigrants, the Germans of Block at times used the voters' assembly and theological issues simply to air the dislikes and personal disagreements prevalent in the community.[33]

In 1890, when Pastor H. C. Senne came to Block, he immediately introduced "rules of order on how meetings should be conducted." The men must have been grateful for the structure, for "the congregation praised the pastor's work."[34] Pastor Senne undoubtedly was a rather remarkable man with a powerful presence; according to the minutes he had rules for every church event and a strict code of conduct for laity. According to *Protokoll,* he gave lectures on "how the two sexes should behave together" (not be too friendly at Sunday socials), how parents should educate children (strictly, not sparing the rod), how and where laity should sit during the church service (men on the north side and women and children on the south in front),[35] who should come to confession and how often (always before communion and other times when the pastor felt it was necessary), and finally on the theological definition of a "middle thing" ("a middle thing is something one could do without sinning [gossip] but a middle thing could become a sin if one would give 'public nuisance' "). German-born Senne had a profound effect on the community's German culture, cementing it to the most conservative tendencies of the Lutheran Church–Missouri Synod.[36]

Even with an organized approach in meetings, disciplining members always proved to be difficult and controversial. For most offenses, shame and guilt were used to admonish and control church members. Dancing, parties, drinking, sexual misconduct, or being a public nuisance caused the most problems in the nineteenth century. A "public nuisance" was the term used to describe anyone who publicly denounced the pastor or fellow members to others in the community.

The pastor and elders reprimanded members and often expected public apologies in the voters' assembly or public announcements from the pulpit on Sunday mornings. Most disciplinary action followed a similar pattern. If a member was accused of committing an offense he or she was first addressed privately by the pastor. If the individual was not repentant or felt unjustly accused, a male would be asked to come to the voters' assembly to discuss his case publicly. If the accused was a female, she was not allowed to attend the assembly, but a male would serve as her proxy during the meeting when her case was discussed or else she would have no representation at all. If the individual would not attend the meeting or if the issue was still unresolved, the pastor and elders or sometimes just the elders would make a visit to the individual's home. Again the accused would be asked to come to the voters' meeting to apologize publicly although letters of apology were sometimes used in lieu of a personal appearance. Only in extreme disagreements between the pastor and one or more of the members was the district synod asked to mediate.[37]

Although many members resisted and resented attempts to regulate and control their behavior, the pastor and the congregation typically "won" the argument and the member completed the process of penance. The longest and most controversial case involved a dissatisfied member who had moved out of Block for a brief period in 1895. Pastor Senne was to write a letter of recommendation for his acceptance into another congregation in another county. The dissenting member had left Block because he had been feuding with another member of the congregation; because of this feud, Pastor Senne refused to write a letter on the man's behalf, and they exchanged angry correspondence for three years. The pastor finally wrote the letter of recommendation, but the man did not like it, so he returned in 1898 and vandalized the church pulpit and walls. The voters' assembly backed the pastor and asked the man to repent and pay the damages. The controversy continued until the man returned again to Block in 1906. Still angry with Pastor Senne, he threatened him with a gun and nailed a copy of the church's constitution upside down on the pulpit. To the humiliation of the pastor and the congregation, they felt compelled to ask the county sheriff and county attorney for assistance. Admitting the need for outside secular intervention must have been difficult for the community to accept; they must have felt truly threatened to ask for such help in an affair that was perceived as a private church matter.[38] Incredibly, the controversy did not end until 1927. The man had returned to Block in the 1920s to continue the quarrel with church officers and a different pastor. Thirty-two years after the matter began, the man wrote a letter of apology, and the church accepted it and "forgave" him. Although this case was highly unusual, the moral certainty and determination of the man and the congregation speak for themselves.

Women were rarely involved in controversial or disciplinary cases, but they had little recourse for direct action either to make charges or to defend themselves against accusations. The concept of the patriarchal family forced brothers to defend (or choose not to defend) sisters and husbands to defend wives and children. The male head of the house was expected to keep his household under control and behaving appropriately. Women rarely received the opportunity to defend themselves except to the pastor directly or to the elders privately. Sometimes they were not dealt with directly at all.

One early case is particularly interesting because it demonstrates a woman's lack of visibility but also her ultimate power to persevere. In July 1878 a synod representative attended the voters' assembly to mediate some difficulties between the pastor and the congregation; Mrs. Block had been accused of slandering the pastor to others in the community.[39] Since women could not attend the meeting, her son-in-law, Louis Timken, served as her proxy. "He said with conviction that it was not true that she had talked in a suspicious way . . . and had not caused trouble here with talk." The pastor continued to assert that he had been verbally attacked by Mrs. Block, reporting that he had not asked her directly about the incident but had written a former pastor from Block, asking him to verify charges against her. Discussion continued for quite a while before the synod representative "showed [the pastor] he had made a mistake in not talking with Mrs. Block first." The pastor "confessed his mistake" to Mrs. Block's male proxy and agreed to write a letter of apology to the former pastor.[40] The pastor never saw or dealt directly with Mrs. Block since the church considered females "silent" in the church.

Although controversies continued to occur, they became less virulent and arose less often in the twentieth century. Graebner sees a similar trend in other denominations in the twentieth century and attributes this tendency to the decline of the community's power to control and retain its members because of the continued pressure of Americanization. There also seems to be a correlation between the increase in lay activity and the decrease in disciplinary action against individuals:

> Members of a closed and cohesive immigrant community might risk or endure discipline at least partly because psychologically they had no other place to go. After the language transition in the synod . . . it became much easier to find another Lutheran congregation quite happy to receive unaccredited a fellow believer. . . . For a highly mobile laity . . . church discipline lost the deterrence it once possessed.[41]

Ladies Aid gathering, May 28, 1923.

At times, individuals and families did leave, but most endured, going only later when economic conditions forced families off the farms and into other employment.[42]

For forty-four years the voters' assembly functioned as the only formal church group and served as the primary network for male adults in the congregation. Men exercised their perceived "God-given rights" to direct, control, and make the church into the religious institution they truly believed it should be. Not until 1912 did the adult women in the congregation create their own organization to recognize female contributions and activities formally.

After 1900 *Frauenvereine* ("Ladies Aid clubs") began to appear in some Missouri Synod churches. A few had organized decades earlier, particularly in St. Louis, to sew, mend, wash, and iron for seminary students. Unlike their nineteenth-century Protestant sisters, Missouri Synod women spent little time in women's groups, either secular or religious, partly because of the synod's attitudes toward women's status as subordinate to the concerns of husband and family. Another reason, however, stems from the German-Lutheran view of women's philanthropy: Luther effectively closed the nunneries in Protestant Germany and emphasized "clerical marriage," in which women were to provide charity and giving within the male-headed family only. Not until the mid-nineteenth-century did Lutheran women in Germany begin to create a place for female charity, when the German deaconessate began to function as a means for women to become nurses and later teachers. Similar in structure to a patriarchal family, the deaconessate provided a place for women to live together under the supervision of a married couple; thus single women had an opportunity to leave home and work outside their immediate family.[43]

Since the synod was created in the United States, church leaders in America had no direct experience with this institution in Germany; no precedent existed for female lay activity even in the form of charity or welfare work. Yet as the synod's welfare ministry slowly increased so did the need to allow women to aid in providing traditional female domestic services and domestic production for hospitals, orphanages, schools for the handicapped, and other welfare institutions.[44]

Compared with women in other Protestant denominations, Lutheran women became involved in the church's organizational work quite late. Mainline Protestant groups had begun to create women's reform societies and other organizations established and operated by women in the early nineteenth century.[45] Missouri Synod Lutheran women, similar to Catholic laywomen, remained excluded from church work except for tasks involving cleaning and caring for the church and its priests or pastors. Clergy and male officials excluded women from organizations or any type of involvement that could usurp male authority in the church. Catholic women, however, had the opportunity to join women's religious orders and to work in a female environment of teaching, nursing, and other social services. Eventually, Missouri Synod Lutheran women and Catholic laywomen created formal organizations within the male domains of church philanthropy.[46]

On May 2, 1912, twelve women under the official direction of Pastor F. D. Droegemueller established the Trinity Lutheran Ladies Aid of Block, Kansas. These second-generation women, most of them middle-aged or older, formed an organized group with the stated purpose "to sew and quilt for orphanages, charitable institutions and such who are in need of help." It is difficult to hypothesize why Pastor Droegemueller created this organization and allowed it to flourish. Like the philanthropic male organizations, Ladies Aid societies had begun first in St. Louis and in other urban settings. Droegemueller may have received strong encouragement from the regional or local synod and finally decided to begin such an endeavor. German-born and highly conservative, Droegemueller was a well-known pastor throughout Kansas and held district synod offices for periods of time while he served the Block community; he may have wanted to set an example for other rural communities to follow. Droegemueller also might have initiated the group because he realized that women's domestic skills were valuable to the church and that such a society could serve as a potential fundraising organization for the church in Block.[47]

The monthly meetings took place on Wednesday afternoons and were opened and closed with prayer. Members were asked to pay ten-cent dues each month.[48] Each meeting included a business session and lunch; the rest of the time was spent sewing, quilting, and socializing. Although the pastor was always in attendance for the business meeting and lunch, the group elected its own officers, and its president ran the meetings. The vice-president, secretary, and treasurer gave reports and served as representatives for the organization. The presence of the pastor throughout the business meeting was normal practice; for men or women, no meetings, committee or otherwise, took place without the pastor in attendance.

Early membership was small but grew steadily. By 1935 the group numbered approximately thirty women, but exact figures before and after this date are difficult to assess.[49] The minutes reveal a steady increase in membership until the early 1920s, when membership reached a plateau, but then it surged again in the early 1930s, a pattern that might be explained by a number of factors. Early membership included mostly women in their thirties, forties, and fifties. Younger women with frequent pregnancies and small children possibly could not find the time or the energy to attend meetings and devote a day a month to interests outside their families. Another explanation could be that since middle-aged women began the group, younger women might have waited to join until their age was more commensurate with current membership. Women, like their male counterparts, seemed to gain status with age, at least until they became much older or dependent widows. Although a few single women attended, married women with older or grown children apparently formed the core of the early group.

Desire, time, and finances seemed to determine membership in the

Ladies Aid members with the founder of the group, Pastor F. D. Droegemueller, shortly before he left Trinity Lutheran.

women's group. Some women simply may not have been interested in such a group; others might have been prevented from attending by a husband's unavailability or unwillingness to take them to the meetings. Some women did join when they were older, but others stopped attending during pregnancy or times of family illness and stress. Many of the third-generation women I interviewed explained that their mothers "just did not have the time" or that their fathers would not allow their mothers to attend or hold meetings at the house. Of course if the family was severely strapped for money even the small dues required of the women made membership out of the question. First- and second-generation women controlled little of their productive labor, so dues had to be taken from household money or generous husbands. Since meetings occurred in members' homes, it is also quite possible that the need to host the group proved overwhelming to poorer women who did not feel capable of having a meeting at their home.

The resurgence of membership in the 1930s demonstrated the desire of third-generation women to become actively involved in the church. Membership, activities, and group autonomy increased in the 1930s

and 1940s. Women took themselves to meetings and were less dependent upon husbands or sons to drive them. Many third-generation
women had worked as hired girls in Kansas City and had the confidence
and experience to balance a budget, purchase necessary supplies, and
sell their domestic production for pay. Compared to their mothers,
third-generation women gained extensive experiences in independent
production and consumption.[50]

As group activities expanded so did the organization's budget. During the 1930s and 1940s, minutes of each meeting revealed a growing
array of money-making activities, including sewing and gifts for church
charities and other needy people, consignment opportunities for dinners, quilts, and blankets, and monetary loans and gifts to the church,
school, and the synod. During the depression years, when male contributions probably decreased, the church budget benefited from monetary gifts from the Ladies Aid. By 1938 the society had its own savings
account at the bank and recording secretaries began signing their names
to the minutes, which were written in English instead of in German.
In the late 1930s, women were no longer identified in the minutes by
their husband's first and last name.

Some interesting differences arise when a comparison is made between the minutes of the women's organization and the minutes of the
men's assembly even though the purposes of the two organizations
were vastly different.[51] The women seemed to take a more personal
interest in each other and devoted meeting time and money to help
each other during times of stress or crisis; also, the death of each member was solemnly recorded in the minutes with a special epitaph for
each. In 1926 this response was written into the record-book at the
death of Marie Block Prothe:

> It was the will of the Lord to take a dear and valuable member of
> the club through death from our midst. The one who died was
> Mrs. Heinrich Prothe. We may hope that she died in faith for her
> Savior. She reached an age of 64 yrs. 6 mos. 24 days. She died April
> 10, and was taken to her last rest on the 12th.[52]

Many scholars have discussed and analyzed the gender difference in
content and structure between the personal writings of nineteenth-
century men and women.[53] Although the recording secretaries of the
Ladies Aid knew the minutes were a public record, the women seemed

to provide a mixture of objective comments (lists of decisions and so on) and subjective remarks. Similar to the private writings of nineteenth-century females, the Ladies Aid minutes clearly show a gender difference from the voters' assembly minutes. The women's minutes record transportation difficulties, illnesses, family catastrophies, and other subjective experiences of the membership and the congregation.

Although *Protokoll* described planning for large congregational celebrations (school picnics and mission festivals), the Ladies Aid celebrated and remembered occasions of births, holidays, and anniversary celebrations of the pastor and teacher. Seminary students from the congregation periodically received clothing or money from the women, and the women did not hesitate to plan family gatherings to celebrate their own organization's anniversary.

The character of the women's activities varied little from the domestic chores they performed for their family or the church; however, as with many women's secular organizations, domestic activities prevalent in informal experiences often were "elevated" to formal status.[54] Typically, interactions among women began in kinship networks, with neighbors caring for each other's children and in sharing domestic tasks at home and at church. Nora Ohlmeier Prothe described a women's tradition performed on the Saturday before Palm Sunday services: "We'd get down and take our bucket, we'd walk to church. There they'd have a black kettle and a heap of water. We'd get down on our knees and scrub the floor and wash the windows in that old church."[55] She went on to describe the activity as a social outing for women and children although the work was arduous and "splinters" plentiful. Even before the Ladies Aid was formed, the women took care of the massive spring and fall cleaning of the church.

The organization of the Ladies Aid gave "women's work" some formal status but also provided an array of activities for women who previously had experienced little opportunity to participate in church affairs. It also gave women a chance to learn new skills; although the organization never challenged male authority, women now had a place to develop skills in leadership, money management, and group interaction. The Ladies Aid also gave individual women the opportunity to spend time away from family concerns, to socialize with each other, and to donate their work to larger charitable institutions outside their local congregation. Their donations and handmade items were sent to national and international synod-affiliated programs.[56]

To women who otherwise had little chance to develop skills outside their homemaking environment, the Ladies Aid offered an expanding educational network of associations. Informal activities provide important educational benefits that often may be ignored or viewed as non-educational. In discussing gender as a historical issue in education, Ellen Condliffe Lagemann proposes closer examination of women's nonschool activities. Since women have been traditionally excluded from formal educational settings and since formal education may not be intrinsically valid to women's own experience, informal educational networks (such as the Ladies Aid) may be more important to continued growth and development, particularly for adult women.[57] German-American women, especially rural women, suffered from a lack of educational opportunities since few women's associations existed outside of immigrant churches.[58]

Although undoubtedly influenced by the presence of male clergy and male governing bodies, the Ladies Aid gained autonomy as it continued into the twentieth century, and this group experience may have eased the transition to women's secular groups. In the 1930s and 1940s some of these women also participated in Red Cross work, other quilting groups, and the Farm Bureau Auxiliary. The autonomy and the budget of the Ladies Aid steadily increased, and third- and fourth-generation women made an easy transition to the group after experiencing a formal youth program (the Walther League), begun in 1924.

After World War I, Trinity Lutheran Church organized a formal youth group for adolescents and young adults. Before the organization of the Walther League, some young men and women at Block participated in a loosely organized young people's group called *Jugendverein*; this group of single young adults met intermittently for social activities, but the unstructured organization never gained much local support.

Like the Ladies Aid, the Walther League developed years after the national synod had begun promoting the organization in urban areas. By the 1890s the Missouri Synod recognized that to maintain the support and interest of its young people after confirmation, an organized church program was needed to keep its youth "safe from secular influences."[59] From its inception the organization was coeducational since the morality of young girls was as great a concern (if not greater) as that of young boys. The *Lutheran Witness* began publishing articles about "Why Girls are Ruined," which discussed the secular corruption of "girls in bloomers and boys with bare arms."[60]

Jugendverein *"youth group," 1912.*

Although some all-male youth groups existed in the late nineteenth century, the Walther League was initially organized in a St. Louis church in 1893. Sanctioned and supported by the synod, the idea spread nationally; by 1923 the number of groups had increased by four times the number in 1918. The perceived threat of liberalized social attitudes of the 1920s spurred local congregations to create their own Walther Leagues and the group at Trinity Lutheran in Block officially began in November 1924.

A number of factors probably led Block to integrate its young people into the Americanized version of *Jugendverein*. World War I had left the Block community shaken and in some ways had forced it into increasing Americanization. Consequently, third- and fourth-generation youth in Block participated in the most Americanized of the three formal church organizations. The Walther League allowed young people to socialize, but even from its begining it had a clear educational purpose. Since few adolescents in Block attended high school in the 1930s, young people who remained in the home and did not hire out needed a transitional situation to help them mature and remain religiously integrated into the community until they married. The youth of Block typically joined the Walther League around the age of fifteen and often stayed in the organization until they were married. In fact, so many young adults participated that Block eventually had a junior and a senior group to separate the adolescents from the young adults.

The Walther League of Block had as its educational objectives, "(1) to assist in keeping our young people with our church; (2) to encourage the systematic study of the Bible; (3)to furnish opportunity for education . . . pertaining to the Lutheran Church; (4) to foster Christian fellowship; (5) to provide wholesome entertainment; and (6) to assist in the charitable endeavors of the church." Offices and committees carried no gender barriers, and any young and single communicant church member was allowed to join the group.[61]

For young girls in Block fifteen and older, the Walther League provided a unique opportunity to participate in a formal church organization and to have equal voting power with boys—an opportunity adult women did not share. Girls were elected as officers and as committee members and served as debaters and lecturers on an equal footing with boys of comparable age. One night a month the young people met in the schoolhouse for their business meeting and the presentation of an educational topic. On another night during the month they came together for a social evening with entertainment of their own choosing. Typically, entertainment included wiener roasts, ice-cream socials, guest speakers, and plays presented by the young people. As with all Missouri Synod churches, music was part of any evening's entertainment.[62]

Of course, the pastor and teacher were present and actively took part in the meetings. The young people periodically invited the congregation and used these socials as a way to make money for their organization. Of the three church organizations, the Walther League formed last and had the benefit of an American-born teacher and pastor to lead the group. From its inception the Walther League's structure and activities resembled many other American church youth organizations, its youth assimilating most readily into American social life.

For the youth of Block, most of whom were third- or fourth-generation German Americans, the league provided a valuable opportunity to interact socially but also to develop skills in leadership, organization, and communication. Its secretaries during the 1920s and 1930s meticulously recorded all committees, all educational topics, and which member was assigned to each. Every month a young person presented a topic, sometimes of a biblical nature and sometimes of a more secular concern. In March 1924 Block's league president spoke on "Was There Harm in Dancing?" In 1930 the local newspaper described a Walther League debate: "Resolved, That education is more desirable than wealth." Ada Prothe and Anna Rodewald of the affirmative defeated Joe Minden and Lawrence Windler, who argued for the negative.[63]

Encouraged and supported by the synod's publishing house in St. Louis, the league purchased many educational pamphlets and books. The Walther League of Block maintained a small library in the schoolhouse, and speakers were expected to research their topics before they made their presentations. These social and educational activities were particularly important since most of these young people did not attend a public high school and had little opportunity to develop these skills elsewhere.

The Walther League also provided a way for young people to mingle in mixed-sex groups. Walking or driving to and from meetings afforded privacy for young couples who often had no other excuse to see each other. Regional rallies and meetings exposed the youth of Block to other young people from other congregations. These regional meetings meant trips to Kansas City or drives to other rural congregations often hundreds of miles away. One female interviewee said that these large gatherings were the most fun because she could "meet all the boys from other places" and see what other churches did differently.

Although the Walther League operated under the auspices of the congregation, the pastor, and the teacher, it afforded young people the opportunity to develop many important skills and a certain amount of independence as a group and individually. These same young people as adults would go on to fill leadership roles in the church and to take their place in a job market and an outside world that increasingly sent them further and further from the insulated world of their youth.

Trinity Lutheran Church played a major role in educating four generations in the Block community. This institution provided the most continuous, consistent, and pervasive mechanism for training young and old in how to think and how to live. It was the link to the old country even as it was a bridge to the new. As Maxine Seller notes, "The establishment of the ethnic church provided what might well have been the single most important source of continuity in a world changed in so many ways."[64] Clergy played an almost larger-than-life role in this patriarchal and hierarchical setting. Clearly, the German-born pastors who led the congregation for fifty-eight years reinforced and maintained the German language, culture, and conservative Lutheran doctrine. When combined with the parochial school, the church became a formidable power that withstood two wars against Germany and the pressures of the outside world for over seventy years.

3
SCHOOL

Considering the parochial school an agency for ideal Christian training, a bulwark for church, home, and state, a necessity to preserve true confessionalism and practice, the Missouri Synod made its schools a matter of conscience with laity and clergy alike and thus succeeded in developing and preserving against great odds a system unique in American education.[1]

The importance of the parochial school, especially the elementary school, to the synod and to individual congregations cannot be overstated. These schools in the nineteenth and early twentieth centuries served three major purposes. First, the school was used to inculcate Lutheran confessionalism and *reine Lehre* ("pure doctrine") in children. Church fathers emphasized that the parochial school was "essential to preservation and inculcation of sound doctrine."[2] Children from age six to fourteen daily studied and memorized Lutheran doctrine and beliefs, and on Sunday in church, they heard a repetition of the doctrine that was taught Monday through Friday in their classroom. Lutheran theology, as interpreted by the Missouri Synod, stressed the inerrancy of the Bible and the importance of each believer's faith and acceptance of Scripture and the Lutheran confessions. The acquisition of Lutheran doctrine required the student to articulate, often in the form of rote memory, Lutheran articles of faith and biblical directives. Writing in *Der Lutheraner* in 1873, church leader C. F. W. Walther stated his philosophy on school to his lay and clerical readers.

May God preserve for our German Lutheran Church the gem of parochial schools! For upon it, humanly speaking, primarily depends the future of our church in America. . . . The continued utmost care of our parochial schools is and remains, next to the public office of preaching, the chief means of our preservation and progress.[3]

Jay Dolan compares the nineteenth-century German Lutheran policy to the Catholic church's resolve to educate their children in the faith and language of their European heritage. Like the German Lutherans, Roman Catholics from a variety of ethnic backgrounds filled nineteenth- and twentieth-century parochial schools. Warned by American bishops as early as the 1860s, Catholic leaders feared the effects of Protestantism in the public school system, and many Catholic immigrants resented the public school's focus on Americanization. Dolan stresses the important role that parochial schools played in "handing on the faith" to future generations of Catholics.[4]

An important component of sound indoctrination involved the inculcation of moral values. Clergy and parents representing various religious faiths insisted that the schools participate in the moral education of children. Early schools in the United States, secular or religious, included the teaching of moral values as part of the academic curriculum. For immigrant children, a new "unsettled environment" offered more temptation, and "immigrant parents turned to schools to help instill basic rules, ways of life, moral concepts, and proper social patterns." No school, or a school providing the wrong moral message, could mean a life of sin, wrongdoing, and indigence.[5]

Besides providing religious indoctrination and moral education, the Lutheran parochial school functioned to maintain German culture and language. Most scholars agree that second-generation children "Americanize" more quickly when thrown into public school environments. Indeed this rapid assimilation process often caused a generation gap between the children and their first-generation parents or grandparents who attempted to maintain old-country ways in the home, which sometimes resulted in conflicts, resentments, and alienation.[6]

Most second-generation Missouri Synod children avoided the public school melting pot, with the parochial school bridging the gap between old and new.[7] Before World War I, Missouri Synod elementary schools taught religion and some other subjects exclusively in the German language. German religious holidays, music, and traditions coexisted with American cultural traditions such as spelling bees, school picnics, and box suppers; the schools were essentially bilingual and bicultural.[8] Thus the parochial school, particularly rural schools, did not compete with old-country ways, an important factor since most children lived and worked only with adults and peers who shared similar backgrounds and beliefs. Robert Toepper discusses the importance of the German language to the Missouri Synod:

> Intimate contact with the German language in grade school made possible the continuation of German-language worship services much longer than ordinarily would have been possible. Thus, long-established immigrants as well as their progeny, together with newly-arrived Germans, had the means of communication necessary to facilitate good rapport.[9]

The Trinity Lutheran school at Block in many ways typified most nineteenth-century rural schools in the Missouri Synod. When the congregation at Block called its first pastor in 1868, he also assumed the duties of teacher for the children; few congregations could initially afford a pastor and a teacher. From Monday through Friday, the church building functioned as the schoolhouse, but in 1884 the old church building became the schoolhouse when a new church was built beside it. Pastors at Block served as teachers until H. Fischer was called to teach in 1890. The congregation built Fischer a three-room house two years later, which completed an array of buildings that included a parsonage, church, cemetery, schoolhouse, and teachers' residence only one-half mile south of Block Corners. The church grounds and the commercial center of the village stood in close proximity, symbolic of the connections between the German Lutherans and the community's institutions. Community and church activities often took place in the schoolhouse.[10]

In rural America, the school served as a hub for a variety of community activities. Although social activities were often held in the school building, the parochial school may have played an even more powerful role in an insulated and religiously conservative community such as Block. Children and adults viewed the pastor and the teacher as the main religious role models of the congregation. As caretakers and leaders of the church and school, the pastor's or teacher's presence reminded the community that the purpose of the buildings was religious in nature; school had a religious as well as an educational purpose and was to be taken seriously at all times. Church, school, and home united to send a powerful educational message concerning religion,

Trinity Lutheran School in 1905, at which time only one male teacher was hired to teach all ages of children. (Kansas Collection, University of Kansas Libraries)

learning, and behavior. Even in a social setting, children and adults were immersed in community values, rules, and culture.

Steady immigration and a high birth rate resulted in the Block school's continued growth throughout the nineteenth century. By 1900 the school served seventy-two children in eight grades, and the number of pupils increased as the church steadily grew in the early twentieth century; in 1916 eighty-five students filled the one-room schoolhouse and church annex. But with the addition of the daughter congregation in Paola and because of lower birth rates, the school population decreased during the 1920s; by 1930 sixty-three pupils were attending, and by 1945 only forty-eight students were listed on the roster.[11]

Parents received extensive pressure to send their children to the Lutheran school. The minutes from early voters' meetings reveal pleas and warnings by early pastors urging reluctant or uninterested parents to take better care of their children's spiritual and educational welfare by sending them to the parochial school. In 1871 Pastor Zschoche exhorted the voters, "It is not a small sin against their children when [the father] lets them grow up without instruction in the word of God."[12] In 1889 the voters' assembly was told that their "children would thank parents at their graveside for school."[13]

Just as New England Puritan clergy had done, Missouri Synod pastors compelled fathers to take the major responsibility for their children's education.[14] Fathers not only paid tuition and administered the school, they, along with male teachers, carried the major responsibility for their children's attending the parochial school. *Protokoll* contains extensive lectures on the importance of fathers' responsibility for their children's education. As heads of the patriarchal family, the men of Block functioned as leaders and authorities on all religious or educational issues. The pastor educated the males so that fathers could educate the children.[15] For mothers, St. Paul defined the prescribed role, "And if they learn anything, let them ask their husbands at home."[16] Clearly, the church regarded a mother's contributions as minimal to children's religious education. She was, of course, to be a role model but always subservient to her husband.

Some men resented the additional fiscal burden of financing a school, but the pastor constantly justified the necessity of providing for the parochial school. Even as late as 1911 *Protokoll* recorded yet another exchange between the pastor and a layman. The parishioner asked, "Why do we not send our children into the free schools which are nearly empty and which also have to be [paid for] by us?" The pastor answered immediately

> that we cannot and are not allowed to do so. All of our children belong to the school of the congregation because we have put them through baptism into the arms of the Lord Jesus because they belong to him. In the free schools our children [have] too many temptations and are brought into danger to be misled especially at the age of five and six years.[17]

Some families who sent children to school inconsistently or who chose not to at all may have been responding to the difficulty of transporting their children across rivers or to the danger of sending small children alone to walk the required distance. Another factor may have affected first-generation parents in their reluctance to send children to school, however. Census records show that many immigrants in Block were illiterate or minimally literate, having received little formal schooling in Germany.[18] These individuals may have seen little value in schooling when children needed to be prepared to perform farm and domestic labor, just as the generations of family members before them had. For some immigrant families, the time away from work and the hazards of traveling to school may have outweighed the perceived benefits.

Although most parents in Block wanted to send their children to the parochial school, some families were forced to make special arrangements if traveling to the school forced children to walk many miles or when swollen creeks impeded travel altogether. An oldest child might have been sent to a public school for a year or two until a younger brother or sister could make the journey to the parochial school also. Elsie Prothe Dageforde told of attending a nearby public school for her first two years until she and her younger brother could make the long journey (four miles) to the school at Block together. "We were too young to be driving a horse. And of course, dad couldn't take us every day. And it was so far to walk. We had almost four miles."[19]

It was not unusual for families to make special arrangements for the children with relatives who lived close to the school. Irene Minden Prothe stayed with her aunt and uncle during the week to attend school, and her mother brought the family "ham and potatoes" and other food to compensate for keeping Irene. When Irene was older she drove a horse and buggy to take herself and her four younger siblings to the school at Block.[20]

The most perilous school travel befell the children who lived west of the Marais des Cygnes River, which could be extremely dangerous; crossing the swollen stream to attend school resulted in many close calls. Minnie Cahman Debrick, who traveled to school in a two-wheeled, horse-driven cart, recalled an experience her husband, Ed, had as a boy living "across the river."

Sometimes it rained alot and it would just pour down . . . then they would have to pull the boat up and get the water out of the boat before they could go across. . . . I know he said that his sister . . . [would] get so scared and she would stand up, and that was the worst thing you could do in a boat. They'd have to get her kind of quieted down, and I guess her dinner bucket came open, it was full of water, and sometimes water was almost lapping in the boat.[21]

External view of Trinity Lutheran School, 1930s.

Even with travel difficulties and long walks and rides, the children came to the school in Block in large numbers from September through June. The one-room and later two-room schoolhouse resembled rural public schools, with hats, coats, and dinner buckets lining the back walls. The heating stove was centrally located, with maps, globes, reference books, and chalkboards along the walls. The desks surrounded the stove, and in the winter the children closest to it smothered and the ones farthest away froze. The teacher's desk, elevated on a raised platform, filled the front of the room. Each room featured a small organ that was used by the teacher and students daily.[22]

The curriculum of the school clearly separated it from the district rural schools in the county. Philosophically, the Missouri Synod schools attempted to teach children "to think consistently in harmony with their theology." Moreover, Lutheran teachers and educators were asked "to critically evaluate their educational theories and practices in light of this philosophy."[23]

To ensure the "theocentricism of all things" the synod in 1870 proposed a policy to publish its own schoolbooks. Concordia Publishing House printed a steady flow of prescriptive materials, which told children and adults how to think and behave and described the synod's opinions on religious and secular topics. Nineteenth- and twentieth-century clergy used the publications to warn members against potential secular threats such as birth control, divorce, women's suffrage, labor unions, secret societies, and dancing. Children's textbooks emphasized Lutheran values and beliefs. Synod leaders knew that they had a powerful tool to educate young and old, warning them to shun unorthodox and American secular beliefs.[24]

The school at Block, however, like many other parochial schools strapped for money, used some public schoolbooks for reading, spelling, grammar, arithmetic, geography, and history. This practice increased dramatically after World War I until secular books were used for almost every subject except religion. Oftentimes the school would buy these secular books secondhand from a public school that had purchased new ones.

The daily curriculum focused on religious instruction in the mornings and on other subjects during the rest of the day. Although no teachers' reports or lesson plans survived at the school in Block, the synod's guidelines for curriculum provide examples of weekly routines. Since all synod teachers received the same training, Block's weekly routine was probably similar to the synod's recommendations. In 1890 and 1928 the synod proposed a weekly time schedule suggesting the number of minutes per week that should be spent on each subject.[25]

	1890	1928
Religion	375	360
German	300	optional
English	300	615
German writing	120	
English writing	120	105
General science		15
Geography	120	175
History	120	75
Civics		15
Health		30
Drawing	60	30
Arithmetic	300	300
Singing	60	60

A look at the recommendations for the pre- and postwar years provides some interesting contrasts. Although the 1928 recommendation stated that the teaching of German was optional, the Block school did not discontinue the German language until 1937.[26] As the German language was being phased out, civics, health, and general science were gradually being added to the curriculum. Time for English instruction doubled in 1928, and time for geography also increased. Although religion was still emphasized, it lost fifteen minutes, probably in order to accommodate the additional subjects. Interestingly, history received less emphasis after the war, but the reduction may have been related to the introduction of an American civics class. Only arithmetic and singing remained unchanged. Possibly these two subjects were considered so "value neutral" that American jingoism and adverse legislation had little effect. The importance of music remained; the synod would not give up singing time to accommodate other curriculum changes.[27]

As in most public schools, the "hidden curriculum" abounded in gender differentiations and division of duties.[28] Following the pattern of their parents in church, boys and girls sat on opposite sides of the room; at recess they participated in single-sex games. The teacher assigned boys to bring in wood and coal and to keep the stove ablaze; he expected girls to clean blackboards and floors. Sometimes this task meant coming to school on a Saturday for a fall or spring-cleaning day, just as their mothers made the pilgrimage to clean the church.[29]

Recess included all kinds of ball games and particularly baseball for the boys. Although "the boys always pushed us off the field," the girls also played ball but had their own version, called "tomball."[30] Other girls played "jackstones" and "house," using string and yarn to wrap around twigs strategically placed in the dirt to separate imaginary rooms. Popular games played by both sexes included fox and geese, hide and seek, ring-around-the-rosy, and drop the handkerchief.[31]

Gender definitions showed up subtly but consistently. Minnie Cahman Debrick described a special marching drill the children performed as they practiced for the annual school picnic:

> We'd practice and we'd practice, and the boys carried the flag and we carried a broom over our shoulder and we'd walk. . . . I don't know why, I guess because the boys had the flags and the girls had to have something. So since girls done the housework . . . if you can figure out that puzzle, you can do more than I can.[32]

Discipline seemed to be another area in which gender definitions affected the behavior of both teacher and students. Interviewees consistently told me that boys were disciplined more severely than girls. Disciplinary action was exercised not just to control a child's inappropriate behavior but as a punishment for not knowing the lesson. Although guilt was used to control children, the teacher also used shame as a powerful method of punishment.[33] Corporal punishment was common, and usually the offender would have to go outside, find a stick, and bring it back to the teacher to use in front of the other children. If a child was disciplined at school, then he or she could often look forward to discipline at home as well; parents rarely challenged the authority of the pastor or the teacher in disciplinary practices. Marie Dageforde Monthey said that

> fathers didn't argue if the teacher punished somebody, they didn't go and make the teacher apologize for punishing that kid. They punished that kid themselves when he got home, because somebody told on him that he got a punishment at school and he deserves one at home. So you better not squawk on him.

Some children developed ways to avoid or at least to lessen the corporal punishment. Monthey described a technique the boys used to avoid the teacher's or the pastor's wrath:

> South of the church there's a big hill where it goes down to the valley. [The boy] was sent to get the teacher a switch so he could paddle him. So he got a switch, but every so often [the boy] would cut a little notch in it so that when the teacher go to paddle him, the stick broke in pieces. Oh, I tell you. Those boys used to play tricks on the preacher and the teacher.[34]

Even with the threat of severe punishment, the children of Block, like children everywhere, pushed the limits and took risks to have fun at the expense of an adult. While waiting for the pastor to arrive and begin catechism class, Elmer Prothe and a friend climbed up to the elevated church pulpit and began mimicking the pastor, much to the delight of their giggling peers. "One morning Ed Pope and I sneaked up to the pulpit and preached like [the pastor] did. And while we were a preaching and a preaching all at once [the pastor] walked in. We dropped down [behind the pulpit] and crawled under the table to our seats. We

School chums Theodore Neu and Louis Schultz, 1910. (Kansas Collection, University of Kansas Libraries)

didn't get caught.[35] For Elmer and Ed the stakes were high if they had been caught in such misbehavior. More often than not, the teacher or pastor did catch the prankster, and a young man would receive severe punishment. To receive his whipping the boy was required to bend over a bench and place his head underneath it.

Girls also received physical punishment, and although it appears that fewer girls were punished, the degree of punishment was equally harsh. One angry teacher threw erasers at whispering girls, and others resorted to whippings although the girls were struck on the back instead of on the buttocks. One irate pastor struck a girl so hard with his paddle that "the buttons on the back of her dress flew off." Marie Cahman Debrick told a story about her sister's punishment and their father's intervention:

[The teacher] whipped black and blue streaks on her. And she never told anything, but when she took her bath, my mother noticed it, and so my Dad went and talked to him about it. First [the teacher] was kind of sloughing it off a little bit like it was nothing. . . . I guess Dad told him if he would ever do that again, he would hear from him.[36]

Because of current attitudes toward corporal punishment, it is difficult to put these stories into historical context. Research on nineteenth-century schools shows that male teachers generally used corporal punishment more frequently than female teachers, and children in Block certainly received their share of it.[37] Most of the teachers at Block were male, and the pastor used similar disciplinary methods with older children in confirmation class. The pastor and teacher clearly functioned in authoritarian and sometimes abusive ways. Their behavior, however, was similar to the treatment that some children experienced in the home setting and was commensurate with definitions of male authority and of the biblical directive not to "spare the rod." In discussing their own experiences, interviewees saw nothing wrong with corporal punishment but felt at times that it was far too harsh or excessive.

Much was expected of a teacher in Block and in any other synod school. Besides teaching all ages of children, a teacher functioned as an accomplished musician capable of playing the organ for school and church, as choir director for all choirs, as a role model for adults and children, and in Block's case, as an educated church official serving as secretary for the voters' assembly.

From its inception the synod considered the teacher's position important to the growth and development of each congregation. Until 1857 synod teachers received the same training as pastoral candidates,[38] which was significant since many early pastors taught schools until the congregation could afford to call a teacher or until a teacher became available for service. In Germany, teaching achieved a high degree of respectability, and church fathers encouraged young men to enter the profession in America. Germany had a long tradition of males in the teaching profession, and church fathers continued this tradition in their adopted country. Unlike their male peers in nineteenth-century public schools, Lutheran teachers chose this profession as a permanent career, not as a transitional one.[39] To enhance the teacher's position, the synod's constitution awarded him status as an advisory ministerial member of the synod. After graduation, like the pastoral graduates, a teacher received a "formal call, a Diploma of Vocation," consecrating him to his office for life. He was to be installed by the parish pastor in a formal ceremony before his new congregation.[40]

Until the 1920s the teachers' colleges of the synod made no attempt to parallel the methods of training in secular institutions. The early curriculum focused on religion, reading, and math skills, with an emphasis on music. As in the parochial schools in each parish, teacher training used both German and English.[41] Around 1920, anti-German legislation and public pressure forced the synod to comply with state boards of education in accrediting its teacher-training institutions.[42] The synod also installed district superintendents, similar to those in the public schools, to oversee and to help standardize the widening array of urban and rural parochial schools supported by local congregations.

Supported and directed by the Concordia Seminary faculty in St. Louis, Missouri Synod teachers attempted to dignify their calling by holding yearly teachers' conferences in each synod district and by publishing a professional journal, *Das Evangelische-Lutheran Schulblatt*. Beginning in 1865, the *Lutheran School Journal*, as it came to be called after 1921, published methods, essays, lesson plans, catechizations, and courses for teachers.[43] Controlled and edited by the seminary faculty, the journal demonstrated once again the homogeneity of thought and behavior prevalent in the synod's training of both its pastors and its teachers. District and national teachers' conferences provided a forum for additional input on curriculum and methods.[44]

Until 1890 (and even thereafter if no teacher was available), the pastor at Block also functioned as the teacher. The congregation tried as early as 1885 to call a teacher, but a teacher shortage prevented them from receiving a graduating student. In 1889, at the prospect of losing their pastor, who was called to a smaller congregation with fewer teaching duties, the congregation tried assiduously to obtain a teaching candidate. Although their pastor did accept another call, the congregation received a teacher in 1890; H. Fischer came to Block as its first installed teacher.[45]

With a new pastor and a new teacher in 1890, the church and school at Block entered an extensive period of growth that lasted until 1921, when the daughter church in Paola was organized. Meanwhile, as the numbers of students increased, so did the demands on the teacher. During this thirty-one-year period four different male teachers worked at the school, and nine different assistant teachers or primary-grade instructors taught as many as eighty-five children in eight grades.[46]

Besides teaching, serving as secretary to the voters' assembly, organizing a young people's club, and directing the choir, some of the teachers found time to give private organ lessons to young schoolgirls. Like the Catholic sisters who taught in parish schools, Lutheran teachers gave music lessons to supplement small yearly incomes.[47] During the late nineteenth and early twentieth centuries, many school girls took organ lessons from the teacher.[48] The community actively used and appreciated the musical background of its teachers. When Teacher Fischer left Block to accept a call from another school, the Paola paper called him "one of the best teachers in this county [and] the finest musician this vicinity ever had."[49]

Because of these extensive duties and the growing number of students, in 1906 the voters' assembly made a significant decision—to hire a female teaching assistant to teach the primary grades. By the turn of the century women teachers were the norm in public schools, but the synod had consistently warned against such a practice. In 1872, J. C. W. Lindemann wrote a highly controversial article in *Das Evangelische-Lutheran Schulblatt*, claiming, "Never do we want to or can we employ female teachers in such numbers as they [Catholics] do; we can never entrust our more mature male youth to 'schoolmistresses'; but we might very well use them for the lower classes."[50] Besides the concern about handling large boys, the synod found itself in a theological dilemma. St. Paul's edict on women being silent in the church and the sanctified calling of teachers made the use of women teachers impossible to justify. Only males could hold a sanctified position as a church official, and women were forbidden to teach and were required to remain silent and subservient to males.[51]

Because of economic constraints and changing attitudes, Lindemann's ideas met with widespread resistance throughout the synod's congregations, and in 1906 economic considerations forced Block, along with many other synod congregations, to hire a woman teaching assistant. This decision was "discussed thoroughly," and eventually the pastor's unmarried daughter, Anna Senne, was hired to teach "the two lower grades for one year with a salary of $100."[52] From 1906 until 1945, the school at Block had nineteen teaching assistants besides the

Trinity Lutheran students with male and female teachers, 1940.

teacher who had been called. Eight of these assistants were women, and each taught in the primary grades, working under the male teacher who also served as principal of the school.[53]

Block hired women teachers when men could not be called or when finances prevented adding an additional "called" teacher. Meanwhile, the national synod continued to wrestle with the dilemma of female teachers. Although the doors to one teaching institution officially opened to women in 1919, they were allowed to enroll only in small fixed ratios compared to male enrollment.[54] Writing in the *Lutheran School Journal* in 1925, John Eiselmeier viewed women teachers as a danger to "manly qualities in boys" and to the development of "feminine qualities in girls."[55] He did not elaborate on how male teachers were to develop "feminine qualities" in young girls; it was simply assumed that they would do so. Throughout the first half of the twentieth century the synod's churches continued to hire women as teachers even though the synod refused to train them, except in small numbers, in their own institutions.[56]

Although community values are difficult to assess, the parishioners at Block seemed to have far less difficulty in adjusting to women teach-

Classmates at the end of formal schooling, eighth grade and confirmation class, 1925.

ers than did the male clergy, locally and nationally. Hiring the pastor's daughter served as a safe way to begin this experiment. According to interviewees' comments, the women teachers were well liked and appreciated; interviewees described "warmer" and "kinder" interactions with them. Students who had had women teachers in the public setting or in the early grades of the school at Block remembered feeling less fear and anxiety, emotions that often accompanied interactions with male teachers. Irene Minden Prothe proudly displays a treasured gift given her by a woman teacher, and many other female interviewees spoke fondly of some of their women teachers. For young girls who had few female role models other than mothers and relatives, women teachers served an important function in their lives, providing the first or one of the few interactions they had with a woman who was not confined to domestic chores and family. In a world of stern male authority figures, women teachers provided a welcome friend and role model.

Although the parochial schoolteacher functioned as the main role model for children, the pastor always made his presence felt, particularly with the two oldest classes. There was little doubt that authority in church and school was male. According to Alan Graebner, the elementary teachers determined much of the child's attitude toward religious authority: "Authoritarian legalism received a powerful and early inculcation when not only were 90% of the teachers male but when so many Pastors had such close contact with the children in their parishes."[57]

Even if pastors did not teach the elementary school, their influence was a constant; each day the two oldest classes would walk to the church and participate in catechismal instruction, which consisted of recitation of Lutheran articles of faith and biblical passages. Luther's *Small Catechism* served as the most important instructional book, and children memorized it in its entirety. The pastor asked the rhetorical questions, and the students responded with the prescribed answers.

The Missouri Synod described this educational instruction and the resulting confirmation as a way to keep youth involved in church activities and safe from outside secular influence.[58] Slow, consistent instruction was deemed the superior method of inculcating doctrine in youth, and the synod made no attempt to hide its disgust with and suspicion of Protestant denominations that increased their membership through emotional appeals and tent revivals. "Emotional religion" and the "female illumination of emotions" in revival meetings horrified church fathers and were antithetical to Lutheran doctrine and practices.[59]

Confirmation was never automatic, and only the pastor determined if the child was ready to be confirmed after the two-year instruction course. Although it was unusual, some children were held back. The pastor's word was law, and he, like the teacher, did not hesitate to use verbal or physical punishment to make a point. Marie Dageforde Monthey told of one boy whom the pastor refused to confirm after his two years of instruction and described how the pastor publicly chastized the young man in front of his peers. " 'You've been going coon hunting too much or you've been hunting skunks. I think you ought to study your catechism better. You better lay your songbook and your suit back. You can use that next year.' And that was all he told him. And he already had his confirmation outfit ready."[60]

To prepare the children for confirmation and to ensure that they studied their lessons, the congregation at Block, like most other synod churches, practiced *Christenlehre* ("religious instruction"). Typically remembered with anxiety or terror, *Christenlehre* functioned as a type of Sunday school drill that was performed after the sermon each Sunday morning. The two classes receiving instruction were lined up in the front of the church and required to answer doctrinal questions in the presence of the congregation; an incorrect answer caused acute embarrassment and was not soon forgotten by the humiliated child or parent. Minnie Cahman Debrick described her feelings about *Christenlehre*: "And so many times I'd dream about that, and I'd dream that I didn't get my lesson. I'd just have an awful time. And how embarrassing if you didn't know your lessons. And I know I didn't miss one question when I was confirmed, but brother did I work hard to get that."[61]

After two years of instruction class and *Christenlehre*, the fourteen-year-olds were confirmed on Palm Sunday in the presence of the congregation; they received their first communion on Good Friday. The confirmation ceremony signaled an end to childhood and formal schooling and functioned as a rite of passage into adulthood, its responsibilities, and full communicant membership in the congregation.

After Palm Sunday confirmation, most children never returned to school since the confirmation class was permanently dismissed. If children wanted to complete their eighth-grade year and receive a diploma, they finished at a nearby public school. The purpose of the parochial school was to provide religious education and to prepare the child for confirmation in the church, not to bestow a diploma. Robert Slayton describes this same tradition in Chicago's Polish Catholic neighborhoods. Like the Lutherans of Block, Polish Catholic boys and girls attended school in equal numbers, and formal school ended with confirmation when they were between twelve and fourteen years old with or without a grammar school diploma.[62] After confirmation, children in rural Block and urban Chicago were expected to begin their labors in the work world of their parents.

Since very few boys and girls from Block went to high school until the late 1930s, confirmation marked their entrance into more adult-related activities and concerns at the tender age of fourteen.[63] For girls, this meant taking on more domestic tasks at home or going out to work as a hired girl, either in a relative's or a nonrelative's home.[64] For boys, confirmation meant doing more farm work at home or working as a laborer for a relative or a friend. Illustrating the importance of confirmation as a rite of passage, *Protokoll* contains examples of parents' special requests to have a child confirmed early because of economic or

Confirmation class on confirmation day with the minister, Reverend O.C.J. Keller (left), and the teacher, A. P. Wolters (right), 1928.

family concerns. After the unexpected and early death of her husband, Doris Wilkens Clausen asked the voters' assembly if her oldest son Herman could be confirmed after one year of instruction class, thus freeing him to take on his father's workload on the farm. The request was granted when the pastor agreed that Herman "had the necessary knowledge," and Herman was confirmed, not expecting to complete his seventh-grade year.[65]

Elsie Gerken on confirmation day, 1927. It was common practice for students to have a special picture taken in their new dress or suit.

Trinity Lutheran Church took great pride and interest in its school, and *Protokoll* contains many references to school activities and purchases. The Ladies Aid provided materials and needed supplies to the teacher and students. Parents knew what to expect from the school and accepted the authority of the pastor and the teacher in most decisions, just as they accepted the sometimes harsh authority of the church. For children, lifelong friendships and animosities began in the schoolroom at Block; many students met and courted their future marriage partners there.

The parochial school stood with the church as a highly visible institution educating the young in the values and beliefs of the church and community. For most children, the authority and discipline of the church and school simply reinforced and maintained the cultural values espoused by the family and the community at large. Children learned important lessons for life, lessons that encompassed gender roles, authority, religious imperatives, literacy, and their place in the adult world. Formal education was pervasive, authoritarian, traditional, and total.

4
FAMILY

Initially the ethnic family of the mid and late nineteenth-century America represents a transplanted, adaptive, primary social unit engaged in the business of conserving and rebuilding ethnic culture, and through a distinctive socialization process, of centering new generations in the image of the old.[1]

The German-Lutheran family played a primary role in the lives of all its members—young and old—and along with the authority and prestige of the church and parochial school, the family served to define, reinforce, and maintain cultural values and beliefs. The family also provided a place for all ages to interact, work, and play out socially and religiously prescribed roles and duties.

Because of the rural setting of the Block community, the family farm functioned as both an economic and a social unit. Age, gender, and kinship determined educational networks of association. Nineteenth- and early twentieth-century families in Block depended on each member to perform certain roles and duties to ensure the overall welfare of the farm and home. In discussing this interdependence Kathleen Neils Conzen explains,

In communities characterized by family farms, stages of family life—from the initial formation of the conjugal unit, to the appearance of small children, to their maturation as part of the family work force, to their departure and the aging and death of the original pair—vitally affected the productive capacity of the agricultural unit, and thus the needs of the farm in turn helped shape the family.[2]

The Henry and Marie Block Prothe family, 1911.

This economic interdependence melded together with the Missouri Synod's worldview of family life and of each person's place in and contribution to the family. To paraphrase sociologist Heinrich Mauer's description of this nineteenth-century Lutheran worldview: Society is organized on the order of the patriarchal family. Each individual has his or her place and calling, but whatever that position, the individual is a splinter of a larger whole and subject to a higher natural law. The essence of that law is relationship and interdependence. Each person has a function or a job to carry out and make the best of for God's sake. "Life is a faithful and resigned stewardship in God's inscrutable world."[3]

For most families at Block, "God's inscrutable world" meant living on semisubsistence farms and raising crops and animals for market. Families resided in two-story, wood-frame houses located on 40–160 acres. Almost every house had a large garden nearby and a shed or barn to house animals or hay. Although most first- and second-generation families were large, most houses included only two or three rooms downstairs and one or two bedrooms upstairs. Personal space was limited, and privacy for adults or children was rare. Houses stood one-half to three or four miles apart, so individual families spent large amounts of time with each other in work and in interpersonal relationships.

Most people accepted the crowded conditions as a part of life. Lydia Prothe Schultz came from a successful farming family, but she and the other seven Prothe children shared a house with both parents, a live-in adult cousin, and an elderly grandmother. Ten-year-old Lydia had a choice of sleeping with her grandmother or her two older sisters. She avoided the hairpulling and kicking administered by her sisters and chose to sleep with her elderly grandmother even though German folklore viewed this practice as unhealthy for the child.[4]

German cultural values and Lutheran doctrine emphasized authoritarian and orderly households; coming from a highly structured society, German Lutherans espoused the importance of duty and order. Just as in the settings of church and school, the family was also to be an institution based on patriarchal authority, discipline, and orderly behavior.[5] For children, this worldview usually meant unquestioned obedience in church, school, and home.

In *Growing Up in the Country*, Elliott West decribes rural disciplinary practices in the West as "contrary to the common impression of parents' harsh rule," stating that many parents administered "moderate, even lenient" discipline. Unlike West's informants, who rarely spoke of discipline, specifically of corporal punishment, informants from Block spoke often of disciplinary practices. Ethnic and religious imperatives provided an adequate justification for the use of corporal punishment. The Block community expected and condoned its use and importance in school; therefore, it is reasonable to assume that most home settings accepted this traditional view of child discipline.[6]

Although childrearing practices varied widely among families of Block, discipline was usually administered by both parents. In recalling their childhoods, interviewees often described their fathers as "stern" and quite willing to use corporal punishment in response to inappropriate behavior. "Whatever dad said to do, we did it—now." Although spankings were a part of most childrens' lives, fathers also used other less physical means to teach children a lesson. Frieda Timken Baumgardt described her father's response after her ten-year-old brother, Martin, stole some of the family's eggs to buy chewing tobacco at George Reifel's general store in Block.

It wasn't long before Martin was deathly sick so he hightailed it home and climbed into the loft of the barn and proceeded to get sick. Dad happened to be below and he heard. He said, "Martin is

Lydia Prothe Schultz, age five.

that you? Why are you sick?" Martin told him and [Dad] told Martin to go tell George [Reifel] what he had done and tell him that "you will work for him until he figures he has been paid for that plug of tobacco."[7]

Although fathers seemed to respond harshly to childrens' misbehavior, mothers were described as often talking with children and using a more "tender-hearted" approach. Marie Dageforde Monthey told a story about her mother's response to her and her misbehaving brothers and sisters: "She took us out into the kitchen. She said 'You've all got me today yet but many a little child would be happy if they could have me as [their] mother.' We all broke down and cried."[8] Such dramatic discussions of death were not idle threats during the first fifty years of the Block community. Young children at Block saw their mothers physically weakened by giving birth every two to three years, and most children experienced the loss of one or two siblings through miscarriage, stillbirth, and childhood infections.

Possibly because of the ever-present fear of death, children and parents also forged strong bonds of affection, despite stringent disciplinary methods. Elliott West argues that "mellowing the exercise of authority was another trait fundamental to the modern family — the open expression of companionship and affection among wives, husbands, and children."[9] Although family disciplinary practices were hardly "mellow," families in Block did exhibit expressions of affection and genuine caring for each other. Lydia Prothe Schultz fondly remembered her father's typical behavior of coming into the house and putting his arms around her mother as she cooked dinner. Mildred Block recalled the special Christmas when her father made a surprise gift of a rocking chair just her size; he told her Santa Claus had delivered it to the Block store. And Minnie Cahman Debrick described her mother's special "small" Christmas tree that she had decorated and hidden as a surprise for Minnie on Christmas morning. Minnie felt it was her mother's way of working through the grief of losing an older daughter earlier that year.

These families, in conjunction with the church and the school, taught their children that obedience and authority were primary in everyone's life and that those who did not conform should expect punishment, sometimes severe. But many families also maintained a bond of devotion and caring that incorporated love and affection with punishment when children did not do what was expected or needed.

Although a child's growing-up experiences varied from family to family, children discovered early the importance of work and of duty to family. Because of economic and religious exigencies, children learned vital lessons that prepared them for eventual adult responsibilities and roles in the family. Children provided important sources of labor for the farm, and in turn, the family setting supplied the arena in which crucial lessons in gender expectations and responsibilities were defined and acted out by parents and extended kin. Karin Hausen describes the nineteenth-century German farm family: "The fact that the sexual division of labour tradition plays a central functional role in the organization of family and household must also be taken into account, as must its decisive influence on the socialisation of children, the theory and practice of which it thoroughly permeates.[10]

As part of helping around the house, it was not uncommon for boys to help care for younger siblings.

Although gender work roles were prevalent in families of Block, typically this sexual division of labor did not become polarized until puberty. Young children of either sex often helped their mothers in domestic and household-related activities. Young girls and boys helped sweep floors, wash clothes, carry in coal, weed gardens, milk cows, and care for the small animals that remained their mother's responsibility. Lack of physical strength often kept young boys doing household-related activities until they matured and could participate more fully in heavy farm labor. Elmer Prothe was the youngest of eight children; he laments the hours he spent working with his older sisters helping to clean the kitchen while his older brothers worked in the fields. Besides the cleaning, he recalls the teasing of his sisters and how as the youngest he "was picked on by the girls."[11] Yet an illness or the death of a parent could drastically accelerate a child's entry into the responsibilities of adult work.[12]

Herman Clausen was eleven in 1895 when his father became ill with lung fever and died. Herman's son, Clarence, related a story his father had told about his new adult responsibilities. "And he went to school

Young girls helping with the fieldwork.

another year and then he started farming. And he said he sat there and cried when he couldn't get his harrow onto his sled . . . he wasn't strong enough to. . . . He said he cried, and he'd go ahead and do it and he'd get done. But, you know, he just didn't have strength to do the job."[13]

Besides parental illness or death, a young child's duties might change or be determined by birth order or the number of male and female siblings. As the oldest child, Elsie Prothe Dageforde often worked with her father in the field until her younger brother became old enough to help with the farm work.[14] Work priorities were clear: If her father needed help in the field, a young girl was expected to help if no boys or men were available. After her brother died, Minnie Cahman Debrick was expected to stop her household tasks, hop on her horse, and ride to the field whenever her father's steam tractor stopped and needed to be restarted.[15] And Marie Dageforde Monthey recalled, "I was the oldest and a lot of times Mama would have liked to have had me in the house, but if Daddy needed me, then I would have to help him chase the horses or cows or take care of the sow with the little pigs or something like that."[16] For preadolescent children, age, birth order, and gender played critical roles in determining their work responsibilities.[17]

Although puberty signaled the end of schooling and the beginning of confirmed membership in the church, it also provided the entry into more adult work responsibilities and usually meant paid employment. If not needed by their mothers, young girls began working outside the home, performing domestic services in the home of a relative. Caring for the ill, helping women before and after childbirth, and cleaning houses proved to be the most viable employment for adolescent girls.[18] Boys continued to work with their fathers or hired out as the girls did, working for uncles or other male relatives. These experiences enhanced skills, solidified the gender division of labor, and served to strengthen ties with extended kin. Lutheran doctrine and nineteenth-century ideology espoused *Geschlechtscharakter* (the "complementary nature of the sexes.")[19] By adolescence, children in Block clearly understood the gender-defined cultural and religious messages reinforcing and maintaining patriarchal authority, the subordination of women and children, and the "status" of male work compared to female work.[20] At this stage, both sexes were in a holding pattern, honing their gender-defined skills and preparing themselves socially and economically for courtship and marriage.

For most adult women, marriage and motherhood placed them firmly in the core of the family domain. A woman's role within the family centered on supporting the farm economy, childbearing, childrearing, and providing continuous services to feed, clothe, and nurture all family members. In discussing nineteenth-century German women, Juliane Jacobi-Dittrich describes woman's role of housekeeper, wife, and mother as "deeply embedded in German society."[21] Immigrants in Block had brought these concepts with them, and the German church fathers of the Missouri Synod continued to reinforce woman's role in the home.[22]

Throughout their life cycles, the women of Block continuously contributed to food production for family consumption as well as for sale. Scholars of rural America estimate that Euro-American women were involved in one-third to one-half of the total food production on family farms.[23] Third-generation women of Block described their mothers and themselves as tending huge gardens, performing all cooking and baking tasks, canning, butchering, rendering lard, making apple butter, and seeing to the production of milk, butter, cottage cheese, and eggs. The list of food-related activities is so extensive that the contemporary mind boggles at the amount of skill and toil needed to accomplish them.

Besides overseeing this massive production of food, women provided support services to facilitate male labor. Elaborate meals were prepared for large threshing crews, and hot and cold meals were sent out to the men in the field, usually delivered by one of the daughters. Three to four meals were routinely prepared each day, based on the season and the men's working schedules. Although many female responsibilities were part of a daily routine, women's activities had to remain flexible to accommodate the overall needs on the farm. Some women tried to avoid inconveniencing the men even during childbirth. Marie Dageforde Monthey recalled a story her mother had told her. "It was threshing time and a woman was expecting a baby and that morning she fixed dinner and everything when the men folks came in; well, she went to the door and showed them her [newborn] little baby. She didn't have any midwife, was all by herself. She had her little baby, she dressed it and fixed it up for the threshers."[24]

Besides food production, the women produced nonfood items needed for daily use. Until the 1940s women typically made soap and many clothing items for all members of the family. Without electricity and indoor plumbing, ironing and housework were all-day affairs.[25] Although housecleaning was monotonous and difficult, historically women and particularly German women have been judged on their ability to have a "clean" and "orderly" house.[26]

Often ignored and undervalued but vital to the farm economy was the fieldwork done by the adult women or their oldest daughters. Typically, women in Block worked in the home or around the grounds of the house and barn; however, if the need arose, women filled in for unavailable male labor to aid in the production of cash crops. If they did not work in the fields during times of necessity, certainly their daughters did. Ida Minden Peckman and her four oldest sisters "all had to work in the fields if [father] needed help," shocking wheat, picking corn, and stripping cane.[27] In discussing the stereotypes and realities of nineteenth-century German women in Missouri, Linda Pickle writes, "Peasant women expected to do hard physical labor and were praised for it. . . . [They came from a] high and long standing tradition of industrious homemakers [who] cleared fields and split logs."[28]

Much like the tasks of children of either gender, women's work was based on the overall needs of the family farm. These farmwomen were not Victorian ladies attempting to adapt gender ideology to expand their legal, vocational, or social sphere; with centuries of German peas-

Minnie Cahman Debrick and her cousin prepare to milk the cows, 1918. (Kansas Collection, University of Kansas Libraries)

antry behind them, they worked because the job needed to be done. Their worldview revolved around function and survival. Duty, family, and necessity formed their realities and determined their behavior, which most often encompassed gender-defined roles; but gender differences became irrelevant when crops had to be harvested, animals fed, and "male" work completed.[29]

Besides the arduous and demanding work of providing food, clothing, and various household items, the women of Block gave birth, reared children, and provided continuous support and nurturance for their families. The experience of motherhood and childbirth defined adult womanhood and its duties and responsibilities. First- and second-generation women in Block had large families, many with seven to ten children.[30] These women typically gave birth every two years and could expect to lose one or two children through miscarriage or stillbirth or because of childhood accident or disease. Second-generation

women averaged 6.5 childen, but birth rates dropped dramatically by
the third generation; these women averaged 2.5 children. This dramatic change in fertility patterns reflects the increased assimilation
and Americanization of third-generation women and men. Notably,
most third-generation women worked as live-in domestics outside of
the community, many working in the Kansas City area. Third-generation males also had wider access to the outside world and assimilated
at a faster rate than their fathers or grandfathers. Fertility patterns reflect some specific generational differences, and before the third generation reached adulthood no consistent attempt to regulate fertility is
apparent.[31]

Regardless of the number of children in a family, almost all of the
third-generation interviewees reported losing a sibling or two. The
physical strain on women who had so many children, combined with
the hard work of food production, must have been debilitating. Even if
these first- and second-generation women did not complain, their
daughters and granddaughters saw the strain and commented with awe
and sometimes sadness about their mothers' health. Lydia Prothe
Schultz, eighth child in a family of ten, recalled that she constantly
worried about her mother: "I was always so close to mother. I always
thought something would happen to her and I didn't want it to. She
wasn't too well, having ten kids . . . I'll tell you, and then losing two."[32]

Traditionally, rural families have always had more children than urban families have had; a large labor source, or a lack of it, could make
or break a farm. Espousing the ideological imperatives of unrestricted
motherhood, the Missouri Synod clergy actively discouraged the use of
birth control until the 1930s. The synod felt contraception "perverted"
and "subverted" the purpose of marriage, making the marriage bed "far
filthier than a pigsty."[33] On the issue of women's health, synod clergy
severely attacked women, stating that "in nine cases out of ten [the
plea of health] is a mere subterfuge to mask female selfishness."[34]

The effectiveness of the prescriptive literature is difficult to assess;
however, third-generation women, like other American women, had
fewer children than their mothers or grandmothers. After having her
fifth child and while still lying in her childbirth bed, Lena Prothe
Koelsch reportedly told her husband, "Now listen, this is five girls and
the next one you're going to have."[35] Exactly how women limited their
fertility is a subject not openly discussed; as in other women's informal
networks, the educational information was probably passed verbally

from one woman to another. The local midwife, first-generation Gesche Mahnken Block, held the most knowledge on fertility and birth, but either she did not have enough information or she simply felt God's will should be done. She told her granddaughter that nursing would decrease the likelihood of pregnancy, but no other information was provided. Gesche Block had five children, and some of her daughters had as many as ten.

As women gained control over their reproductive capacity they lost control of the birthing process and the birth room. Midwifery was extensively practiced in Block until Gesche Mahnken Block died in 1911. Highly respected and affectionately known as Grandma Block, she emigrated from Germany as a young wife in the 1850s. Until her death at eighty-seven, Grandma Block delivered most of the babies in the German-Lutheran community. Described as a neat, tiny woman and blind in one eye, Grandma Block traveled to farm houses on horseback until her advanced age restricted her to buggy travel. She would pack a small bundle of clothing and leave the house on a moment's notice or, if necessary, she would arrive two or three weeks ahead of the expected birth and stay until the baby was safely delivered. She left when the new mother and child were out of danger.[36]

Her expertise was unquestioned by members of the community, and apparently her skills were also respected by the local doctors. Unlike many hostile doctor/midwife interactions, the relationship between Grandma Block and the local doctors seems to have been a good one. Local doctors were at least seven miles from the Block community, so Grandma Block's skills in treating the ill and in midwifery were critical to the early generations in the community. She alone decided if a doctor was to be called, and doctors knew to come immediately if she asked for assistance. County commissioner August Frank honored her in her obituary by saying, "In cases of sickness, she was usually the first to offer her services. She will be sadly missed in our community. Grandma Block was one of the noblest women I ever knew."[37] In 1879 Herman Timken was born prematurely and was seriously underweight; his daughter, Louise Timken Mammen, passed the story on: "When my dad was born he weighed barely a few pounds. [Grandma Block] made a bed in a cigar box and used a man's handkerchief for a diaper. She fed him with an eye dropper. Others said he would never make it and she said, 'Oh yes he will.'"[38]

Although Grandma Block was remembered mostly for her midwifery, she also passed along folk remedies for various ailments; often these remedies would be used as part of her midwifery skills in treating newborns and mothers. Folk medicine and midwifery were highly respected and used in Germany, and Grandma Block was simply carrying on a tradition that had been practiced for centuries in her native country. In his research on German-Russian midwifery, Timothy Kloberdanz describes the German midwife as a woman who learned her skills from her mother or another close female relative, making it a family-based tradition. The midwife apprentice would work beside an older midwife, and the training period depended on the types of illnesses the apprentice wanted to treat. Kloberdanz found that sometimes treatments included "laying on of hands and singing."[39] Although there is no information about Grandma Block's training, since she came to America as a young married woman, she probably learned her trade before emigrating. Like European midwives, Grandma Block accepted gifts of food or other items besides monetary compensation. Describing her grandmother's status and expertise, Frieda Timken Baumgardt recalled that Grandma Block was gone a lot, visiting the sick and delivering babies; when she was home, she was an avid reader of German medical books. "That's all she ever wanted to do. When people got sick they would call her and she would go there. . . . One of the doctors said if she couldn't handle it she could call him. She was just about as good as he was."[40] Although women continued to help other women during childbirth, the availability and prestige of American male doctors discouraged young women from taking over from the aging midwives of the nineteenth century.

Many scholars have written about the slow and difficult transition from the reliance on midwives to the use of male doctors.[41] An interesting statistic suggests that even a small community like Block may have suffered during this change from a female- to a male-controlled birthing room. Within three years of Grandma Block's death in 1911, women in Block delivered seven stillborn babies; this number is significant when contrasted to the four stillbirths recorded during the first forty-two years of the community.[42] Having no one to replace the skilled midwife, women may have been hesitant to call a male doctor. More important, Grandma Block's prenatal care for mother and child may have prevented potential stillbirths, and her expertise in "knowing when" to call a doctor may have minimized birth complications that could kill a child in the womb if proper assistance was lacking.[43]

Grandma Block epitomized the type of informal networking among women of all ages in the Block community. Women and girls shared tasks and helped each other within families, among neighbors, and across generations. The female network in Marie Block Prothe's family provides an excellent example of how this networking expanded in nuclear families and intergenerationally. Marie raised four daughters and four sons and cared for her aging widowed mother and elderly cousin; she also performed most of the cooking tasks while her oldest daughter, Lena, sewed for the rest of the family. Lena continued to sew for the family even after she was married, making two confirmation dresses and other items for a younger sister, Lydia; in turn, Lydia helped Lena with the housework in her home. Because Lydia's next oldest sister died at ten, she became her mother's main helper in the kitchen and the house. Another daughter, Laura, stayed with an older married sister, Sena, to help with housecleaning chores. Although Marie cared for her aging mother, it was her mother's task (as long as she was able) to care for any family members who became ill. By the time all the women married, the task-sharing network had expanded to include female members of married kin and three or four generations.

Severe illness or childbirth in a family often meant a young adolescent girl would be hired to come and assist. Young girls were exposed to childbirth, childrearing, severe illness, and death, not just within their own families but in the families of kin and neighbors. Older and widowed women were called upon to help prepare food, clean house, and nurse the sick during times of crisis in the families of kin and sometimes of nonkin. In fact, this informal networking and task sharing was so predominant in many women's lives that participating in a formal organization such as Ladies Aid must have seemed unnecessary or like a "luxury" compared to the busy, ongoing networks among female family members and married kin.

Whether women participated in formal or informal networking with other women, such a highly educational setting included young and old and provided a primary arena for the exchange of skills, emotional sustenance, and support. As rural historian Joan Jensen writes,

> The oldest and most persistent form of community activity has been the development of and participation in women's support networks, networks that women have created for giving assistance and understanding to other women. . . . This fabric of support

August and Katie Windler Prothe and daughter Linda, 1936.

was important both to the women it helped and to the society
they served.[44]

Adult women in Block clearly needed and desired the presence of
other women to share the workload, and young females learned gender-
defined social and occupational skills in the kitchen and at the bedside
of female kin. In a religious and ethnic world that powerfully supported
and maintained the patriarchal family, these women created and controlled their immediate environment that, although restrictive, provided a bulwark against male interference or control. As third-
generation women entered the outside world, these well-learned skills
and lessons provided the necessary basis for their expanding independence and self-esteem.[45]

Just as their wives, sisters, and mothers worked together, men in
Block shared a parallel educational network centered on work and family life. With few exceptions most males in Block farmed, some in conjunction with small businesses, but most devoted their lives to living
off the land and providing for their families through the sale of cash
crops and farm animals. Ethnic ideology and religious imperatives
helped to define and create the roles for males as well as females in the
family setting.

Nineteenth-century German culture deemed patriarchy the most effective and "natural" system for families, urban or rural. Since the family farm was also an economic enterprise, the control and rule of the husband/father was perceived as vital to family organization and productivity. In fact, some scholars argue that the "small family enterprise" reinforced and maintained male authority and dominance.

> In such cases the family members would be thrown into almost constant interaction . . . family loyalty, respect for the family name, the adjudicating of squabbles and conflicts within households, or perhaps in the context of extended kin circles, and a rather pronounced authoritarianism were typical organizational features that kept the head of the household in a dominant position.[46]

In Block, as in many other rural settings, the balance of power and control revolved around gender-defined tasks; for most men this meant seasonal work and hard physical labor throughout much of the year. The farm year opened with the spring thaw, when land had to be cleared, manured, and plowed. As summer approached, hay was cut and crops nurtured for fall harvest. In the summer and early fall, men picked corn and cut, bound, and shocked grain; fall also included extensive woodcutting, butchering, and the storing of vegetables for winter. Winter work focused on repairing fences, machines, equipment, houses, and barns. During a slow period, male relatives hunted to provide wild game as well as to relax; hunting paired an economic necessity with a highly social event. Even elderly men who continued to labor in the fields rarely missed an opportunity to enjoy hunting with sons or grandsons. Marie Dageforde Monthey recalled this story about her elderly father:

> In the evenings, my dad, no matter how hard he worked, if the boys wanted to go hunting, he'd carry the lantern. Clear around this section or wherever it was, they could always see where Grandpa was and that way they wouldn't get lost. Regardless of how old he was, he always had to see the boys where they went hunting.[47]

Farm animals had to be cared for throughout the year, important work that most men attended to themselves. Clarence Clausen described the gradual transition from horses to machines:

> There were some tractors that came in with automobiles but most of them weren't successful. The old horses they stayed . . . they'd have a team walking around and there was a big tongue on it and [the horses] would walk in a circle and they'd have it geared down so they could run a threshing.[48]

Until the advent of gasoline tractors in the twentieth century, men depended extensively on horses, mules, children, and women to aid with the farm labor.

Although females of all ages and young boys crossed gender-defined work roles when necessary, first- and second-generation males in Block rarely ventured into women's work, but apparently there were exceptions. An eldest child, Elsie Prothe Dageforde clearly remembers her parents working together on many tasks. Not only did her mother help in the fields but her father "would help with the gardening and with things around the house" if he had no fieldwork. Marie Dageforde Monthey described one highly unusual incident that occurred during her temporary job helping a family during and after the birth of their fourth child. Struggling with two large washtubs full of dirty bedclothes, seventeen-year-old Marie was shocked to have the father assist with the "messy" task. "He helped wash them, all those dirty clothes. Yeah, he helped me with the clothes and he hung them on the line and everything. It was very unusual. He was one out of a hundred that done that." (She immediately added, "You don't need to put that down, because that's one out of a hundred.")[49]

Although steam tractors and threshing machines greatly reduced the need for work animals, sheer physical strength was still a vital ingredient in successful farming. Adult men feared becoming physically incapacitated and being unable to carry on their heavy work. After the turn of the century, Henry Prothe's chronic physical problems became unbearable, and he became a "cripple," forcing him to acquire a "hired man" to help with the work. Diagnosed as having a form of rheumatism or arthritis, he sought help from local doctors and specialists in Kansas City. When nothing helped, he desperately began sending out for patent medicines advertised in the local papers; one of these medicines

A threshing crew at work, 1920.

"worked," and he resumed his heavy workload, thereby assuring the security of his farm.[50]

Sons' labor played an important role on the family farm and affected its financial well being. Henry Prothe had four sons, but when his illness struck they were still too young to take over his responsibilities, so he had to hire help. His brother, William, had similar health problems, but his sons were able to take over the farm duties and a hired man was unnecessary. Although boys and girls attended school in equal numbers, a young boy's primary responsibility during spring and fall planting took precedence over school attendance. A boy's father and male relatives provided the first important lessons for a future farmer.

Work sharing was not uncommon for men at Block. A family first drew its labor from its immediate kin, and then, if necessary, a hired man would be employed. Adolescent boys were the primary work source, working with fathers, brothers, and uncles. Just as in the female network, three generations were often involved in farm production. Young boys learned their skills from male relatives; if their fathers did not need them, they often hired out to uncles for wages and room and board. Grandfathers and older men continued to work although usually at less physically demanding tasks, eventually assisting sons who took over primary responsibility of the farm.

During times of crisis, wages were not exchanged, and work was shared by male relatives and neighbors to help a man save his crops. If a man became ill or incapacitated, he could count on family and friends

Paul Prothe clearing land with his team of horses, 1920s.

to keep the farm running temporarily; even after a death, arrangements were made to keep the family solvent if there were no sons to take over the farm. Dick Block, Jr., forty-five years old, died unexpectedly in 1894. His one son was far too young to work the farm, so a male relative agreed to rent the land and pay Block's widow a percentage of the cash crops. Combining the income with her domestic produce, the widow was able to keep her house and provide enough money to support her five children.[51]

Even with good health and the help of neighbors and friends, men in Block faced the continuing stress of unpredictable Kansas weather and other natural catastrophes inherent in farming. From 1860 to 1936, ten droughts severely damaged the farm economy of the state.[52] The young immigrant farmers in Block received a particularly destructive blow in the early days of the community.

One day in 1874 the elder Prothes and their sons were plowing the corn. They stopped at noon to eat. A cloud covered the sky. The cloud was grasshoppers. It became so dark that candles had to be lighted in the house to see. When they returned to the fields, the corn that had been so green and pretty was all gone. The other crops were devoured as well as were the leaves on the trees. A little prairie and vegetables were all that could be gathered that fall.[53]

Besides dealing with the heavy workload, stress, and economic responsibilities, the men participated in family matters and male kin networks. In defining the husband/father's religious and social responsibilities, the Missouri Synod had much to say; men were to function as "lord of the house" and were essentially responsible for the behavior of the entire household. "But when according to God's pleasure, children see their mother listening to their father, they will respect their father as lord of the house, and they will obey their mother, the weaker vessel, because of her loving humility toward her husband, who is also her protection."[54] As provider, protector, leader, and disciplinarian, males in Block had extensive social and religious prerogatives over other family members. In addition to representing the congregation in voters' meetings, they were to rectify any problem occurring between church/school authorities and any member of their households. As head of the household, each man was encouraged and privileged to keep order in the family in the best way he could.

Although family styles varied widely, it is reasonable to assume that some husbands and fathers may have abused their power, but there is little data to substantiate if or how often abusive situations occurred. Because this is a sensitive family issue, few people were willing to discuss it. Only recently has contemporary society begun to deal more openly with types of child or spouse abuse. Women and children in Block worked extremely hard, and it is not unreasonable to assume that their labor was at times exploited by insensitive husbands and fathers. "Power over" other family members also may have allowed and encouraged physical abuse since corporal punishment was an accepted fact. Historians who investigate the nineteenth-century German family confirm that wife and child abuse was not an uncommon feature of German family life; in fact, the legal system and German society accepted and expected a certain amount of physical abuse as an important means of family control.[55]

Although to a lesser degree than the women, the men of Block helped care for sick children and wives; some men went to the house of a male friend to provide assistance and nurturance during times of sickness or grief, particularly if physical assistance was needed to clean or to transport an ailing person. Before telephone service began in 1905, male relatives or friends rode out day or night to find a doctor for an ill person or for a woman in childbirth. Traditionally, men sat with a corpse throughout the day and night before burial, dug the grave, and transported the casket to the cemetery. Although men's predominant educational networks were

Two generations: Herman Wendte and his wife, Anna, their son-in-law Louis Schultz, and their daughter Meta Wendte Schultz.

based on economic and occupational associations, the men were never far from the constant social and personal interactions of their immediate families and extended kin.

Similarly, the interactions of grandparents and extended kin expanded the circle of the nuclear family and created an extensive web of connections.

> Uncles, aunts, and cousins interpenetrate the social life of family members, serving as sources for affection, support, advice and to a less extent control. . . . The family remains adult-centered and maintains a place in the sun for the elderly, whose contributions to the household continue so long as they are able to help, and who serve as storehouses of wisdom, legend, and lore, cautionary and exemplary tales all part of the cultural heritage.[56]

Grandparents played an important role in most families in Block. If both grandparents were living, they would maintain a separate household from their children; however, when one died, typically the surviving grandparent would then live with one or more of his or her children. Whether the surviving grandparent was female or male, a son or daughter assumed responsibility for the parent's care and well being; in most cases, however, daughters and daughters-in-law assumed or were expected to assume the burden of care. The exception to this practice occurred if there was an unmarried adult child, who it was assumed, would live with and care for the surviving parent.[57]

Even if an elderly parent lived with one child, other children were expected to help. Sometimes an older person would move from one household to another and visit all of the children for short periods of time. Whatever the arrangement, older people continued to have a major role in the family. Commenting on her grandfather, Michael Walz, Ida Minden Peckman described his routine in the last years of his widowhood.

> He always came over on Mondays when I washed. He'd say, "My, you've got a lot of socks on the line." He'd stay a while and talk and then he'd go on again in the buggy. . . . Then I think he went to Meelie, my little sister, and he just [went] around to talk to everybody and to see everybody. He was real interested in everybody.[58]

For many children, the hired help, particularly hired men, became an important role model for children. Although hired help often filled only a temporary need, some larger farms required the daily services of hired men. These farmhands ate meals, socialized, and sometimes boarded with the family. Children often saw them as surrogate family and at times the hired men reciprocated, bringing candy from town to children, telling them jokes, teaching boys important farming skills, and playing out gender roles with young girls.[59] When ten-year-old Lydia Prothe Schultz made her first pie, the hired men joined her father in a taste test; the men laughed, teased her, and told her it was "flaky but [they] might need more than a fork to cut it."[60]

Sunday afternoon family dinners regularly became social events for extended-kin networks. An entire family would visit another household and typically three generations came together for relaxation, recreation, and conversation. Children played with siblings, cousins, and sometimes nieces and nephews (this was a time when children were encouraged to play and stay out from underfoot). Women prepared a huge meal, and the adults ate while the children played outdoors; only after the adults finished were the children allowed to eat. The men adjourned from the dining room to gossip, argue politics, or play cards, horseshoes, or croquet. The women fed the children, washed dishes, and exchanged stories and talked. Toward evening a light supper would be served from the day's leftovers, and families would return home before dark or soon after.

Sunday afternoons were fondly remembered by residents of Block, and the tradition continued well into the mid-twentieth century. For serious, work-minded people, Sunday afternoon socials created an atmosphere of light-hearted fun and conversation. Families who were isolated throughout the week suddenly found themselves immersed in a relaxed atmosphere where food, conversation, and people were plentiful. This weekly activity firmly bound families to each other, and each new marriage expanded the family network.

Still, for the first and second generation and for many of the third generation, Sunday afternoons maintained age and gender barriers. Children ate only after adults; they played outside and were expected not to be a "bother." Men talked politics, baseball, and played games only with other men, while women prepared food, cleaned up, and even as they chatted, engaged in sewing or mending. Most of the third-generation interviewees recalled few times that their mothers did not take mending with them on family outings. Only by the third generation did socializing become a coeducational activity for adults, and women no longer felt a need to take "work" with them during social visits. Sunday afternoons provided a respite for individuals to interact with others besides the immediate family and allowed women and men the opportunity to relax, using levity and humor in the safe environment of single-sex groups. The interviewees remembered that the best jokes and stories were told in the absence of the opposite sex.

Besides the traditional Sunday afternoon gatherings, three major events of the life cycle linked families together and marked the passage of the generations: Baptism, marriage, and funeral ceremonies celebrated the beginning, maturation, and passing of individual members in the community. When any of these events occurred in Block, all ages within the community attended the ceremonies and witnessed these transitions in individual lives and families. For an ethnic community, "family rituals, ceremonies, and group participation in sacred and pragmatic acts" take on added significance. "At most central family events, such as weddings, during sickness and at burials, immediate neighbors continued to be assigned distinctive functions and roles."[61]

Baptisms, the most common event in the Block community, signaled an infant's birth not just into the community but into spiritual life.[62] Lutherans accept the idea of original sin, so in their doctrine to die without baptism is to die without redemption; therefore they believe a child should be baptized within a few weeks of birth. During the winter months, weather might have delayed the ceremony, but parents took children to be baptized as soon as the child could be taken safely to the church.[63]

The family and the community looked on as the pastor baptized the infant in a special ceremony during the Sunday worship service. The child often had an outfit made just for the occasion and frequently a dinner and celebration would follow the service. Usually this was the child's first outing, so the parents took the opportunity to "show off" the new baby to family and friends.

One of the most important aspects of the baptism was the choice of sponsors (godparents) for the child. Since the child was too young to answer the questions of faith posed by the pastor, the sponsors brought the infant forward to be baptized and accepted and affirmed the faith for the baby. The duties of the sponsors were important and clearly specified in Lutheran doctrine. They were to be more than witnesses; therefore, Lutheran doctrine asked parents to choose sponsors already confirmed in the Lutheran faith. Sponsors were to testify that the child had been properly baptized, to assist in caring for the child's Christian education, especially if the child lost its parents, and to pray for the child.[64]

Customarily a child had three sponsors, although after 1930 most children had only two. The sponsors represented both sexes, but usually a boy would have more male sponsors and a girl more female sponsors. To disperse responsibility and provide security, the three sponsors were often from three separate nuclear families, although they were usually related to the child in some way. The infant's uncles and aunts seemed to be the preferred choice of most parents.

The child's name was formally announced during the baptism, and sponsors were bonded to the child through the naming process. Until World War I, a child was given three Christian names. The first names of the sponsors were usually used for the child's three names, as well as the name of the same-sex parent. In 1876 Jacob Georg Louis Heinrich

Evelyn Schultz soon after baptism, 1914.

Arthur Kettler was baptized and given the first names of his two male sponsors, his father's first name, and two additional names of male relatives.[65]

With a child's identity firmly established through baptism and naming, he or she grew up bound to family and to older members in the community. As the child grew, sponsors participated in celebrating birthdays and eventually the child's confirmation day. Confirmation reestablished the affirmation of faith first made by a child's adult sponsors and signaled the entrance to adulthood. On confirmation day sponsors gave special gifts of Bibles, prayer books, or hymnals to their godchildren. The pastor chose and recorded a specific Bible verse for each confirmand, which served as a guidepost for adult life and was solemnly recorded into the church recordbook.

After confirmation the young person began preparing for the next significant life-cycle marker—marriage, the visible ritual that bonded individuals to each other and to their adult responsibilities within the community. The Lutheran Church—Missouri Synod considered marriage the "normal state for the average adult" for the purposes of "lifelong union, sexual intercourse, procreation of children, and cohabitation for mutual care and assistance."[66] For social and religious reasons most young people at Block expected to be married sometime during their twenties. Young girls in Block typically worked after confirmation, saving money and buying and making items for a trousseau; young boys also began saving money, preparing to take over a family farm or to rent or buy property of their own.

During these years of economic semi-independence and maturation, adolescents began spending time with the opposite sex for socials on Sunday nights. Before the coeducational activities of the Walther League in 1924, young people spent Sunday nights at each others' houses playing games, talking, sharing refreshments, and walking each other home.[67] These walks were most important, for they provided the one opportunity for privacy with the opposite sex. Esther Prothe Maisch discussed these social activities and said, "[We] had a lot of fun around fifteen, sixteen, and seventeen years old. . . . Then [we] would get kind of serious around twenty or twenty-one."[68] "Getting serious" meant making a final decision on a marriage partner. The average age of marriage for females was 22.3 years and for males 26.6 years.[69]

The Missouri Synod had rigid definitions concerning the behavior of young people before and during their engagement.[70] Pastors in the Block community supplied the synod's rhetoric to young people and admonished inappropriate behavior. Marie Dageforde Monthey said that early pastors were particularly concerned about young people, and "if they kept company very long, it was time to get married." After several dates couples were considered "going together," and if the couple decided to break up after seeing each other regularly "that was just as bad as a divorce."[71]

Although couples were scrutinized until officially engaged, it was the marriage ceremony and the activities associated with the wedding that involved community participation. Before a wedding, the residents in Block practiced an old German custom; the ride of the *Hochzeitsbitter*, which provided added excitement and color to the announcement of the betrothed couple. Usually a male relative of the groom, the *Hochzeitsbitter* went door to door inviting families to the upcoming wedding. Riding on horseback and wearing a hat full of colored ribbons, he yelled greetings to each household and sometimes recited a short poem to invite each family to the wedding. Nora Ohlmeier Prothe remembered the excitement of his visit. "He had a hat on whenever he came to invite you [and] you would pin a ribbon on the hat. Then the day of the wedding, he rode ahead of the couple, the procession. They acted crazy; they whooped and hollered and the ribbons would fly."[72]

The wedding ceremony itself was longer than most Protestant weddings, the religious service including participation by the congregation in prayers and sometimes in singing. The attendants were initially all male, but by the 1880s weddings in Block resembled American weddings, with two female and two male attendants for the bride and groom.

Traditionally, the wedding reception was large, with lots of food and drink. During wedding receptions, the Germans of Block seemed to reinforce the stereotype of jovial, fun-loving revelers, as the serious business of everyday life was temporarily forgotten. In 1891 when August Prothe married Katie Windler, the local paper provided an interesting description of the reception held at the groom's home. "There were over 300 guests, and a happier and better lot of people we never saw together. 'The tables fairly groaned under the weight of good things.' . . . After dinner many different games and amusements were indulged in, in which young and old participated in." The merriment continued and eventually someone suggested a collection be taken for the widows and orphans; the hat was passed, and Pastor Senne took the donations and thanked the group. The narrator went on to describe the vast array of presents given to the bridal couple. "The presents were so numerous and it seemed to us very beautiful and useful articles were there, from a small boy's reminder in the shape of a mouse trap, through all the category of parlor and kitchen paraphernalia to a fine span of horses."[73]

Weddings in Block were truly community affairs for all ages. Because of the synod's strong attitudes against outsiders (non-Lutherans), most marriages united two local families. Thus, endogamy served to slow down the assimilation process. Block practiced a type of "regional endogamy" common to German-American communities; if young men or women found no one in Block to marry, it was completely acceptable for the young person to marry a German-Lutheran from another community.[74] Many young men and women from Block (Miami County) married young people from Linn-Palmer (Washington County). As

Henry Wendte and Manda Prothe wedding party, 1914. The man in the center, with the ribbons on his hat, was the groom's brother John who served as Hochzeitsbitter. *(Kansas Collection, University of Kansas Libraries)*

third-generation boys ventured out to work with relatives in Iowa, Illinois, and other states, they often married young German-Lutheran women from their work communities. Before the 1920s most young couples resided close to Block and began farming, but after 1920 economic and personal reasons took some couples to the nearby town of Paola or elsewhere to begin a new life.

Death was the final marker that played a predominant role in uniting families and community. In the early days of Block, funerals served to remind residents of their mortality and the fragility of life. Not until the second decade of the twentieth century did adult deaths equal the number of children lost (anyone twenty-one or older was considered an adult). Between 1868 and 1915 three rows out of six in the church cemetery were devoted solely to children, but this statistic can be explained in part because the Block community was founded by young and middle-aged adults. Thus for the first few decades of the community, children simply outnumbered the elderly.

From 1868 to 1920, the community lost an average of fourteen infants (twelve months or younger) each decade; the average number of children (including infants) who died each decade was twenty-five.[75] Children watched siblings and friends die, attended most funerals, and participated in family rituals where the deceased was always kept at the house. Children served as flower girls, leading the procession to the cemetery, and the schoolchildren were expected to sing at the funerals of their peers.

In addition to the fear of losing children, the adults of Block had to deal with the death of peers and the inevitability of their own demise. Although many men and women lived to advanced ages, the men lived longer on the average. Until the 1920s the average female in Block could expect to die ten to sixteen years sooner than her male peers.[76] Childbirth, childbirth-related problems, and the physical strain of chronic childbearing may have affected the difference in longevity significantly.

Regardless of the sex or age of the deceased, death and funerals brought forth extensive support from family and friends. Women typically prepared the body for burial and brought food to the household for the three days following the death. Nora Ohlmeier Prothe described a scene she witnessed as a young child after the death of an elderly neighbor. "They said they had washed him. He had underwear on, and they had laid him on a board. They always said that was so they'd keep straight. I never will forget that man that laid there. They'd go and buy a coffin and put the man in, they couldn't hold him very long."[77] Men came over to do chores and to sit with the deceased until burial; they also served as pallbearers and gravediggers. The deceased would be taken care of by the family, and after two days the pastor held a short service at the house before the body was buried in the church cemetery. Following burial, family and friends adjourned to the church for a funeral service.

After the turn of the century, the burial procedure changed. Undertakers came to the home and embalmed the body there or would transport it seven miles to Paola, embalm it, and return it to the home. Not until 1921 did the voters' assembly allow coffins to be brought into the church and then only if bodies had been embalmed.[78] Alma Clausen Debrick remembered that in 1932 her deceased grandmother was taken from the home and returned the next morning after the embalming in Paola. She explained that the ever-present fear of mice or small animals coming into the house prevented people from ever leaving the body alone.[79]

The cemetery at Block provided the final resting place for all members of the community, and a unique feature there typifies the community's belief system. An individual was buried not in a family plot but in chronological order of death. In the early decades, when many more children died than adults, the children had their own rows, alternating with adult rows. Four nonchurch members are in a separate row from the congregation, but with that exception, the graves mark the chronological passing of people and time. Since this pattern is not a German custom, one can only speculate that the community once again simply chose the most functional system to bury those who died in the faith. In a larger sense, however, one cannot overlook the possibility that the community viewed death and the spiritual realm as unifying and equalizing phenomena. For those who died in faith, family affiliations paled in comparison to community and religious bonds.[80]

Death completed the family cycle for each resident of Block. The ceremonies and rituals shared within the family and community visibly symbolized the life cycle and connectedness of men, women, and children in every facet of family life. Combined with the economic interdependence of farm life, family interpersonal relationships remained close-knit and structured and served as the most vital of educational experiences. Although each individual had a role to play based on both gender and age, residents of Block lived lives that required cooperation and continuous interdependence within and among families.

The dynamics of family life are complex and difficult to assess since the obvious interdependencies of work and nurturing seem so pervasive. How individuals in a family perceived their roles and their satisfaction with the family unit is often obscured because people are frequently unwilling to put their own interests ahead of the larger family unit. Moreover, historians of the family have often ignored or misunderstood the obvious and subtle areas of tension among family members.[81]

Adult males in the family certainly had an opportunity to pursue their own interests since the social, legal, economic, and religious aspects of patriarchy allowed and encouraged such behavior. Women and children were not to question a husband's or a father's decision and were expected to serve and to tolerate male relatives living with the family. Fathers-in-law, uncles, and male cousins required the same deference and housekeeping services as fathers.

Individual family members acquiesced to patriarchal authority for a variety of reasons. Some individuals probably felt a strong sense of family loyalty and duty, and the German tradition of duty and honor to family would have effectively silenced many potential dissenters. Others saw no alternatives and either left the family unit or silently complied. If the practices of the all-male voters' assembly were any indication of how conflict was resolved, then family members who disagreed probably left their homes and the community if they had an opportunity. A dissenting verbal minority was rarely tolerated; individuals were expected to be silent and acquiesce or to leave. Since compromise was rare, dissenters often left the community out of frustration or simply repressed their opinions. Still, within a family unit, passive resistance caused stress and tension.

The possibility of coercion cannot be ignored in any hierarchical system. Sons needed to wait patiently for a father's monetary assistance or for their inheritance; daughters and wives were financially dependent, and both human and divine sources espoused female subservience. Interestingly enough, third-generation interviewees consistently felt that their mothers and grandmothers tolerated "men bosses" far better than their own generation did. Most of the interviewees saw their own marriages as "more equal"; and although they certainly would not think in terms of a "balance of power," they acknowledged a qualitative difference in husband-wife relationships in their own marriages and even more so in the marriages of their daughters.

By the third generation, families in Block could no longer follow the traditional prescriptive roles for men, women, and children. Job opportunities and the outside world provided new horizons and challenged the traditional family's balance of power. Pressures created by technology, lack of land, urban opportunities, Americanization, and the crises of World War I combined to challenge if not to threaten the beliefs, values, and behavior of the first two generations. Supported and reinforced by the church and school, family life at Block had been the predominant educational experience, but the family remained protected and insulated only until the "outside world" could no longer be ignored or rejected.

5

THE OUTSIDE WORLD

The resentment of German farmers, burghers, and small-town intellectuals against "the world," against the techniques of a competitive society,
attained a religious and ethical meaning. Loyalty to a set of traditional
attitudes became loyalty to a truer faith, obedience to a higher law.[1]

Writing in 1928, sociologist Heinrich Mauer was attempting to describe how religion and ethnicity affected "social accommodation" to
American society. Ethnic and religious biases against the "outside
world" established a powerful bulwark between German-Lutheran
communities and American society. The Missouri Synod tried desperately to shield its members from "the world" through conservative doctrine and the use of the German language in church and school;
preservation of the "true faith" demanded constant and unrelenting
stewardship. "Thus, no matter which way he turned, the German Lutheran immigrant leader saw hostility and harassment, real or imaginary. . . . Every possible social, cultural, and theological weapon was to
be wielded in this battle for survival in a hostile environment."[2] The
term "outsider" was reserved for individuals not in the Missouri Synod
fold, and synod leaders as well as local pastors warned the laity against
interacting with nonmembers. Mildred Block reported a story that her
second-generation mother had told her. "Pastor taught Mom and them
in the school that if you weren't a Lutheran you shouldn't have anything to do with them [outsiders] or go to Hell. That was his philosophy.
Wasn't that something?"[3]

Small rural congregations such as Block successfully insulated most
of their membership for decades, but advances in transportation and
communication made this process more and more difficult, particularly in work-related and economic activities. Moreover, the limited
amount of inheritable or salable land forced some members to seek jobs

and economic opportunities away from the core community. Finally, World War I and its aftermath made attempts at total isolation dangerous and undesirable, both for the synod and for its congregations.

Contact with the outside world proved to be the most important educational factor in promoting Americanization for individuals and families in Block. For rural communities like Block, the transition into the economic, political, and social realm of the outside world proceeded in a slow but steady manner. Initial movement into that outside world usually resulted from economic needs, and in the case of Block, from the production and sale of agricultural goods. First and second generations depended heavily on local markets, and economic life revolved around production for family consumption and the sale of crops and livestock. Neighbors and local merchants in Block, Paola, and other towns in the county had provided the primary market, but by the late nineteenth century farmers in Block were shipping crops and livestock to the regional markets in Kansas City. Small neighboring mills and merchants still did business but to a lesser extent, particularly after automobiles and expanded railroad service made transportation of crops, livestock, and people affordable and routine.

For families in Block, the expanding markets of large-scale commercial agriculture brought changes for every member: "The decisions to respond to economic exigencies, strategies of coping and surviving, were ethnic specific, most often made in the family context or with implications for the family as a first consideration."[4] Gender, age, and generational differences determined each family's response to the changing economic environment. For males in Block, early contact with the outside world revolved around activities related to the sale and purchase of crops, animals, machinery, and land. Men handled cash, made legal transactions, and negotiated prices with local men and businesses throughout the county. Their travel included trips to banks, railheads, mills, mines, creameries, and dry-goods stores. Although the German Lutherans at Block did indeed make every attempt to trade with a fellow Lutheran, if one could not be found then another German would do. If trading with another German was not possible then the men in Block simply traded where they could receive the best price for goods.[5]

The church certainly reinforced trading with other German Lutherans, and first- and second-generation men preferred to trade with someone they knew and trusted. Finding German merchants and businessmen became important for the men in Block if they were uncomfortable about making transactions in English. As businesses in Block lost trade with the growing use of the automobile, German-owned businesses in Paola increased their trade.

Peiker's clothing store and Wishropp's grocery store served the needs of the families in Block who chose to "come to town" to do their shopping or to sell their goods. Both German-born, F. O. Peiker and A. Wishropp began a store together in 1893 on the square in the neighboring town of Paola. When the men separated their business into two stores, Peiker sold clothing and Wishropp groceries. Both men cornered the market on trading with German clientele in the county and hired boys from Block to work for them. Wishropp's grocery store included an upstairs restaurant that often became the highlight of a visit to town. These two men, although not active members of the church in Block, provided an open door for German Lutherans in Block who chose or needed to trade outside the Block community. They also supplied a needed economic link for the community since both participated in the larger, heterogeneous mainstream of "town life."[6]

The economic dealings of the men in Block offered them the opportunity to go out into the world when they chose to do so. In the early days of the community men formed cooperatives; they would alternate in making weekly trips to town to buy for themselves and the others.[7] Although first- and second-generation males worked and interacted mostly with extended family and friends, these economic interactions also afforded men the opportunity to talk, interact, and observe people who did not come from similar backgrounds. Even warnings from pastors could not interfere with the basic economic necessities associated with agricultural work and business. Before the Americanization brought about by World War I, the synod adamantly warned members against bank loans (interest charges were preceived as usury), life and fire insurance, pensions, the stock market, and labor unions, but by the early twentieth century, synod leaders and local clergy had already lost most of their power to determine "business ethics."[8] Most important, economic necessities gave males a justification to socialize with outsiders. Male acquaintances and friendships were formed from these business networks, and as the twentieth century approached, more men from Block became involved with outsiders in political and social functions as well.

For the women the journey to the outside world occurred more sporadically than for their male counterparts. The agricultural economy of the family depended extensively on women's productive capacities and labor—not just for home consumption but for outside markets. Women's production of butter, eggs, cottage cheese, and garden vegetables provided a steady cash income during times of financial stress and in between annual or semiannual sales of farm products and livestock.[9] Marie Block Prothe's white leghorn chickens produced thirty dozen eggs a day, which, along with butter and cottage cheese, brought cash weekly for material, dry goods, or children's shoes.[10] Christina Bergman produced four hundred pounds of butter during 1875.[11] Esther Prothe Maisch reported that in one day she canned as many as twelve quarts of peas from her own garden for home consumption and to sell.[12]

The point here is not to document that rural women worked hard and productively—historians, sociologists, and the women themselves have already done so.[13] The critical factor to examine is the way in which the women in Block connected to the outside world and the way that this world served to educate them. Recent analyses of women's work have focused on the separation of women's and men's work spheres; however, for rural women, the artificial dichotomy of private/public work ultimately does little to assess the amount of work done, the value of that work, or even how women felt about their work.[14] By continuing to evaluate rural women's economic contributions based on public visibility and the amount of monetary exchange, researchers create a "false status" that tells little about what women did and the importance of that work to the family, community, and the outside world.[15]

To compound the problem, historically both women and men tended to underrate and misrepresent the production and exchange of domestic goods. For example, in the early days of the Block community, women used spinning wheels to make wool thread and later wove the thread into garments.[16] According to the 1865 Kansas State Census, Rebecca and Catherine Beckman of Block listed their occupation as "spinner" and Rebecca's daughter Catherine as "weaver," but in later census reports, the three women were simply referred to as "housekeeper." It is quite plausible to believe that these women made garments for others as well as for their families and that some form of barter or exchange was used. And it is quite implausible to believe that after the 1865 census they no longer functioned as spinners and weavers as the census label indicates.[17] These labels, "housewife," or "housekeeper," not only imply a lack of productivity as it was normally measured but also devalue and misrepresent women's contributions and interactions with the outside world.[18]

In her study of women's contributions in dairy farming Nancy Grey Osterud uses the term "valuation" instead of "value" to describe how men and women perceived and thought about women's labor; such a comparison allows historians to note differences between the value (real worth) of women's labor as opposed to the valuation (perception) of it. The reality of women's worth is usually far greater than the perception. Osterud goes on to argue that mechanization and capitalistic expansion reinforced the importance of large market exchange, which increasingly *devalued* women's work.[19] Interviewees from Block remarked on the importance of women's labor on the farm and viewed women of the community as "hard workers." Yet as Osterud and other scholars have demonstrated, women often viewed themselves as "helping out" even when they had completed their daily domestic duties and then supplied farm labor whenever their husbands needed them. Women's labor was flexible, constant, and oftentimes rendered invisible.[20]

Although their labor was often devalued in the family setting, women in Block directly participated in the economic sphere of the outside world. These women produced goods for their families, neighbors, and friends, with the surplus going to Block, Paola, and neighboring general stores that sold their products to consumers. At times the demand for domestic goods may have outstripped the supply.[21] Sometimes goods were bartered; at other times cash was exchanged. The sale of women's domestic production was a reciprocal exchange that took place so often, usually weekly, that money was rarely deposited in banks or documented in legal transactions. Women, unlike men, were not involved in exchanges of large amounts of cash that resulted from annual harvests or the periodic sale of livestock. Although women's domestic goods brought in small amounts of money, the value of women's production lies in the fact that it provided a steady, continuous income.

Women in Block remained important producers and connected directly to the economic sphere well into the 1940s, with the depression of the 1930s only reinforcing the importance of their production. Minnie Cahman Debrick sold cream, "but if I made it into butter, I got a few pennies more."[22] When the demand for domestic production decreased, women's temporary wage labor usually replaced it during times of financial stress.[23] In discussing rural women's economic contributions Joan Jensen asserts that

> although the purpose may have been preindustrial, that of providing for the family, the means were commercial. And the work was of major consequence in providing an economic infrastructure for the expansion of industrial capitalism. Farm families, like urban families, could join in the new era of consumption. The difference was that rural women remained producers as well as becoming consumers of the new industrial age. And that was an important distinction.[24]

Certainly, their economic contributions allowed some women in Block visible entry and exposure to people and places outside the Lutheran community. At first, their connections to the outside world were often indirect, with their husbands serving as middlemen in economic exchanges. Husbands and fathers initially took the domestic goods to market, although many first- and second-generation wives went along, and the task was performed together. How often women traveled to neighbors and to town to sell their own produce varied among families. Often female travel was affected by the age of their children, weather and road conditions, and the quantity of goods to be sold. When men went alone to sell their wives' products, typically the women sent a list of deliveries and items to be traded or purchased in exchange for their products. Irene Minden Prothe recalled that when her mother was "too busy" to make the weekly trip to town she would write up the bill for her goods and make a list of needed purchases; then her father made the trip and returned with the necessary items and groceries.[25]

First- and second-generation women never went to town alone; either they went with their husbands or the husbands went alone. Some first- and second-generation husbands insisted on taking the produce to town themselves and procuring orders for their wives to fill. Marie Dageforde Monthey recalled:

> Mama knew that he had different ones that wanted [produce] and she tried to provide it for him. And the kids stayed at home and helped with the work. Mama didn't often go to town. . . .

> My daddy, he was kind of a salesman like that. He went [to town]
> by himself and we all stayed at home and worked. When he
> came home we'd better have the work done or else he'd give us
> a cussin'.[26]

Age and generational differences clearly mark a transition in these
trips to the outside world. Contrary to the popular conception of large
rural families coming to town on Saturdays, residents of Block told a
different story. In the late nineteenth and early twentieth centuries,
even if both parents went to town together, often older children would
be left at home. The wagon simply could not hold everyone, and children were expected to stay at home. For parents, leaving the children
at home allowed a rare opportunity for privacy and time away from
their family; for children, lack of town travel increased their isolation and provided further insulation from the temptations of town
and outsiders.

For most third-generation women, particularly those who married
around 1920 or later, the automobile provided the opportunity for taking their own goods to town, to barter or to collect the cash themselves.
After purchasing a new car, fathers taught all their adolescent children
to drive — girls as well as boys. The experience of Lydia Prothe Schultz
typifies the transition between second- and third-generation women in
Block. Lydia's father taught her to drive the family car when she was
seventeen, and she often ran errands to town alone. Her mother never
learned to drive a car nor did she drive the family's horse-drawn wagons.
Fathers taught daughters to drive not to instill independence (which it
certainly did) but for far more functional reasons; driving enabled them
to run errands to town for fathers and brothers who could continue to
work in the field until the necessary items arrived.[27] Recent scholarship has suggested that the widespread use of the automobile fostered
dramatic changes in rural women's interactions with the outside world,
both economically and socially.[28]

Advances in transportation and communication also connected the
Block community to the outside world in other work-related ways.
Nonagricultural jobs procured by residents of Block provided temporary and sometimes permanent entry into the outside world. Small
numbers of men worked in local businesses, but most men had to go
elsewhere if they chose not to farm or were unable to rent or buy farm-
land. By the third generation, land became more difficult to divide

Young men at a social gathering, circa 1919.

among sons or sons-in-law.[29] Also, military experiences in World War I
and advances in technology and communication opened doors for some
men in Block, and they no longer chose to farm. Martin Prothe man-
aged a small restaurant in the train depot in Paola. Lou Schultz worked
on his uncle's ranch in Wyoming before returning to live in the county
as a mechanic on the Missouri Pacific railroad. Most men who chose
to leave the farm or were compelled to in order to make a living moved
to nearby towns to acquire work. Paola, the county seat, received most
of these men, and the railroad, small businesses, and shops provided
the employment.[30]

As residents moved from the community, the outside world could
no longer be ignored, and many former residents actively wished to

embrace town living and all its potential influences. By 1921 enough
Lutherans from Block were employed and living in Paola that a daughter church was organized. First Lutheran Church of Paola began with
only a few families (mostly young couples) but grew to rival its mother
church in size and influence. A parochial school opened immediately,
and for decades First Lutheran had only German surnames on its membership roles.[31]

The relationship of the country church and the town church provides some insights into other social aspects of the Block community.
With the exception of one charter member who was in his sixties, the
town church was founded by young and middle-aged men (in their
twenties to forties). Most were third generation and had either moved
to town or chosen to associate themselves with town life. Their mo-
tives are uncertain but probably a number of factors precipitated the
move. First, the Block community had undergone a difficult period
during World War I. Initially, these young married couples may have
chosen to Americanize themselves by living and working in town; land
ownership may not have been available to them even had they wanted
to farm. Second, English was always spoken in the town church, and
from the beginning these couples wished to appear separate from Block
in their male voters' assembly, the Ladies Aid, and in other church activities. Third, male leadership in Block stayed firmly entrenched in
second-generation older males, so the new church may have been one
way for younger men to assert their independence and their willingness
to Americanize.[32]

As with all parent-child relationships, the two churches experienced competition as the town membership grew and gained more
members from the rural church. Still, each church invited the other
as guests for important activities such as Mission Festivals, school
picnics, Walther League activities, and dedication ceremonies. Although the town church appeared less conservative, particularly in
language issues, each church needed the other's support since outsiders were still suspect as new Missouri Synod members.[33]

Even as some married couples willingly began to move away from
Block, limited employment opportunities forced young single men and
women to look for work outside of the community. In the 1920s and
1930s, young unmarried men who wanted to farm but had no land or
source of employment often traveled to another state or German-Lutheran community to find temporary work as farm laborers. Northern

Iowa, Washington County, Kansas, and Garfield County, Oklahoma, offered German-Lutheran communities and employment opportunities for some of these men. Elmer Prothe explained that young men worked in certain locales because they had a relative there or knew someone in a particular German-Lutheran community. Often many of a young man's friends followed him to acquire employment. During times of peak labor (corn-picking season in Iowa), "if one boy knew someone then they'd all go."[34] Travel, new work surroundings, and a chance to make good money sent many young boys to these out-of-state communities. Sometimes boys had to travel farther from home to obtain work. In 1935 the local paper reported that "Lorenz Prothe wrote from Wenatchee, Washington, that he and other Block boys are picking apples in an orchard there." Although most of the young men returned to Block, a few married and stayed, buying land or renting from male relatives or fathers-in-law, which reinforced and maintained the practice of German-Lutheran endogamy well into the twentieth century.[35] These experiences provided the third-generation males with new experiences, although much about their "new" surroundings remained the same—ethnicity, religion, and rural living.

For young single girls in Block, domestic service offered a steady means of transition into the outside world, providing a far greater contrast in lifestyle than that experienced by their male peers. After confirmation and graduation, most adolescent girls began an apprenticeship, initially honing domestic skills by working for the immediate family or relatives in the community. By the end of the nineteenth century, the neighboring town of Paola began advertising for live-in domestic servants or "hired girls." This experience in a young girl's life became a rite of passage prior to marriage. Girls from large farm families hired out to middle-class town families to work for weekly wages and to improve their domestic skills as future wives and mothers.

The importance of this exposure to the outside world cannot be overemphasized, particularly its power in assimilating young girls into American culture. Some scholars convincingly argue that because of this live-in experience, young German-American girls had better English skills and assimilated more quickly than their brothers.[36] Other scholars maintain that domestic service reinforced female stereotypes and dependency and exploited young women with its low wages and monotonous drudgery.[37] But for young girls from Block this hiring-out experience provided an opportunity for increased self-confidence, financial independence, female networks, assimilation into American society, socialization, and technological competence.[38]

Hiring out fit well with the ethnic and religious prerogatives of the Lutheran Church–Missouri Synod. Young girls had been working as domestics for centuries in Germany; synod leaders saw this activity as an appropriate and a "safe" way for a young girl to hone domestic skills in preparation for future family life.[39] Yet synod leaders initially failed to see that this experience would place young girls in the homes of non-Lutherans and thus accelerate the assimilation process.[40]

A close examination of the group of young women who hired out from the Block community reveals some interesting patterns. Sixty-three percent of the young girls confirmed between 1913 and 1937 worked as hired girls.[41] At age sixteen or seventeen, most girls hired out to nonrelatives to begin live-in domestic work. Although the very poorest girls did not hire out, a parent's property holdings did not seem to determine a daughter's work experience, but other factors were significant. Birth order played an important role in determining which daughters worked as hired girls: In Block, 74 percent of all first-born daughters hired out; in contrast, only 49 percent of last-born or only daughters did. Nora Ohlmeier Prothe was the oldest of three girls in a family of eight. When asked why she worked out, she answered, "If you had a couple of girls at home why you couldn't all stay at home."[42] A mother's health also helped determine which daughters hired out. A last-born daughter might have stayed at home to help an ailing mother whose health had begun to fail after many pregnancies and the rigorous demands of the family farm. Lydia Prothe Schultz was the third of four daughters and she hired out for three years but returned home to help her mother when her younger sister married and left the home.[43]

Most of the interviewees reported that they made the decision to hire out. Although pressure to avoid a financial strain and to begin adult responsibilities was great, it is likely that both parents agreed with the daughter's decision to stay or leave since the decision affected the entire family. Before Irene Minden could leave for her Kansas City employer, her parents decided that she needed a new coat to "work in the city." She recalls,

And I never will forget when I was old enough to go to Kansas City to work, and I needed a coat, my Dad had to sell a load of wheat that I could get that coat. And here I thought to myself that I had

Hired girls in Paola, 1918. (Kansas Collection, University of Kansas Libraries)

four brothers and sisters and Mamma bought me that one coat — it took a load of wheat.[44]

This family-decision process supports Virginia Yans-McLaughlin's research on Italian Catholics in nineteenth-century Buffalo. McLaughlin states that family values acted as independent variables on occupational opportunities and that girls and women would find appropriate work that did not challenge cultural values.[45] In the case of girls from Block, financial needs merged with ethnic and religious imperatives concerning gender socialization and work.

Although one less person relieved pressure on the family budget, hired girls from Block were not viewed as additional sources of income for their families; unlike their Irish and Scandinavian peers, girls from Block controlled their money and were not expected to send it home. Wages bought clothes, trips home, or items for their trousseaus. Every hired girl interviewed stated adamantly that she kept her own money and either saved it or bought items for herself. The family did not expect their daughters to send money home, but the young women were expected to care for their own financial needs and purchases.

For $3.50 a week hired girls in Paola did the cooking, housecleaning, washing, and ironing and were expected to babysit if the need arose. If they had evenings free they would make arrangements to spend time with each other, meeting downtown or in one of their rooms. Ida Minden Peckman remembered "going with the girls around the square" on Saturday afternoons because "you always met somebody you knew."[46] Lydia Prothe Schultz remembered times spent with seven or eight girls from Block who worked in Paola around 1918. "We played cards, ate, and talked. We called each other on the telephone. Two or three girls worked at a boarding house and they were given permission to entertain all of us in the hotel dining room."[47]

For young girls coming of age after 1920, domestic service in Kansas City provided a chance for higher wages and educational opportunities in all facets of their lives. The contrasts in urban and rural lifestyles loomed large for young girls who had rarely if ever been away from the Block community and their families. Girls from Block worked for some of the wealthiest people in Kansas City.[48]

Irene Minden Prothe described her fear and excitement when at sixteen she took a job with a family in Kansas City. Some friends met her at Union Station and took her from her first train ride to her first streetcar ride and then to her new job. "Oh my goodness, I will never forget that. I had to wear this apron [uniform] and I had to serve and cook the meal. Things you don't [know], everything was so fancy, and [her employer] had a menu all made up, and there was things on there I had never heard of before."[49] Older girls from Block helped Irene to adjust to her new surroundings, taking her to movies, shops, parks, and to church on Sunday. Driving a car, using a streetcar, and catching a train became routine events for many hired girls. For the young women from Block, attending Emmanuel Lutheran Church in Kansas City opened doors to new people and social activities. Emmanuel Lutheran be-

*Irene Minden Prothe with friends she met at Emmanuel
Lutheran Church in Kansas City, September 2, 1928.*

longed to the Missouri Synod, but in many urban churches the transition to the English language and to Americanization occurred much
sooner than in rural churches. All the women from Block in Kansas
City attended Emmanuel Lutheran and participated in the social activities. A young church member remembered that "they fit in just beautifully. They may have been a little shy, here and there. . . . Mostly they
knew that they belonged."[50]

Train travel home once a month provided a link with Block and the
family. Although some young woman returned home after two or three
years in Kansas City, 64 percent stayed and married men there. Others
came home to care for ill parents, to help the family, or to marry local
men. This hiring-out experience undoubtedly gave young girls from
Block new perspectives about themselves and the outside world. The
combination of urban lifestyle, financial independence, and the chance
to live in homes of non-Lutherans afforded them a broad, rich edu-

Six Block hired girls enjoying a free Sunday after-
noon in Kansas City, 1928.

cational experience unparalleled in the lives of their mothers or
grandmothers.

This generation of women from Block was the first to control their
fertility, the first to take an active role in selling their own domestic
goods, the first to have extensive exposure to wealthy, urban, non-German Lutherans, the first to have independent banking accounts, and
the first to gain experience with the latest in communication systems,
electrical appliances, and transportation. Most important, this educational experience may have facilitated change in their expectations and
behavior. Most women's experiences were similar to Irene Minden
Prothe's: "I learned a lot and I cried a lot because I didn't know how to
do things. . . . I learned."[51]

Work and economic opportunities forced the Block community to
connect with the outside world. Ethnic and religious misgivings about
the secular world could not erase the need to be a part of the economic
system. For men, these economic interactions often laid the ground-
work for networking with outsiders in the political system as well.

In Block, male political behavior in many ways mirrored the voting
patterns and political behavior of the Missouri Synod nationally. In the

nineteenth century, C. F. W. Walther encouraged "political quietism," and pastors were actively discouraged from engaging in any political activity from the pulpit.[52] The distinct separation of church and state was held in high esteem by the synod, and members were encouraged to respect the dictates of the state unless spiritual concerns were under attack.[53]

Although more Missouri Synod Lutherans affiliated with the Democratic party in the nineteenth century, party associations changed according to the controversial issues of the time. Alan Graebner describes two major worries that could galvanize the synod into political activism: fear of Roman Catholicism and fear of moral and social reforms. Missouri Synod Lutherans had an immediate aversion to any person or any issue that appeared to expand the power—real and alleged—of the Roman Catholic church. Legislation sponsored by Protestants that attempted social amelioration proved equally repugnant, particularly Sabbatarianism, prohibition, and women's suffrage.[54] Ironically, nativistic legislation enacted before and after World War I forced the Lutherans and the Catholics into an uneasy alliance to save the parochial school system.

Nineteenth-century Block voted strongly Democratic, and a few residents joined in political activity in the late 1870s. Frederick Luebke's research on German-American political activity provides some possible explanations as to why nineteenth and early twentieth-century Block voted as it did. Luebke concludes that many "religious Germans" resisted the strong anticlerical rhetoric of prominent German-American leaders; also, the early Republican leadership was associated with the antiforeign Know Nothing party.[55] Because the Democrats of the mid-nineteenth century were perceived as more favorable to the immigrant, the Democratic party in Missouri had the support of many German Americans, including conservative Lutherans and the majority of Catholics, who would not join a party that was perceived to harbor attitudes that prompted their worst fears about lack of religious freedom and ethnic intolerance.[56] Block's large Missouri contingency and its religious conservatism probably determined the strong Democratic support.

Although the majority of males in Block did not actively pursue political interests, some individuals ignored synod dictates and enthusiastically embraced American politics. Initial political activity was rare, but interest increased as the Block community expanded to include the bulk of East Valley Township. Soon, males in Block ran for township offices and attended county political conventions, and in 1877 Dietrich Block was elected constable for East Valley Township.[57] All elections in the 1880s, 1890s, and early twentieth century showed solid Democratic votes in the township. In 1880 a county vote on prohibition was soundly defeated forty-nine to eight in East Valley Township.[58] Frustrated with his Democratic constituency, a non-German resident of the township complained to the editor of a county paper that he wanted to move because the "damn Dutch" were "too beastly Democratic."[59] In 1904 East Valley Township elected six delegates from Block and five alternates to the county Democratic convention.[60]

The resentment directed toward the Wilson administration after World War I precipitated the gradual downfall of the Democratic majority in East Valley Township. Through the 1920s the Democrats lost support in the township, and in the 1928 presidential election, East Valley Township resoundingly rejected the Catholic Democrat, Al Smith, for the presidency. Thereafter, the township retained a slim Republican advantage for most elected officials.

The early and strong support voters in Block gave to the Democratic party is particularly interesting because it was greatly affected and nurtured by an outsider. B. J. (Barney) Sheridan, a second-generation Irish Catholic, grew up on a farm in Osage Township and had many friends and associates in the nearby Block community.[61] Sheridan became editor of the *Western Spirit*, the county Democratic paper, around 1880. For over fifty years he actively participated in county Democratic politics and significantly dominated the party for many years. Flamboyant and opinionated, Sheridan grew up near the Germans and eagerly courted their votes. He attended weddings, school picnics, and sometimes special musical events or speeches in Block. More important, he gave these events press coverage, attempting to connect Block to the outside world. In contrast, the other Paola paper, the *Miami County Republican*, gave the Block community little attention until the 1920s. Sheridan's obvious attempts to shelter the Block community from anti-Germanism during World War I may have alleviated the potential for violence, particularly in 1918. Although he could be opinionated and controversial, most residents in Block saw a friend in Sheridan. Herman Clausen, a staunch Republican, never subscribed to the *Miami County Republican* but always read the Democratic paper because "he liked to hear about Barney Sheridan."[62]

Besides the established political parties, another male link to the outside world included group membership in a controversial organization that crossed party lines but had a decidedly political agenda. In 1880 a notice in the Paola paper announced the formation of a new male society that called itself the Anti-Horse Thief Protective Association (AHTA), and men interested in joining such a vigilante group were invited to attend the first meeting.[63] This first AHTA in the county represented a national network of associations (mostly midwestern and western) initially spawned in northern Missouri after the Civil War. By the turn of the century, Miami County boasted ten lodges and some ladies auxiliaries, and Paola hosted the state AHTA convention in 1901. The AHTA was "organized for the purpose of restoring property to its owners" and to "protect private property"; it functioned as a cavalry unit with appointed officers, lieutenants, and riders attending weekly meetings at their appointed lodges. When a theft occurred the local riders gathered at the lodge and then attempted to "arrest thieves and create public sentiment for the observance of law."[64]

Some males in Block wanted to join an AHTA lodge that formed in the community. The vast majority of AHTA men were non-Lutherans, but eventually some Lutherans from Block joined the ranks. Missouri Synod doctrine was adamantly opposed to members joining secular associations, and because the AHTA was also a secret society the organization was inherently "evil" in the eyes of the synod and local pastors. The synod always saved some of its most virulent rhetoric to attack secret societies, which were seen as particularly threatening because members mixed with outsiders and because secret societies often had rituals and prayers. The synod considered such activities heretical. Indeed, Freemasons and other lodges were blamed for much of the nativistic legislation enacted in the late nineteenth and early twentieth centuries; the lay magazines constantly warned members about joining such groups.[65]

In January 1901 at the quarterly voters' meeting, Pastor Senne confronted the men who had joined the secret AHTA, stating that the "oath that one takes and the secrecy are against God's word." At the special meeting called later in the month, the pastor reminded the men that the church constitution they had signed clearly stated that oaths and secret memberships were a "sin." A few of the men apologized and said they would leave the AHTA.[66] One year later some men still remained in the group, and the pastor gave them an ultimatum — quit the

AHTA within the next three months or be excommunicated.[67] Most men rejected the AHTA and remained in the church; however, a few resisted and subsequently left the church. One interviewee told me that her grandfather refused to give up the AHTA and never returned to the church at Block, although his wife attended with her children every Sunday.

Certainly the temptation was great for some men in Block to be a part of a secular organization that wielded power for over four decades. The AHTA was simultaneously feared and supported by people in the county. Although little if anything was ever recorded in the local papers, the vigilantes did more than threaten to find and arrest thieves. Marie Dageforde Monthey described a scene her mother had witnessed as a young schoolgirl. A horse had been stolen approximately three miles east of Block, and the AHTA was called to find the thief.

> [The horse owners] notified the neighbors that they knew [the thief] and [AHTA] all got together and took that man to the barn and hung him in a tree besides the barn where he stole that horse. . . . And when he was dead, they put him on that wagon without sideboards and drove right past the [public] schoolhouse and the teacher let all the kids get out to see that. They wanted the kids to see what the AHTA did to people that didn't behave themselves.[68]

Although secular and secret organizations were forbidden, two church-sponsored activities eventually brought the outside world to Block. Mission festivals and school picnics initially had functioned strictly as church events, but both activities gradually expanded, allowing access first to other Lutherans from outside Block and then to non-Lutherans or outsiders.

The first mission festival documented in the church records at Block was held in fall 1888, although the local paper mentioned a "mission meeting" in 1886.[69] The purpose of the festival was to have a special Sunday service devoted to raising money for Lutheran missionary work. The festival imitated a secular celebration (*Volksfeste*) held in Germany that had begun in the late eighteenth century; the first American mission festival was celebrated in Edwardsville, Illinois, in 1855. Held outdoors, the morning worship service was followed by a dinner and another service in the afternoon.[70]

Block's mission festivals, held in late summer or early fall, grew dramatically when other Lutheran congregations were invited and friends and relatives made special trips to attend the celebration. Families brought blankets and basket dinners and were excited about the opportunity to hear two visiting pastors speak. The festival also provided an opportunity to visit with out-of-town friends and relatives rarely seen the rest of the year. Henry Block's grove, west of Four Corners, provided the outdoor setting that became a yearly favorite of many. Nora Ohlmeier Prothe remembered the scene. "All day, we'd go to the timber. Take our dinner, go all day and have two visiting ministers talk. [They] had seats and a platform where the minister was. They'd take an organ over there . . . That was a great day."[71]

The local paper covered the event in 1893 and pronounced it "grand entertainment," with the sermons "beautifully delivered."[72] In 1900 the mission festival changed a key ingredient that opened the event to non-Germans; beginning in that year one of the two sermons was always delivered in English.[73] In the 1920s and 1930s the local paper always covered the event and never failed to mention the upcoming festival, announcing the names of the ministers and the time of the English service.[74]

Although this event may sound similar to the Protestant revivals that occurred throughout the Midwest, the mission festival operated differently. The purpose of the mission festival at Block was to provide reaffirmation of the faithful, not to convert the outsider. The event never included faith healings, emotional outbursts, speaking in tongues, or dramatic conversions typical of many Protestant revivals. Indeed, initially only German Lutherans were encouraged to attend; certainly any emotional outbursts by the audience would have horrified the clergy, who expected their audience to be silent and docile.

Along with the mission festivals, the school picnic provided an even larger space for outsiders to enter into Block's world and interact socially with members in the community. The "children's feast" began in 1904 and was similar to the mission festival, with a service in the morning and a program prepared by the schoolchildren in the afternoon.[75] By 1910 a six-member committee was preparing the annual school picnic and outsiders were not only welcomed but encouraged to come. The schoolchildren prepared an elaborate program and performed on a platform for parents and friends; songs, marching drills, recitations, and plays were part of the entertainment. Although the

Trinity Lutheran School picnic in Block Grove, 1920s.

picnic had more of a secular than a religious bent, the "Germanness" remained. In 1914 the front page of a local paper reported the celebration and described the scene. "Arriving at 2:00 the Paola Ladies Band surprised the picnic and played music. . . . [a] concert for the Germans with whom a great hit was made by playing 'The Watch on the Rhine' and other airs of the fatherland."[76]

The war changed the character of the picnics, and the celebration in 1918 revealed no German influence but overflowed instead with American patriotism.[77] Like the mission festivals of the 1920s and the 1930s, the annual picnics were well advertised and well attended. In 1925 the local paper reported that the event was "attended by many Paola merchants and families"; the 1932 coverage stated, "A year without the Block picnic would be blank indeed . . . [the picnic was] a country gathering where good order, good will and wholesome enjoyment ruled the hour."[78] Throughout his life Barney Sheridan, editor of the *Western Spirit*, rarely missed a school picnic at Block. In announcing the upcoming picnic in 1935, he wrote a fitting tribute to the community and this yearly event.

The Block community along with the baseball experts and the scientific horseshoe pitchers never fail to put up an interesting and instructive program. The amusements are all lively yet moral, and it reflects the religious, educational, and industrial elements of the German colony which has contributed so abundantly to the good name and progress of Miami County.[79]

Although the mission festivals and school picnics gave the Block community a chance to welcome outsiders on its own terms, other social events enticed community members into town or out to the county for other means of social activity. With few exceptions, most social contact with the outside world occurred after World War I, but one activity, inherently American, lured the men in Block into weekly summer encounters with outsiders. Baseball came to Block's school playground in the 1890s. Although the parochial schoolteacher introduced the game to the children, adult men soon began to play the game in organized leagues, putting them at odds with the pastor, who did not want the game played on Sunday. This was one disagreement the pastor lost since the community was adamant about its team.[80]

From May to September, young men worked six days a week, went to church Sunday morning, and then played baseball in the afternoon. By 1913 the "Block Grays" played teams throughout the county and in western Missouri. The Paola newspaper announced the upcoming games and often printed box scores and descriptions of previous games. The newspaper loved to describe the team's games in ethnic terms: "The Germans from the country have a nifty little ball club and will welcome a game with any of the leading teams of the county." Often called "the bunch from the settlement" or "the Germans," Block's team had supporters "in great numbers."[81] Although described in ethnic terms, the team "spoke American" when it came to baseball. A young man might have been born Heinrich August Herman Wendte, but a great fastball transformed him into "Lefty" Wendte when he walked to the pitcher's mound on a Sunday afternoon.

Until the United States entered World War I the Block team and fans continued to make weekly trips throughout the county, challenging any community with a team. After the war, Block's baseball team disbanded for a while, and the local paper said little about the team in the 1920s. But by the 1930s Block was fielding a strong team once again, and the local papers continued to publicize its exploits.[82]

Block baseball team, circa 1912, first known as the Block Blues and only later as the Block Grays.

Although some women attended the baseball games, this activity was predominantly male. Because men had more social independence and mobility as well as more economic and political contacts, their presence in the outside world typically preceded women's involvement outside the community. Before the 1920s, with the exception of baseball games, the men and women of Block uniformly stayed close to the community, particularly for social activities, but the local and national events brought about by the war and the needs and interests of young adults coming of age during or immediately after the war made isolation undesirable for many individuals in the community. Advances in transportation and communication also made continuous isolation impossible; the third-generations' mobility forever changed the isolationist attitudes within the community.

As members of the community moved to town and as Block's young people found employment farther from home, the residents began to interact with outsiders in secular groups and organizations. School-children became involved in county spelling bees and contests, and families took trips to visit relatives out of state. Both men and women traveled to town more often than their parents or grandparents had. The men joined the Farm Bureau, participated in American Legion activities, and played in sporting events. Women joined "mixed groups" for quilting and service projects, and the Ladies Aid began to serve dinners for auctions and other secular affairs. Weddings, anniversaries, and birthdays included non-Lutheran guests and visitors.[83]

Although far from being integrated into mainstream American society, Block's residents slowly began to emerge from predominantly religious and ethnic networks. Economic, political, and social encounters firmly connected them to the outside world, where new networks taught valuable lessons in Americanization. Age and gender continued to define interaction, but these outside contacts undoubtedly served as a highly significant educational experience.

Unlike many urban German-American communities, the Block community was effective in maintaining a slow, controlled assimilation. By allowing members entrance into the outside world only after careful indoctrination within institutional and family networks, the religious/ethnic community at Block supported and sustained the "old" even when surrounded by the "new."[84] Only war with Germany greatly accelerated the transition, forcing the Block community and many of its residents into the outside world.

6

AT WAR WITH GERMANY

Don't worry about me. I'm proud to fight for my country. But, when you write, don't put a single word in German for it will hurt me and you too. Our letters are read by our officers. English is the best language anyway.[1]

When Will Schroeder wrote this letter from France in 1918, he identified the most difficult adjustment that his community at Block faced during World War I and in the following decades. German culture, especially the German language, was under attack at a national as well as at a local level in the United States. The war with Germany in 1917 and its aftermath profoundly affected the Block community's institutions of church and school. Families and individuals in Block found themselves in an ambivalent struggle to maintain the old and to institute the new. No longer could the community limit its interactions with the outside world; that world had come to Block and would not be deterred. The advent of World War I and its ramifications opened a twenty-year struggle over the use of the German language and its eventual demise in the church and school at Block.

At the national level, it was the Missouri Synod's "Germanness" and its religious exclusivity that threatened American superpatriots and fueled anti-German rhetoric and behavior. The synod's exclusive use of the German language, its pro-German stance before 1917, its rigid definition of the separation of church and state, and its aversion to ecumenical fellowship with other Protestant groups made it an obvious target for charges of un-Americanism.[2] Missouri Synod congregations and pastors received a large share of the abuse from the anti-German behavior precipitated by World War I.[3] Fortunately, in the Block community violence played a minimal role during this controversial time, but other effects on the community and its people were significant and permanent.

Events during World War I and the following two decades clearly demonstrate the ongoing struggle of the Block community as it confronted its religious and ethnic distinctiveness. Responding to external pressure, the church and school in Block, like most Missouri Synod institutions, began a series of transitions designed to avoid potential conflict. The threat of violence from the outside, however, did little to lessen the internal struggles of each local congregation as painful changes became necessary when national and local pressures intensified.

Although nationally the Missouri Synod defended itself against a number of charges of un-Americanism, Block, along with many local synod churches, suffered most from the issue of language. After the United States entered the war in 1917, continued use of the German language was a visible sign of behavior that many Americans perceived as suspiciously unpatriotic. The telephone switchboard in Block resounded with German, all church services were still in German, and the parochial school taught much of its curriculum in German.[4]

As the Allied war effort deteriorated in summer and fall 1917, the church and school in Block made no formal changes to accommodate the mounting pressures. Local county papers that had printed some pro-German essays and articles before April 1917 escalated their anti-German editorials and essays.[5] Certainly some residents of Block found themselves in a quandary and had to censor their comments while in town. Elsie Prothe Dageforde remembered that some residents "kinda upheld Germany in a way, since they originated from there. But I don't think they really said too much because they were afraid to."[6]

In winter 1917–1918, the anti-German rhetoric peaked locally and nationally, and the Missouri Synod could no longer ignore a serious crisis. The *Lutheran Witness* discussed the "turn of affairs" and the pending "disaster" that awaited the synod's institutions if the membership failed to show "outward evidence of goodwill and American spirit."[7] Regionally, midwesterners experienced harassment and violent acts against German Americans. Missouri Synod churches and schools throughout the Midwest were vandalized, burned, and forced to close. German-Lutheran churches came under heated attack, particularly in Nebraska. In describing the problems throughout the Midwest, Frederick Luebke postulates that Kansas had fewer violent incidents because the State Council for Defense was coordinated by Missouri Synod Lutheran Martin Graebner, a professor and clergyman

Two soldiers from Block in 1918, Martin Prothe (above) and George Dageforde (left).

at St. John's College. The Nebraska Council as well as other state councils included "superpatriots" and newspaper publishers who continued to bombard the public with anti-German and inflammatory rhetoric.[8]

Although the church in Block was not vandalized, the community took these threats and the regional vandalism seriously. New Lancaster, located seven miles from Block, seemed to pose a particular threat, and some men from Block spent evening hours guarding the church grounds from vandals. Marie Peckman Wendte recalled,

> We had to be careful [in Block]. New Lancaster people were against us because we still had German in church and school. [We] had people stay up all night to watch the church so they wouldn't burn it down. [Men] kept an eye on it. We had to quit teaching in school for a while. The teacher had to use the American language to make peace.[9]

These external pressures and an important series of events in 1918 convinced the Block community to act. In February and May 1918 the local county papers printed front-page articles on the required registration of "Alien Enemies," and many men and women in Block were forced to register and to be photographed and fingerprinted as potential enemies of the government.[10] In response to local pressure and to pressures from the district synod offices, Block's formal church and school organizations acknowledged and began visibly to support the American war effort. In March 1918 the Ladies Aid openly assisted the war effort by donating ten dollars to the Red Cross.[11] In April the male voters' assembly took its first decisive action in recognition of the war when it voted to accommodate to "war time" by changing the scheduled meeting time of its church and school. In this same voters' meeting, a proclamation read from the national synod gave permission for the men in Block to join the Farmer's Union and encouraged them to do so as a sign of patriotism. The pastor also read a letter from the United States government asking for voluntary troops.[12]

Not until a special meeting in May 1918 did the voters' assembly openly discuss the crucial issue of language. Although the men refused to relinquish the German language, they encouraged the teacher to use more English in the school. The group also ordered five hundred copies of Theodore Graebner's *Testimony and Proof Bearing on the Relation of the American Lutheran Church to the German Emperor*, a thirty-two-page tract commissioned by the national synod's president to alleviate fears about the Missouri Synod's loyalty to Germany. The assembly then decided to buy a "service flag" and to put "Trinity Lutheran" in English on the front of the church building.[13]

The July assembly voted to have the pastor read a letter from the "patriotic committee" after the church service on Sunday and agreed that the annual school picnic was to be a totally patriotic picnic, with the proceeds going to the Red Cross.[14] The schoolteacher, H. F. Klinkermann, played a key role by coordinating the school picnic and the children's activities to create the patriotic theme. He personally led the campaign for Red Cross donations, and even more important, he took a public stance on the necessity of providing signs of American patriotism in the school and community.

The local paper covered the picnic in detail, making much of its patriotic nature. A non-Lutheran and an army chaplain were invited to speak; County Judge C. F. Hensen spoke on "Patriotism as Taught in the Lutheran Schools," and the Lutheran chaplain from Camp Funston was particularly praised: "[The chaplain] made a fine address along patriotic lines. . . . He advised all his hearers to generously support the war savings stamp campaign, liberty bond campaigns, the Y.M.C.A., the Red Cross and all beneficial war work."[15]

    With the war continuing, in October 1918 the voters' assembly post-
poned the fiftieth anniversary celebration of Trinity Lutheran Church
in Block. Another letter from the "patriotic committee" was read,
which advised congregations to discontinue the German language in
the school and to begin the use of public schoolbooks except for religion. Additionally, the voters approved a donation for the Army/Navy
Board sponsored by the Missouri Synod.[16] Although the war ended a
month later, the changes in language policy would continue to dominate voters' meetings for two more decades.

    Given the difficult circumstances, why was the Block community
so reluctant to make changes in its formal institutions of church and
school? Although the reasons are complex and varied, some hypotheses
can be examined. Nationally, the Missouri Synod defended itself by
reciting the importance of the separation of church and state, but the
Block community probably resisted less for political than for personal
reasons.[17] First and foremost, the Block community was composed of
immigrants whose religious and ethnic traits never allowed them complete access to the American mainstream. They were accustomed to
being different from their American and non-Lutheran neighbors and
took a certain pride in their separateness. Their religion stressed and
encouraged this distinctiveness to ensure *reine Lehre*. Alan Graebner
describes this attitude of resistance as a "siege mentality" that affords
the Missouri Synod Lutheran the will to resist even in the face of overwhelming opposition.[18]

    Outsiders both as immigrants and as religious separatists, the resi-
dents of Block, much like the synod itself, observed an "official silence" as long as possible while attempting to insulate themselves
from outside intervention. Religiously and ethnically, the stakes were
high; a defensive posture was not unusual for the Block community if
it felt threatened. The German language was so bound to German culture and religion that to sever language ties was to sever values and
beliefs as well. For some individuals, Americanizing was not particularly threatening or unwanted, but many residents strongly resented
being dictated to or forced to institute change because of pressure from
secular groups or even from the national synod.[19]

    Although there were religious implications that justified Block's re-
sistance to change, people may have opposed it for several other reasons. For many residents, the war was completely unrelated to their
ethnic, religious, and cultural life; families had personal ties to Ger-

many, not political ones. Residents defended their language and culture because they saw them as ultimately unconnected to the war; the community viewed their church as devoid of political connections. Clergy rarely if ever used the pulpit for overtly political reasons. Many individuals in Block viewed the attack on their church, school, and language as a personal affront unrelated to their American patriotism, which, they assumed, they should not have to demonstrate.[20]

Block's institutions and formal organizations eventually responded to external pressures to change, and another important factor facilitated these transitions. The war had a direct impact on families and individuals in the community, forcing some residents to confront their "Germanness" and religious exclusivity in personal ways. Gertrude Krause was a hired girl working in Winfield, Kansas, and attending classes at St. Johns College; she expressed her personal and spiritual anxieties in a letter to Lydia Prothe Schultz in 1917.

> That we are now in war you know without doubt already. Will Martin and Ernest go also? From here over hundreds go into the war, also some of students go into the war. The whole city is crowded with soldiers. Oh, this horrible war! Now nearly all the world is in war. Then maybe the (last day) will come. Don't you think so too? I just feel like that.[21]

Gertrude's letter portrays the ambivalence, frustration, and anxiety felt by many German Lutherans in the Block community. Even as she realized and understood the personal cost of American intervention, she felt frightened and totally overwhelmed by the future such a war might bring.

When the war began in Europe, many families still corresponded with their German relatives and subscribed to German-American newspapers. These two activities connecting Germans in Block to the old country were effectively decreased if not eliminated entirely by 1917 when the United States became involved in the war. Families who had maintained connections for decades suddenly stopped communicating, never to correspond again. The German-American newspapers that carried many national events about Germany and German culture were typically no longer obtained and read in Block's homes.[22]

Besides this severing of European and personal and cultural ties, families experienced the double bind of watching their sons leave for mil-

Camp Funston, near Ft. Riley, Kansas, existed as a boot camp for new recruits during World War I.

itary service, possibly to fight against relatives and friends still living in Germany. Will Schroeder's letter (p. 136) provides insight into the type of indoctrination many third-generation men from Block experienced in the military. German-American men confronted direct and indirect hostility and suspicion in the army; their very names encouraged the special scrutiny of officers or peers. By summer 1918 seventeen men from Block had been drafted into the U.S. Army and sent to Camp Funston, Kansas, for training. The young men, who had rarely if ever been outside Miami County, found themselves thrown into the army's melting pot where their German accents and names often caused them embarrassment or forced them to demonstrate their patriotism.[23] While in camp some men from Block probably observed firsthand the treatment of those men who failed to perform their patriotic duties. Kansas had a large contingency of German Mennonites who were ultimately drafted and sent to Camp Funston. Being German American and conscientious objectors placed a particular burden on Kansas Mennonites, who considered any type of military work as un-Christian. The men from Block witnessed the repercussions when twelve German-American Mennonites refused an order to cut down a sunflower; the twelve were placed in confinement, court-martialed, and sentenced to twenty-five years imprisonment for refusing to work.[24]

In 1918 the outside world came to Block in the form of an executive order from President Wilson, and some women and men experienced a marginal status based on both gender and ethnicity. In February the local newspapers announced Wilson's order requiring the registration of "alien enemies," or all German-born men who did not have citizenship.[25] In June the newspaper announced registration for "alien females"—German-born women without American citizenship or any woman married to a German-born male without citizenship.[26]

This presidential act caused renewed suspicion to be cast on the Block community, as twenty men and eighteen women were required to be photographed, questioned, and fingerprinted at the Paola post office. Stunned and confused, the Block community was appalled that some of its members were subjected to such treatment. Some of the women were particularly indignant since one-third of those required to register were second-generation, American-born and had received full citizenship at birth; their crime was to be married to German-born, first- or second-generation men who had no citizenship. The women, like their male peers, were threatened with immediate deportation if they did not comply with this registration. Esther Prothe Maisch reported that her American-born mother was so angry about the registration that she refused to give the family extra copies of the required photo even though they pleaded for one as a keepsake.[27] Even an eighty-four-year-old grandmother, Rosena Debrick Schultz, was required to be interrogated, photographed, and fingerprinted.[28]

Although the men complied with the required registration, confusion and resentment abounded. Dick Ohlmeier had applied for citizenship papers soon after coming to Miami County, voted in all elections, and assumed he was a citizen; he was startled to discover he was not an American citizen because he had not completed all the required papers.[29] Martin Gerken had farmed in Block for over fifty years after coming to the United States in 1859; when questioned by authorities about his citizenship papers, he replied, "I served three years and three months in the Union army during the rebellion, and till the close of the war. . . . I always understood that made me a citizen.[30]

With sons being sent to war and with trusted and important members of the community being labeled "alien enemies" by the government, the Block community received a boost in morale from a young woman raised

Alien registration photo of eighty-four-year-old Ro-sena Schultz, 1918.

in the community. Elizabeth Block, granddaughter of midwife Gesche Block, provided a much-needed example of American patriotism, honoring the community in an unusual and a dramatic way. Independent and unmarried, Elizabeth had left the community to attend nursing school in Denver, Colorado, graduating in 1911 and then working for five years as "chief nurse" in Santa Rita, New Mexico. When the United States entered the war, she immediately volunteered to go to France to serve in a Red Cross hospital. For months her request was rejected by the government because her parents were German-born. Her loyalties were scrutinized at length, but local county officials, including *Western Spirit* editor Barney Sheridan, lobbied on her behalf. The schoolteacher, H. F. Klinkermann, and others in the Block community wrote letters attesting to her good character and loyalty. Sheridan and Klinkermann had been important promoters of Block's patriotism and realized the symbolic value of Elizabeth Block's service to the war effort. Finally, after months of delays and government investigation, she sailed to France in summer 1918, serving there for one year. The only Miami County woman to serve in France, she was steadfastly honored by county officials and became a symbol of Block's loyalty during the anti-German crises of 1918.[31]

Even as the draft and alien registration noticeably singled out citizens of Block, a more subtle pressure was exerted during spring 1918. In late 1917 and early 1918, county officials began encouraging all citizens to buy liberty bonds and to support the Red Cross. In the eyes of many county leaders, support of the Red Cross and bond drives symbolized patriotic fervor and pride; in fact, donations to either effort usually meant an individual's name and monetary gift would be published in the county papers.

With few exceptions, members of the Block community had not participated in either of these activities throughout 1917. As pressures mounted over the language of the church and school, individuals in Block were growing anxious about their personal safety and thus more cautious about their behavior. Anti-German rhetoric was escalating nationally and locally, so citizens in Block typically kept a low profile, particularly while in town. Elsie Prothe Dageforde explained that "a lot of the people in town were against the German people, so we had to be very careful what we said, particularly if you were in town."[32]

In fall 1917 the *Miami County Republican* reprinted a scathing anti-German article: "The only difference between German Germans and American Germans is that they are 3000 miles apart . . . it would be better if all Germans lived in Germany."[33] The following spring even the *Western Spirit*, whose rhetoric typically had been less inflammatory, reprinted an article written by an "American author of high character and world wide renown," who encouraged his readers to "wipe out the last vestige of sentiment in favor of anything that is German. . . . The German language shall neither be taught nor spoken in America, and every German book must be destroyed. German songs must be cast aside and forbidden and the very name of Germany must be condemned. . . .The word German must be eliminated and the government of Germany destroyed."[34]

It is probably no coincidence that alien registrations in February coincided with the largest bond drive ever in East Valley Township. B. J. Sheridan published a special article complimenting Block's war efforts and praising the residents' patriotism.

There are no more loyal citizens in Miami County to-day than those living in the German settlement of Block, southeast of Paola. . . .The [liberty bond] response was immediate, almost two thousand dollars being raised in one month and still the good

work goes on. Word from there now is that many are already fig-
uring on investing in the third liberty bonds.[35]

In April almost all names listed as new donors to the Red Cross were
from the Block community, and the May and June donation lists from
East Valley Township were replete with German names.[36] Editor Sheridan listed every activity in support of the war that occurred in Block
throughout 1918, usually giving it front-page status. His willingness to
publish and praise Block's war efforts in 1918 probably played a significant role in preventing violence and vandalism against the German-
Lutheran community and its people. Had Sheridan inflamed his readers, as many Kansas editors did, with anti-German or anti-Block sentiment the consequences could have been devastating for the
community.[37]

Many historians labeled the war as the most important single event
in promoting the assimilation of Germans into American culture, but
the Block community continued to spend the next two decades struggling with the language issue.[38] Nationally, the language used in parochial schools had long been a source of turmoil for German-Lutheran
communities and for other religious groups; the Edwards Law (1889) in
Illinois and the Bennett Law (1890) in Wisconsin had attempted to
eliminate foreign languages in all public and private schools.[39] Although these two laws were eventually repealed, World War I brought
a renewed effort to force all private schools to use English exclusively.
In 1919 twenty-one states, including Kansas, had laws requiring English only in public and private schools.[40] States continued to pass
school-language restrictions until two important Supreme Court rul-
ings resolved the issue in the mid-1920s in favor of the parochial and
private schools.[41]

Despite the national and state turmoil, the Missouri Synod continued to uphold the importance of the German language in its schools
and churches. Yet some pastors and laity avidly pushed use of the English language and remained committed to change although conservative powers in the synod refused to budge on the language issue. Even
after the war crises, the Missouri Synod's president "felt the loss of
German language would ruin the school system" and expose the people
"to all manner of American heterodoxy."[42]

The Block community mirrored the national synod's ambiguity on the language issue, and the voters' assembly minutes of the 1920s and 1930s reflect this struggle. In January 1923 the assembly voted for one English service a month to be taught by the "student" who also served as the assistant teacher.[43] The language question was discussed throughout the next two years, but not until January 1925 was another change accepted; the "student" was assigned to teach *Christenlehre* once a month in English.[44]

In January 1929 the voters' assembly initiated a long and controversial process: the translation of the church's constitution into English. For six months, the constitution committee worked to complete the task, only to have it voted down in the next assembly meeting. A special meeting was called for May, but no quorum was present. Finally, in the July voters' meeting, the new English constitution was accepted and read to the entire congregation.[45]

The school received attention in the January 1931 voters' meeting when religious instruction for the three lower grades was discussed to determine whether German or English was to be used. Three changes, all attempting to increase the use of English, were proposed, and all three were voted down. The group agreed, however, that report cards would be used in the parochial school.[46] The April and July meetings that year played a pivotal role in slowing the transition to English. Although the assembly voted for two English services a month, the conservatives won a crucial victory in the July meeting when the proposal was made and accepted that all decisions made by the assembly would require a two-thirds vote instead of a simple majority. Bolstered by the constitutional change, the conservatives attempted to rescind the April decision to have two English services a month. After verbal battling and three different votes, the two English services remained but monthly communion was to be in German in two of every three months.[47]

Each individual change from German to English, whether in church or school, created controversy and compromise, but slowly the pro-English faction found a two-thirds majority to make the changes. In 1932 practicality pushed the voters into changing the Christmas service to English since "there are children who do not know German."[48] Afternoon Lenten services remained in German, however. By 1936 the voters agreed to record their minutes in English but to alternate German and English in the opening Scripture and prayer. Finally, in 1937, after "lengthy discussion and a short recess," the voters agreed that the German language would no longer be used in religious classes, confirmation class, and *Christenlehre*.[49]

Although the institutions of church and school changed slowly, many postwar families and individuals at Block embraced Americanization and made a concerted effort to enter more fully into the outside world. People from Block accomplished the move through wider job opportunities, non-German marriages, secular activities and organizations, and expanded travel opportunities. Young men's military experiences changed perspectives and attitudes, facilitating Americanization. Newborns were rarely given all German names, and radio, print media, and advertising influenced farm and home.

Baptisms and weddings looked less German, and non-German-speaking spouses helped to bring about the necessary increases in English church services. In the 1920s it was not unusual for a new bride to come to church in Block with her husband, take her place across the aisle from him with the other women, and sit through the entire German service not understanding one word of it.[50] Cemetery markers also indicate that the transition from German to English proceeded more quickly among the people themselves than it did in the institutions in the community. Between 1909 and 1919, 48 percent of all grave markers were still inscribed in German; by the end of the next decade, the number of German inscriptions had dropped to 10 percent.[51]

With the creation of a Lutheran church in Paola, town dwellers returned home less and began attending their own institutions of church and school. Young people of the third and fourth generations identified less with the Block community, and some began attending public high school. World War I anti-German sentiments caused embarrassment for community members who wished to embrace American ways; they wanted to prove it was possible to be good Lutherans and still speak and "act" like Americans. Block clearly lost most of its "liberalizing force" to the town church, where the language and cultural changes were rarely controversial. Dissenters from Block simply drove to town for church.

As families and individuals made the necessary transitions and as the church and school slowly Americanized, Germany's war activities in the late 1930s once again forced the Block community to examine its ways. In 1935 the community had the opportunity to hear a Missouri Synod pastor speak on his recent trip to Hitler's Germany; five

Block soldier serving in New Guinea during World War II.

hundred people attended, and the event was covered by the *Western Spirit*.[52] This speech was probably the community's last direct link with prewar Germany.

When World War II began in Europe, the Block community had much less to fear from outsiders and was more unified in its response. Before the United States entered the war, the voters' assembly had approved two "collections" for relief aid and for the Army/Navy chaplains.[53] When young men from Block began to enter the military in 1942, the assembly quickly sent money for the synod's Army/Navy chaplains and voted to purchase a service flag and an honor roll;[54] the Ladies Aid purchased a one-hundred-dollar war bond.[55] However willing the church was to promote public displays of loyalty, the voters of Block still struggled with the language issue within the church. In October 1942 the assembly voted down an attempt to reduce the number of German services to one a month. Although a strong majority (60 percent) voted for the change, once again the requirement

Another World War II soldier from Block, Elmer Maisch, who worked in the army motor pool and drove an ambulance in England.

for a two-thirds majority saved the German language and postponed the transition to English.[56]

By the war's end in 1945, the voters' assembly had taken two more special collections and had resolved to have a special "Thanks Service" in celebration of armistice in Europe;[57] the Ladies Aid bought another one-hundred-dollar war bond in 1944.[58] The effects of World War II on the community were far more subtle than those of World War I; the open hostility and threats of 1918 were gone. The local newspaper in 1942 reported that resident Henry Pagels had received a twenty-five-word message in German through the international Red Cross from his brother in Doverden, announcing the birth of a son, Frederick: "Goes well with all of us."[59] Pagels had immigrated to Block in the early 1920s; his aunt, Dorothea Pagels Rodewald, had paid his way to the United States when she could no longer run the family farm after the death of her husband. Because he had lived in Germany fairly recently, Pagels became an important linguistic force in the community and helped conservatives retain the German language for a longer period of time.[60]

World War II provided the final assault on the old ways, linguistically and culturally, particularly for the elderly in the Block community. Having lived through the early difficulties of World War I, they suffered another loss as German discourse on telephones was discouraged and grandsons and granddaughters returned from the war and war-related jobs far more Americanized than when they had left. As jobs opened for women, young girls from Block no longer felt the need to work as hired girls. Most war veterans returned to Block, never to speak German again.[61] Young Fritz Prothe bridged the cultural gap with honor, having served as tank commander and official translator for his platoon.[62]

Although Block's homogeneity was already weakened and change was inevitable, the United States' entry into World War II struck a final blow to the isolation and insulation the Block community had enjoyed for over seven decades. The slow, painful changes toward Americanization dramatized the depth of ethnic and religious conservatism bred into the community for four generations. Ethnic and religious identity, fostered by years of cultural pride and homogeneity, faded into the past. By 1945 only Block's church and school remained, but the community's people continued to symbolize a strong ethnic past for generations to come.

CONCLUSION

The Block community and its people created networks of association that educated, shaped, and molded four generations of German Lutherans in Miami County, Kansas. Church, school, family, and outside networks each played a role in the transmission of beliefs, values, and culture; age, kinship, and gender defined the networks and taught pervasive and invaluable lessons. The educational networks of association influenced individual and group behavior in a community that closely bonded ethnicity to religion, included a homogeneous population, and had the benefit of rural and regional isolation. These three factors effectively meshed to provide an educational setting that was total, pervasive, and ongoing for four generations.

Of the four networks of association, the church and school functioned as the hub around which the entire community lived and worked, and their interconnection increased their power and influence. Church networks were gender-defined, and age determined the entry and exit patterns of women and men. The hierarchy of authority remained solidly male in a church that firmly believed in the subordination of women and children. The male voters' assembly functioned as the governing body of the church, and in this educational arena men worked out individual and group conflicts similar to those of Jon Gjerde's Norwegian Lutherans in Minnesota; theological discussions often masked personal dislikes and individual and group power struggles within the immigrant community.[1] Unlike Catholics and some Protestant groups, Missouri Synod men called their own pastor, who served at the whim of the voters' assembly. As in other rural and urban immigrant churches, men learned democratic processes, particularly through group meetings, voting, and the financing of church activities.[2]

The church not only functioned as a conservator of German language and culture but as a powerful social control over individual behavior. Like eighteenth-century Puritan institutions, the voters' assembly and pastor in Block served as judge and jury when a member's behavior did not conform to community standards. Early pastors constantly reminded the men to inform others when they observed "sinful behavior." A serious offense often required a public apology in the form of a letter or a personal appearance. This strict control diminished in the 1920s after the conservative, German-born pastors died and when it became apparent that third-generation men would no longer tolerate such clerical control. Expanded mobility and economic options provided the third generation with the opportunity to leave the community or to attend the town church if they disagreed with the pastor or the voters' assembly.

Women and eventually adolescents defined a place for themselves by creating church-related activities that justified separate associations. The organized groups of Ladies Aid and the Walther League operated at the discretion of the men, but in time each group expanded its self-governance and independent actions. The women successfully blended social gatherings with domestic activities, and the youth group combined early Bible study and educational activities with social events and trips. Like their husbands and fathers, women and children developed skills in financing, leadership, group interactions, and independence in general. With true American entrepreneurial spirit, members of each organization learned to parlay domestic and social activities into money-making endeavors that increased each group's prestige and ensured its continuation.

Immigrant churches played a major educational role in rural and urban communities, and of the four networks, the church was affected least by Americanization and the passage of time. For over seventy years its formal organizations, structure of authority, and character of activities changed only by degree.[3]

Trinity Lutheran Church provided a continuous, unchanging, and pervasive mechanism for training young and old in how to think and how to live. It is not difficult to understand the lack of internal change if one remembers that it took the most threatening outside pressures of World War I to precipitate institutional change. In a hierarchical world where men were often reluctant to challenge the authority of the pastor, it is no wonder that change came slowly for marginal groups such as women and children.

Gaining strength through its close association with the church, the school network taught children strong, consistent messages about beliefs and behavior. The education of the young was considered important, not just because the community valued literacy but because it was the best way to inculcate Christian values and beliefs. Young children learned social and gender roles in conjunction with religious doctrine, firmly linking appropriate gender behavior to religious imperatives. Like the church, male authority was unquestioned. Unlike the public schools, the school at Block permitted children to see few female teachers. Girls learned to acquiesce, and boys learned that age and status gave the male teacher unyielding control in the classroom. The melting pot of the public school remained remote and had little effect until children in Block started attending public high school in the late 1930s.

Formal education remained relatively unchanged in curriculum, discipline, and teachers' role models until the fourth generation began attending school in the late 1920s and early 1930s. The aftereffects of World War I and the more assimilated third-generation parents forced the school to Americanize, particularly in curriculum. Female teachers were more commonplace, and all teachers appeared to rely less on corporal punishment as the main method for controlling the classroom.[4]

Aided by rural isolation, Block's protective and insular institutions functioned with unparalleled authority, staving off outside religious and cultural threats to its unity. Even if individuals were tempted by the outside world, Block's institutions remained unwavering in their constancy and "truth." Institutional education was authoritarian, traditional, and total. For some people, the protection was unwanted and resented; but for most, it offered strength, assurance, and unfailing support from birth to death. Unlike some urban ethnic environments that created dissociation and conflict among families and between generations, the rural environment buffered the cultural shock that many first- and second-generation Germans faced in large American cities. As Frederick Luebke, writing about Nebraska Germans, suggests, "it seems that immigrant institutions operative in the rural and small town environment were fairly successful in easing the process whereby the newcomer was assimilated, mostly, perhaps, by slowing it down."[5]

Family networks functioned as productive work units, providing the arena for interpersonal interactions; these work units were typically single-sex and stretched across generations. As scholars have noted, when men and women worked together in other rural settings, women and children were often perceived as "helping out" with male jobs. The patriarchal family educates in specific ways, not only by defining economic and social roles but by teaching its members how to view their roles and status in the family. As Gerda Lerner notes in *The Creation of Patriarchy*, "The family not merely mirrors the order in the state and educates its children to follow it, it also creates and constantly reinforces that order."[6]

Because of the complexity, variability, and privacy of family life, the structures of authority are difficult to assess. Bolstered by religious doctrines, patriarchy was unmistakable; however, the German reverence for and tradition of motherhood placed women firmly in the core of family interactions. Women's public deference to their husbands did not determine the private interactions of husband and wife or parent and child. In assessing women's experience, Claire Farrer decries the importance historians give to public behavior. "Because the public arenas are more readily accessible [for investigation] than private ones, it is too often assumed they are the dominant, if not the only areas where expressive activity occurs."[7]

A strong sense of family pride and privacy required that problems be kept from nonfamily members, and public displays of affection or anger were highly unusual. In German-American families each family member understood the importance of duty and control. Yet as if to balance this self-discipline, family celebrations and religious rituals occurred throughout the life cycle, bonding family members to each other, to the church, and to the community.

As family members ventured into the outside world, particularly those of the third generation, outside networks changed family dynamics, individual behavior, and the expectations of both women and men. Although men journeyed into town sooner and more often than women, outside networks played a large role in expanding the role and activities of the women in Block. The continued need for salable and consumable domestic goods kept women in the mainstream of family productivity. Improvements in transportation allowed young women to work in Kansas City as hired girls, a live-in domestic experience that exposed them to Americanization in a dramatic way, particularly in contrast to brothers who "worked out" but lived at home or in another German-Lutheran community. The automobile gave adult women the opportunity to transport their goods to town to exchange for groceries or cash. Twentieth-century women in Block, like many rural women, functioned as both producers and consumers much longer than their urban counterparts.[8]

The men interacted in work-related networks associated with farm sales and small businesses. Through political and eventually social activities such as baseball and the Farmer's Union, men in Block entered the secular world. The necessity of nonfarm labor and military service also required entry into the American mainstream, encouraging if not forcing Americanization for some individuals. Certainly both wars with Germany, especially World War I, demonstrated the influence of outside intervention and its effects upon the Block community.

The exclusiveness of the church initially insulated and protected the people; however, in the twentieth century this protectionist attitude forced many residents of Block into painful conflicts as change became synonymous with survival. As individuals and families responded to outside pressures, they began to force internal change in their institutions. Although many people wanted the traditional stability and theological certainty, others began to embrace Americanization and demand more freedom, particularly in their personal lives.

Questions remain to be answered concerning religion, ethnicity, and gender. Block serves as an excellent point of comparison for other rural-ethnic communities in the Midwest with its many similarities to other village communities that have been studied. For example, Conzen's German Catholics in Stearns County, Minnesota, Gjerde's Norwegians in Wisconsin, and Ostergre's Swedes in Minnesota exhibit similar family patterns and are examples of communities that grew around an immigrant church and school in isolated regions in the nineteenth-century Midwest.[9] Conzen's description of Stearns County Germans closely correlates with Block Germans.

> Stearns County's Germans were able to develop and preserve a distinctive ethnic culture firmly based on the triad of farm, family, and community, which has to a significant degree endured to the present. Neither the content of that culture nor its survival can be understood without taking into account the extent to which pioneers were able to transplant traditional values supporting family continuity on the land.[10]

As much as this sounds like the Block community, I believe that Block's German Lutheranism, as interpreted by the Missouri Synod, provided a distinctive component to its rural immigrant character. More than just the well-documented German "clannishness" and traditional family patterns defined Block's character; the ethnic-religious bond forged by the synod required Block to retain both its ethnicity and its religious exclusivity longer than other rural immigrant communities. The community resisted assimilation not only for ethnic reasons but for religious reasons; assimilation was a threat to ethnic purity and to spiritual salvation. Because the church thrived in a defensive, immovable posture, only the extreme circumstances of World War I could crack the barriers of Block's isolationism. Certainly the third generation began to enter the outside community for economic and social reasons before the war, but assimilation could have remained extremely slow had not other external pressures been exerted during 1917 and 1918. Even with these pressures to Americanize, it took the community two more decades and another world war before it finally relinquished the German language in its institutions.

In contrast to Germans in St. Louis, Milwaukee, and New York, Germans in Block had the benefit of regional isolation, more homogeneity, and an opportunity to prolong assimilation that the large urban settings rarely had. Even if urban-ethnic communities retained their foreign language or used parochial schools, most of them did not experience the longevity or the religious exclusivity of Missouri Synod churches and schools. In many ways, Missouri Synod communities, like Block, served as a nexus between ethnic groups that sent children to heterogeneous public schools and ethnic communities that created parochial schools but typically had a less homogeneous population.[11]

Although the study of gender remains a difficult task in traditionally male-defined communities, it continues to promise and to deliver rich rewards. Additional methods must be devised to uncover the attitudes and activities of women in a strongly patriarchal community, however. Historian Gerda Lerner asserts that "the true history of women is the history of their ongoing functioning in a male-defined world on their own terms."[12] As a further guideline to gender analysis, Lerner argues that women and women's experiences should be viewed in comparison with men in similar social groups and time; viewing gender in isolation ignores the time, place, and context of a given setting.[13]

Joan Scott's seminal article on gender as a category of analysis provides some additional guidelines for interpreting gender behavior within a given social context. She contends that in order to use gender as a category of analysis the historian must understand that although how women behave in a specific patriarchal context is important, it is probably more important to understand the "meaning" associated with the behavior. Scott also points out that social relationships are indeed reciprocal and that "the direction of change is not necessarily one way."[14] In Block, gender behavior changed over time so that by the third generation, the men and women functioned by choice in more obviously interdependent ways: working on farm produce, taking produce to town, interacting more at social gatherings, and sharing recreational interests (e.g., card parties). The third-generation interviewees emphasize these differences when comparing their marriages to their parents' or grandparents'.

Within the social context of this rural-ethnic community, one must understand that religion played an important role in women's behavior. Women in Block had limited personal and work options, and unlike other Protestant women, they could not resort to evangelical causes or behavior to assert their independence and worth. For women in Block, religion did not offer as fertile an environment for independence as it did for women in most other Protestant denominations.[15] Still, I would argue that women in Block clearly benefited from the Ladies Aid organization because it provided an educational arena for growth in leadership and in fiscal and group-interaction skills. Compared to other Protestant groups, however, the women in Block had fewer opportunities for growth through formal church networks. Power in church and school belonged to the men, and for busy rural women, reform or social welfare societies served little purpose when domestic work had to be produced and families fed and clothed.

Women's networks, whether based on church, school, family, or outside associations, did play a crucial role, however. Based on age and kinship, these networks in sum provided the most important lessons learned by a girl or a woman in Block. Far more than the male-dominated institutions of church and school, family and outside networks functioned in supportive and educational ways. Three generations of women often shared domestic responsibilities in a family. Rooted in this sex-based division of labor, women's support networks extended far beyond the family to interactions in the outside world.[16] Hired girls from Block, particularly those who worked in Kansas City, mothered the newest or youngest girls who came to the city as domestic laborers. As Joan Jensen argues,

The oldest and most persistent form of community activity has been the development of and participation in women's support networks, networks that women created for giving assistance and understanding to other women. . . . It has been the basis for a type of feminism on the farm whose role in allowing women to survive, and at times flourish, under severe pressure has not been given adequate attention by scholars.[17]

In addition to examining the importance of women's support networks, the imperatives of economics and gender-defined work roles need analysis. In the economic sphere of the outside world, numbers alone provide limited information, particularly when much quantitative analysis has been based on male work or on urban female work patterns. Moreover, the often-used public/private construct fails to provide a meaningful format in a discussion of rural or ethnic women's experiences.

Two significant work experiences effected change in the options and behavior of women in Block. First, women's domestic production was vital to the farm economy in Block. Third-generation women, who as adults lived through the farm crises of the 1930s and the Great Depression, continued to function as producers as well as consumers. Rural women's work activities in their gardens or with small animals often kept the family afloat during hard times. Even during healthier economic times, the women consistently contributed to the farm income. Although Jensen and other scholars assert that such participation did not necessarily redistribute the power structure within the household, the women's economic contributions supplied a vital element for family survival, clear evidence of the interdependency of men and women in the economic realm.[18]

A second important female work experience took place outside the Block community. Before settling down to marriage and children, many women in Block, the majority of the third generation, left their homes to become live-in domestics; their new environment taught invaluable lessons and changed the lives of these young women. In this work realm, religion and ethnicity clashed with economic needs and Americanization. Although initially supported by the Missouri Synod, hired girls' interaction with outsiders became a bane for clergy, who saw too late the effects of assimilation on these young women. Twentieth-century clergy blamed hired girls for increases in immoral behavior, the dissatisfaction of young people in the church, decreasing birth rates, and female insubordination. This once appropriate work setting became a contaminating experience in the eyes of the synod clergy. Micaela di Leonardo argues that for immigrant women ethnicity takes second place to economic needs. " 'Ethnic culture' is not an unchanging construct passed down by ethnic mothers, but the living result of the intersection of all members of a particular group with the economy and population of a particular region in a particular time."[19] By working at a gender-defined job (domestic service), young women from Block effectively challenged and in some ways undermined the religious dictates that required "subordination" and "silence" from their sex. The hired girl experience clearly changed their behavior, and more important, their attitudes and expectations about themselves.[20]

How ethnicity, religion, and gender affected women's economic options needs far more investigation and analysis. Although great strides have been made in analyzing women's work experiences, more research must be focused on finding objective and subjective ways to assess rural women's work experiences and attitudes; women must define their own work options and choices. Recently, oral histories and personal narratives have been used effectively to describe women's life and work experiences.[21]

Finally, the significance of education, with its implications for future research, must be explored. In the past, many historians of education have chosen to focus on schools, ignoring the historical richness of culture. Because most educational historians have examined urban environments, I would argue that the variables of ethnicity and class have been integrated into educational historians' research, more than gender, rural, and religious variables. Mary Leach argues that historians of education, whether working from a Marxist, liberal, or revisionist position, share a "serious neglect of the recognition of gender as a central organizing principle in nineteenth- and twentieth-century education." Historians of education have not taken advantage of the vast amount of research "exploring the multiplicity of women's roles and identities and the intersection and contradictions between the roles and identities imposed by race, sex, and class" that can be applied to a wealth of educational issues.[22]

With few exceptions, rural education continues to be ignored even though this setting offers the educational historian the opportunity to explore the educational experience of the majority of Americans in the nineteeth century. Historians of education continue to be fascinated with urban settings, school bureaucracies, and urban power struggles, ignoring the setting that provides the most pervasive and long-lasting examples of local democracy and community control – the rural school.[23]

Like rural schools, parochial schools (urban or rural) need more research; their wealth of resources remain untapped. Recent research on Roman Catholic schools, for example, demonstrates the vast potential for educational historians.[24] Our country began with church-sponsored schools, and although the form has varied over time, parochial schools of all levels have continued to play an important role in educating a large minority of American children. Little comparative work has been done on parochial institutions, and almost no research has examined the interaction and roles of parochial versus public schools in any historical period.

Historians of education need to continue to ask questions about the formal and the informal ways that individuals and communities educate people.[25] For Block, formal education played a powerful role in inculcating values and beliefs, but only by analyzing informal experiences, particularly experiences of family and of the outside world, can we view the Block community as a whole. Formal institutions describe the dominant group (males) and their worldview; informal educational experiences tell about the dominant group but also provide much-needed information about the marginal groups (women and children). The community must be examined in a holistic manner so that these less powerful groups can be understood. More important, examining all types of educational experiences is necessary in order to assess the reciprocity of the community's subgroups. Other conceptual frameworks similar to "networks of association" must be found to avoid projecting oppressor-victim constructs or other dichotomies that ignore interaction and reciprocity among individuals and groups.

The community at Block functioned as an important educational setting, creating individual and community identity in the lives of four generations of German Lutherans. It is tempting for an outsider to view this small parochial world by its limitations, reducing the community to a rural ghetto of sorts. Historian Martin Marty places a community like Block into a larger context, assessing the historical and contemporary significance of such a place. Although he was describing what he calls a "Catholic ghetto," Marty's words fit the "sheltered world" of the Block community.

These days we have to visit any number of these sheltered worlds in order to learn about the America we inherited. In fact, despite intermarriage, rage against old orders, social mobility, suburbanization, mass higher education, mass media, or whatever, most Americans still live in parochial and provincial subsectors of the social economy. They do, at least, if they are fortunate. They may later have identity crises, but they belong to something strong enough to have given them an identity in the first place.[26]

The formal institutions created in the Block community have endured. The church, school, and cemetery stand as monuments to religious faith and perseverance; some fifth and sixth generations still reside on original homesteads. People live and die there and some move away, but the sense of community remains—a link to the past and a symbol of survival for the future.

NOTE ON SOURCES

Any historical or ethnographic study is always defined, and sometimes limited, by the availability of primary sources. Extensive quantitative and qualitative source materials for this research permitted a comprehensive examination of this village church and community. Trinity Lutheran Church of Block, Kansas, has preserved a plethora of primary materials. The official church recordbook registers baptisms, confirmations, marriages, and deaths from 1868 to the present, an invaluable record that includes birth information, school enrollment, marriage age, life-course data, and cause of death.[1] Besides the church recordbook, information from the quarterly *Protokoll* "minutes" from the voters' assembly from 1870 to 1945 provided details on theological and individual controversies, business and monetary concerns, and routine administration of church activities and events. Insights into exclusive female activities from 1912 to 1945 can be found in the Ladies Aid minutes. These monthly minutes provide information on both formal and informal activities of the churchwomen. Minutes of the Walther League (a young people's group) from 1924 to 1938 supplied information on adolescent and young adult behavior and activities.

Until 1936 many church documents were written in Old German script, and Ursula Huelsbergen, an experienced translator who made verbatim translations of these documents, added greatly to the research. Fortunately, the church recordbook had been translated in 1982 by Myrtle and Elmer Thoden, lifelong members of the church and community. Elmer had been taught to write in the Old German script in the Trinity Lutheran school, and he still had his old grammar books to serve as resources if his memory failed.[2]

Oral interviews provided another useful source for this investigation into community life; fifteen older residents or prior residents willingly discussed their lives in Block. The thirteen women and two men interviewed were born in Block between 1897 and 1920. Nine of the interviewees still live in the Block community, and five other interviewees live in the neighboring town of Paola. Only one of the interviewees had lived her adult life outside of Miami County. Their stories, anecdotes, and memories enrich this study and give life to the reams of quantitative and literary material.[3] Photos, personal correspondence, and newspaper accounts also add to the documentation.

Other useful sources of information include state and federal census data; statistical yearbooks, journals, booklets, and magazines published by the Lutheran Church–Missouri Synod; and World War I alien registration documents. During the anti-German hysteria of World War I, President Woodrow Wilson ordered registration of all unnaturalized German-born Americans, and the state of Kansas, unlike most states, did not destroy these fascinating records, which include information on immigration, occupation, literacy, and families as well as fingerprints and photographs.

Sources on material culture provided an added dimension. Many families in the Block community have lived for several generations on the same land. Many community members still farm, and some land and houses have passed through the hands of four generations. Since public documents deal primarily with male activity and experience, women's activities may go unrecognized unless investigated from other angles. The study of material culture such as quilts, furniture, household items, tools, and other items of daily work provides important insight into women's activities and experiences.[4] Presently, many residents in Block have a significant number of objects in their homes that date from their families' departure from Germany. A discussion of those objects during interviews frequently led to interesting information that might otherwise have been forgotten.

These quantitative and qualitative sources effectively mesh to provide a comprehensive and multifaceted portrait of a village community. Although a sense of chronology is important, I have used a topical approach in order to identify the overlapping, reinforcing patterns that characterized education in Block and defined the links between individuals and the community they created.

NOTES

INTRODUCTION

1. These figures are taken from the *Statistical Yearbook of the Lutheran Church — Missouri Synod* (St. Louis: Concordia Publishing House, 1884–1945).

2. Some of the earliest studies were done by Merle Curti, *The Making of an American Community: A Case Study of Democracy in a Frontier Community* (1959; Stanford: Stanford University Press, 1969). For other examples, see Don H. Doyle, *Social Order of a Frontier Community: Jacksonville, Illinois, 1825–1870* (Urbana: University of Illinois Press, 1978); Gordon W. Kirk, *The Promise of American Life: Social Mobility in a Nineteenth-Century Immigrant Community, Holland, Michigan, 1847–1894* (Philadelphia: American Philosophical Society, 1978); and Ralph Mann, *After the Gold Rush: Society in Grass Valley and Nevada City, California, 1849–1870* (Stanford: Stanford University Press, 1982). For a general discussion of midwestern and western community building, see Robert V. Hine, *Community on the American Frontier* (Norman: University of Oklahoma Press, 1980). For studies that focus on ethnic groups or women, see Frederick Luebke, ed., *Ethnicity on the Great Plains* (Lincoln: University of Nebraska Press, 1980); Lorraine Garkovich, *Population and Community in Rural America* (Westport, Conn.: Greenwood Press, 1989); Nancy Gray Osterud, *Bonds of Community and the Lives of Farm Women in Nineteenth-Century New York* (Ithaca, N.Y.: Cornell University Press, 1991); Jon Gjerde, *From Peasants to Farmers: The Migration from Balestrand, Norway, to the Upper Middle West* (New York: Cambridge University Press, 1985); and Walter D. Kamphoefner, *The Westfalians: From Germany to Missouri* (Princeton, N.J.: Princeton University Press, 1987).

3. I am referring to Bernard Bailyn's *Education in the Forming of American Society* (Chapel Hill: University of North Carolina Press, 1960). Since its publication this work has profoundly influenced historians of American education. An example of this continuing influence can be found in John Best, ed., *Historical Inquiry into Education: A Research Agenda* (Washington, D.C.: American Educational Research Association, 1983), an anthology that provides a comprehensive view of potential research in the history of education. Some recent books on the history of education that take a broad view of education include Joel Spring, *The American School, 1642–1990*, 2d ed. (New York: Longman Press, 1990); Henry J. Perkinson, *The Imperfect Panacea: American Faith in Education, 1865–1990*, 3d ed. (New York: McGraw Hill, 1991); and B. Edward McClellan and William J. Reese, eds., *The Social History of Education* (Urbana: University of Illinois Press, 1988).

4. I am using the definition of patriarchy as defined by Gerda Lerner in *The Creation of Patriarchy* (New York: Oxford University Press, 1986), 239. "Patriarchy in its wider definition means the manifestation and institutionalization of male dominance over women and children in the family and the extension of

male dominance over women in society in general. It implies that men hold power in all the important institutions of society and that women are deprived of access to such power. It does not imply that women are either totally powerless or totally deprived of rights, influence, and resources."

5. Barbara Finkelstein first develops her networks of association in her excellent chapter, "Casting Networks of Good Influence," in *American Childhood: A Research Guide and Historical Handbook*, ed. Joseph Hawes and N. Ray Hiner (Westport, Conn.: Greenwood Press, 1985), 111–52. Although Finkelstein creates this framework to discuss nineteenth-century childhood, I find it a useful tool in attempting to view interdependencies and reciprocal interactions among women, men, and children.

6. The omission of race as a necessary category of analysis is not to slight the importance of skin color. Obviously, as white Europeans, Block residents benefited from their race, receiving all the social, political, and economic benefits inherent in being white in America. I have chosen to focus on these other variables (ethnicity, gender, and so on) because they are critical to a description of the community's educational systems and responses to Americanization. When outside contacts bring the residents of Block into mixed racial settings I do discuss issues relevant to race.

7. Robert M. Toepper, "Rationale for Preservation of the German Language in the Missouri Synod of the Nineteenth Century," *Concordia Historical Institute Quarterly* 41 (Feb. 1968):167. The quote cited by Toepper comes from sociologist Heinrich H. Mauer, "The Fellowship Law of a Fundamental Group," *American Journal of Sociology* 31 (July 1925):49–50.

8. For information on the importance of chain migration to homogeneity, see Charles Tilly, "Transplanted Networks," in *Immigration Reconsidered: History, Sociology, and Politics*, ed. Virginia Yans-McLaughlin (New York: Oxford University Press, 1990), 79–95; Kathleen Neils Conzen, "Historical Approaches to the Study of Rural Ethnic Communities," in Luebke, *Ethnicity*, 7–9; and Kamphoefner, *Westfalians*, 70–105. For information on German land-succession patterns and the importance of endogamy, see Russell Gerlach, *Immigrants in the Ozarks* (Columbia: University of Missouri Press, 1976); Kathleen Neils Conzen, "Germans," in *Harvard Encyclopedia of American Ethnic Groups*, ed. Stephan Thernstrom (Cambridge, Mass.: Harvard University Press, 1980), 415; Kathleen Neils Conzen, "Peasant Pioneers: Generational Succession among German Farmers in Frontier Minnesota," in *The Countryside in the Age of Capitalist Transformation*, ed. Steven Hahn and Jonathan Prude (Chapel Hill: University of North Carolina Press, 1985), 259–92; and Frederick Luebke, *Germans in the New World: Essays in the History of Immigration* (Urbana: University of Illinois Press, 1990), 165–66.

9. Outside contacts in the economic and political arena provided the initial interactions for the residents of Block, particularly for the men. These contacts became important in the early twentieth century, and World War I dramatically forced the community into the outside world.

10. This is not to minimize the importance of religious beliefs to Scandinavians, but Scandinavian Lutherans typically belonged to other, more liberal Lutheran synods, particularly the American Lutheran Church (ALC) and the Lutheran Church of America (LCA). A very small minority belonged to the Wisconsin Synod, which has conservative practices similar to those of the Missouri Synod. In present-day Lutheranism, the ALC and LCA have merged with a small (more moderate) group of Missouri Synod Lutherans to form the Evangelical

Lutheran Church of America (ELCA). For an excellent study of Norwegian Lutheran immigrants, see Gjerde, *From Peasants to Farmers*, and Jon Gjerde, "Conflict and Community: A Case Study of the Immigrant Church in the United States," *Journal of Social History* (Summer 1986):681–97.

11. Roman Catholic churches and schools serving German communities may have been less homogeneous than Missouri Synod churches and schools. Rural Catholics might have been assigned a priest of a different ethnic background or have had women religious of different ethnic backgrounds teaching in their schools. In fact, an ethnic difference between religious and laity often caused problems within the parish. For an excellent analysis (although predominantly urban) of German Catholic immigrant parishes, see Jay P. Dolan, *The Immigrant Church: New York's Irish and German Catholics* (Baltimore: Johns Hopkins University Press, 1975), Dolan, *The American Catholic Parish, 1850 to the Present* (New York: Paulist Press, 1987), and Dolan, *The American Catholic Experience: A History from Colonial Times to the Present* (Garden City, N.J.: Image Books, 1987). Chapters 5–12 provide the most pertinent section: "The Immigrant Church between 1820–1920."

12. Although urban immigrants did create subcommunities within their cities, they certainly had little regional isolation compared to rural areas. And even with endogamy, outside influences severely affected the community's initial homogeneity, if indeed it was homogeneous. For examples of excellent urban studies, see Kathleen Neils Conzen, *Immigrant Milwaukee, 1836–1860* (Cambridge, Mass.: Harvard University Press, 1976); Virginia Yans-McLaughlin, *Family and Community: Italian Immigrants in Buffalo, 1880–1930* (Ithaca, N.Y.: Cornell University Press, 1978); Robert A. Slayton, *Back of the Yards: The Making of a Local Democracy* (Chicago: University of Chicago Press, 1986); and Stanley Nadel, *Little Germany: Ethnicity, Religion, and Class in New York City, 1845–80* (Urbana: University of Illinois Press, 1990).

CHAPTER 1. COMMUNITY OVERVIEW

1. Mack Walker, *Germany and the Emigration, 1816–1885* (Cambridge, Mass.: Harvard University Press, 1964), 69. For additional analyses of German emigration, see Stanley Nadel, *Little Germany: Ethnicity, Religion, and Class in New York City, 1845–80* (Urbana: University of Illinois Press, 1990), 15–26; Walter Kamphoefner, *The Westfalians: From Germany to Missouri* (Princeton, N.J.: Princeton University Press, 1987), 12–39; and Kathleen Neils Conzen, "Germans," in *Harvard Encyclopedia of American Ethnic Groups*, ed. Stephan Thernstrom (Cambridge, Mass.: Harvard University Press, 1980), 406–25.

2. Through the use of census data, obituaries, and other family records such as baptism and confirmation certificates, it is often possible to approximate the time of arrival and place of German birth. This is important since by the fourth or fifth generation this information is often lost, misplaced, or simply no longer known by any living family members.

3. Particular works that discuss this emigrant desire to preserve rural German culture include Russell Gerlach, *Immigrants in the Ozarks* (Columbia: University of Missouri Press, 1976); Terry G. Jordan, *German Seed in Texas Soil: Immigrant Families in Nineteenth Century Texas* (Austin: University of Texas Press, 1975); Conzen, "Germans," 412–17. For information on other ethnic

groups that attempted to transfer their "old world village" to America, see Robert Slayton, *Back of the Yards: The Making of a Local Democracy* (Chicago: University of Chicago Press, 1986), 113–19; Jon Gjerde, "Conflict and Community: A Case Study of the Immigrant Church in the United States," *Journal of Social History* (Summer 1986): 682–83; and Charles H. Mindel and Robert W. Habenstein, eds., *Ethnic Families in America: Patterns and Variations* (New York: Elsevier, 1976).

4. Conzen, "Germans," 406–9; Walker, *Germany and the Emigration*, 50–51; Kamphoefner, *Westfalians*, 70–105; and Nadel, *Little Germany*, 15–26.

5. Frederick Luebke, "Ethnic Group Settlement on the Great Plains," *Western Historical Quarterly* 8 (Oct. 1977):412.

6. Gottfried Duden, *Report on a Journey to the Western States of North America* (Elberfeld, Germany: Swiss Society for the Promotion of Emigration, 1829). Duden was a disenchanted German professor who emigrated, toured the Midwest (particularly Missouri), and returned to write his emigration handbook, which was extremely popular in Saxony Province. For more information on Duden and the influence of his writing on emigration to the state of Missouri, see Audrey Olson, "St. Louis Germans, 1850–1920: The Nature of an Immigrant Community and Its Relation to the Assimilation Process" (Ph.D. diss., University of Kansas, 1970), 3–5.

7. For an interesting description of transatlantic crossings comparing early sailing ships to later steam ships, see Edwin C. Guillet, *The Great Migration: The Atlantic Crossing by Sailing-Ship since 1770* (New York: Nelson, 1937). See also Philip A. M. Taylor, *The Distant Magnet: European Emigration to the U.S.A.* (New York: Harper and Row, 1971).

8. Author interview with Clarence Clausen, March 15, 1986.

9. By examining early state and federal census data it is possible to determine the approximate date of arrival by comparing the age and place of children's births; if one child is born in Germany and the next in the United States, this information helps pinpoint the time of arrival. The "Registration Affidavit of Alien Enemy" required during World War I also helps to determine when the emigrants arrived. The documents for Kansas are located at the Kansas City, Missouri, Branch of the National Archives (Miami County, 1918, Box 17). J. Neale Carman, who researched foreign-language settlements in Kansas in the early 1950s, states that the Block area remained linguistically important because of some late immigration in the 1920s. Carman, "Foreign Language Units of Kansas: Historical Atlas and Statistics," (manuscript, University of Kansas Archives), 2:1291–95.

10. Author interview with Nora Ohlmeier Prothe, June 24, 1986.

11. Author interview with Mildred Block, Nov. 22, 1985.

12. Author interview with Irene Minden Prothe, July 18, 1986.

13. This story was taken from "The Kahman Family Tree," in the possession of Minnie Cahman Debrick, who was Eidena's granddaughter.

14. F. W. Bogen, *The German in America: Advice and Instruction for German Emigrants in the United States of America* (Boston: B. H. Greene, 1851).

15. Author interview with Nora Ohlmeier Prothe, June 24, 1986.

16. Author interview with Marie Dageforde Monthey, August 16, 1986.

17. Robert W. Baughman, *Kansas in Maps* (Topeka: Kansas State Historical Society, 1961).

18. Ibid., 79.

19. August R. Suelflow, *The Heart of Missouri: A History of the Western*

District of the Lutheran Church–Missouri Synod, 1854–1954 (St. Louis: Concordia Publishing House, 1954), 174.

20. This story was told to Mrs. John Sponable, who reported it as part of her "History of the Block Community," *The Miami County Republican*, Aug. 17, 1951.

21. Author interview with Marie Dageforde Monthey, Aug. 16, 1986.

22. Charles Tilly argues that the effective units of migration were "sets of people linked by acquaintance, kinship and work experience" ("Transplanted Networks," in *Immigration Reconsidered: History, Sociology, and Politics*, ed. Virginia Yans-McLaughlin [New York: Oxford University Press, 1990], 79–95). As defined by Wilbur Zelinsky in *The Cultural Geography of the United States* (Englewood Cliffs, N.J.: Prentice-Hall, 1973), 29, this type of migration occurs when "a viable ethnic nucleus takes hold in a given location" and positive information induces others to follow. For more information on chain migration in rural settings, see Kathleen Neils Conzen, "Historical Approaches to the Study of Rural Ethnic Communities," in *Ethnicity on the Great Plains*, ed. Frederick Luebke (Lincoln: University of Nebraska Press, 1980), 7–9; Kamphoefner, *Westfalians*, 70–105; and Kathleen Neils Conzen, "Peasant Pioneers: Generational Succession among German Farmers in Frontier Minnesota," in *The Countryside in the Age of Capitalist Transformation*, ed. Steven Hahn and Jonathan Prude (Chapel Hill: University of North Carolina Press, 1985), 259–92.

23. Reminiscence of Michael Schultz, in *History of Churches: Miami County Kansas*, ed. Sister M. Charles McGrath (Paola, Kans.: Paola Association for Church Action, 1976), 62–63.

24. Author interview with Minnie Cahman Debrick, Sept. 23, 1986.

25. Founded in 1855, the county was initially named Lykins after the proslavery missionary David Lykins. When Kansas became a free state in 1861, the county was renamed Miami, presumably after the Miami Indians whose reservation lands encompassed the region. The Wea-Piankishaw, Potawotomie, and Peoria-Kaskaskia reserves were also located within the county. For this and other county history, see George Higgins, *Miami County: The King of Counties* (Paola, Kans., 1868), 8–9.

26. E. W. Robinson, *Sectional Map of Miami County, Kansas* (Paola, Kans., 1868).

27. For the best discussion of German-American agricultural methods and crops, see Jordan, *German Seed in Texas Soil*.

28. Homer E. Socolofsky, "How We Took the Land," in *Kansas: The First Century*, Vol 1, ed. John D. Bright (New York: Lewis Historical Publishing Company, 1956), 299.

29. An excellent source for analyzing and understanding land policy in the United States can be found in Benjamin Horace Hibbard, *A History of the Public Land Policies* (Madison: University of Wisconsin Press, 1965).

30. Kansas, First State Census, "Miami County" (1865), Microfilm, reel #6, Topeka: Kansas Board of Agriculture.

31. Gerlach, *Immigrants in the Ozarks*, 60; Conzen, "Germans," 415; Kamphoefner, *Westfalians*, 70–105; Conzen, "Peasant Farmers," 259–92; and Frederick C. Luebke, *Germans in the New World: Essays in the History of Immigration* (Urbana: University of Illinois Press, 1990), 165–66.

32. J. B. Wilson and Company advertisement in *Western Spirit*, Aug. 12, 1910.

33. German newspapers had the largest readership of any ethnic newspapers in the United States. In the 1920s, there were fifteen German-American news-

papers in Kansas. The closest newspapers to the Block area were published in Atchison, Lawrence, Leavenworth, and Kansas City. For more information on German-American newspapers, see Eleanor L. Turk, "The German Newspapers of Kansas," *Kansas History* 6 (1983):46–64. For information on German-American newspapers nationally, see James M. Berquist, "The German-American Press," in *The Ethnic Press in the United States: A Historical Analysis and Handbook*, ed. Sally Nuller (Westport, Conn.: Greenwood Press, 1987), 131–59, and Carl Wittke, *The German-Language Press in America* (Louisville: University of Kentucky Press, 1957).

34. Sponable, "History of Block Community."

35. The change to some English names probably reflects the dire economic situation during the Great Depression. As in other parts of the farm belt, the dust bowl years discouraged some farmers in the Block area who were forced to pursue or decided on other work options. The English names that appeared on the plat map are those of wealthy town dwellers who bought real estate as an investment, not necessarily as a homesite. Another factor that accounts for the loss of German-owned property may be that third- and particularly fourth-generation males chose other options in preference to farming. As elderly parents moved to town and younger family members decided not to farm, the land was sold.

36. This quote is taken from an interview with Herman Clausen conducted by Jill Denning, *Miami County Republican*, Jan. 1, 1980.

37. The information about the stores in Block has been acquired by piecing together newspaper items and reminiscences of deceased and living residents of Block. Some of the dates are difficult to confirm, but all stores, shops, and mills mentioned did exist, although some for only brief periods of time.

38. Slayton, *Back of the Yards*, 113.

39. Ibid., 114.

40. In the nineteenth and early twentieth centuries, county papers were full of articles, editorials, and letters to the editor about the county road and bridge situation. When males from Block were elected to public office they usually served as road overseers as well as in other offices such as constable and justice of the peace for East Valley Township.

41. For a short period of time, Block was considered as a possible railhead, but probably for political reasons, the community of Henson, named after the family of the county judge, received the coveted honor. Had Block received the railhead, its isolation in the county would have lessened.

42. Reminiscence of George Reifel from an interview conducted in 1951. These reminiscences are from the personal papers of his niece Myrtle Neu Thoden.

43. Although this seems like an incredible number of trains leaving Paola for Kansas City, the newspaper ad clearly makes this claim. Missouri Pacific advertisement, *Western Spirit*, Feb. 19, 1892.

44. Homer E. Socolofsky and Huber Self, eds., *Historical Atlas of Kansas* (Norman: University of Oklahoma Press, 1972), 36.

45. Reifel reminiscence.

46. Notice in *Western Spirit*, May 12, 1905, that delivery for Rural Route 9 would begin.

47. Article in *Miami County Republican*, Nov. 28, 1968, 5.

48. I have been given much anecdotal information about the telephone party-line system at Block. Some East Prussian speakers would use this dialect to keep

most "listeners" from understanding conversations. Although I have no written documentation, interviewees said that during World War I, "some people didn't like" for them to speak German on the telephone; it aroused suspicion and seemed unpatriotic. German on the telephone was discouraged but never discontinued and was used particularly by older residents who remained uncomfortable conversing in English.

49. Many books are available that provide historical information on the philosophical and theological viewpoints of the synod. I would suggest Carl S. Meyer, ed., *Moving Frontiers: Readings in the History of the Lutheran Church–Missouri Synod* (St. Louis: Concordia Publishing House, 1964); Carl S. Mundinger, *Government in the Missouri Synod* (St. Louis: Concordia Publishing House, 1947); Alan Graebner, *Uncertain Saints: The Laity in the Lutheran Church–Missouri Synod, 1900–1970* (Westport, Conn.: Greenwood Press, 1975); and a series of articles written by sociologist Heinrich H. Mauer in the *American Journal of Sociology* 30–34 (1924–1928).

50. Graebner, *Uncertain Saints*, 113.

51. This brief outline of the founding and early history of the synod comes from the following sources: Walter O. Forster, *Zion on the Mississippi: The Settlement of the Saxon Lutherans in Missouri, 1839–1841* (St. Louis: Concordia Publishing House, 1953); E. Clifford Nelson, ed., *The Lutherans in North America* (Philadelphia: Fortress Press, 1975); Ralph Dornfeld Owen, "The Old Lutherans Come," *Concordia Historical Institute Quarterly* 20 (1948):3–56; Meyer, *Moving Frontiers*; and Mundinger, *Government in the Missouri Synod*.

52. The "Old Lutherans" included a number of different Lutheran groups besides this early Saxon group. For a specific description of each group and their religious controversies, see Owen, "The Old Lutherans Come."

53. *Der Lutheraner* was a journal published for both clergy and laity in the synod. Walther realized the importance of communication and publication, and his initiative in publishing served as a catalyst for unification and organization. The journal continued publication well into the twentieth century.

54. Early synod founders and leaders were German educated, most from Leipzig University; many early pastors were also from German universities. After its founding, the synod began creating its own seminaries, established along lines similar to German universities; thus even the early pastors' education stood in dramatic contrast to their congregation's educational background.

55. Alan Graebner, "The Acculturation of an Immigrant Lutheran Church: The Lutheran Church–Missouri Synod, 1917–1929" (Ph.D. diss., Columbia University, 1965), 7–8.

56. Two books provided the most comprehensive information on the school system of the Lutheran Church–Missouri Synod. See Walther H. Beck, *Lutheran Elementary Schools in the United States* (St. Louis: Concordia Publishing House, 1939) and August C. Stellhorn, *Schools of the Lutheran Church–Missouri Synod* (St. Louis: Concordia Publishing House, 1963).

57. Graebner, "Acculturation," 164–65.

58. Frederick Luebke, "The Immigrant Condition as a Factor Contributing to the Conservatism of the Lutheran Church – Missouri Synod," *Concordia Historical Institute Quarterly* 38 (April 1965):22. See also Luebke's *Germans in the New World*, Introduction.

59. This slogan, "No Union without Unity," was a principle of C. F. W. Walther and was used continuously by Walther and later by other theologians to

discourage any religious partnership that did not accept the synod's theological dictates.

60. Erwin L. Lueker, ed., *Lutheran Cyclopedia* (St. Louis: Concordia Publishing House, 1954), 542. This book is one of the best sources available for understanding all facets of Lutheran belief and theological terminology.

61. Allan H. Jahsmann, *What's Lutheran in Education? Explorations into Principles and Practices* (St. Louis: Concordia Publishing House, 1960), 25–30.

62. Almost every book and journal on Missouri Synod theology discusses and maintains the subordinate status of women. The church has made some changes in the late twentieth century but continues to exclude women from the ministry. Concerning "women's place" in church and society, one may examine the nineteenth- and twentieth-century lay magazines, journals, and "advice" books to better understand the Missouri Synod's position.

63. Luebke, "Immigrant Condition as a Factor," 27.

64. I am referring here to the repeal of the Bennett Law in 1890 and the Oregon Law of 1922, laws that threatened to ban the use of foreign language in the schools and to prohibit private schools. The synod joined Roman Catholics and others in actively fighting these laws.

CHAPTER 2. CHURCH

1. Russell Gerlach, *Immigrants in the Ozarks* (Columbia: University of Missouri Press, 1976), 118. For additional discussion of the importance of the German immigrant church, see Stanley Nadel, *Little Germany: Ethnicity, Religion, and Class in New York City, 1845–80* (Urbana: University of Illinois Press, 1990), 96, and Frederick Luebke, *Germans in the New World: Essays in the History of Immigration* (Urbana: University of Illinois Press, 1990), 165–66. For a comparison with German Catholics, see Jay P. Dolan, *The American Catholic Experience: A History from Colonial Times to the Present* (Garden City, N.Y.: Image Books, 1987), 158–94; for a comparison with Norwegian Lutherans, see Jon Gjerde, "Conflict and Community: A Case Study of the Immigrant Church in the United States," *Journal of Social History* (Summer 1986):681–97.

2. The first two years of the congregation are sketchy since early records were destroyed in a house fire of one of the members.

3. The information on buildings and dates is taken from *Protokoll* ("minutes" from the voters' assembly), Book 1, 1–2, 23, 73–76, 105–7, Trinity Lutheran Church (TLC) Archives, Block, Kansas.

4. These figures are taken from the *Statistical Yearbook of the Lutheran Church–Missouri Synod* (St. Louis: Concordia Publishing House, 1884–). My statistics are taken from the yearbooks published in 1884, 1895, and 1920–1945. The numbers of children are approximate, referring to those fourteen years and under who were not yet communicants. One reason for the decline after 1920 was the creation of a daughter congregation (First Lutheran) in the nearby town of Paola.

5. All references to the Trinity Lutheran Constitution are taken directly from the original document approved by the Missouri Synod in 1872. The constitution has been updated, but I will be quoting from or referring to this original document unless otherwise stated. The original document can be found in the archives of Trinity Lutheran Church, Block, Kansas.

6. See Frederick Luebke, "The Immigrant Condition as a Factor Contributing to the Conservatism of the Lutheran Church–Missouri Synod," *Concordia Historical Institute Quarterly* 38 (April 1965):24; Carl S. Mundinger, *Government in the Missouri Synod* (St. Louis: Concordia Publishing House, 1947), 218; and Alan Graebner, *Uncertain Saints: The Laity in the Lutheran Church–Missouri Synod, 1900–1970* (Westport, Conn.: Greenwood Press, 1975), 5–6.

7. Jon Gjerde, "Conflict and Community," 682. Gjerde's community makes an interesting comparison with the church at Block. The Norwegian Synod had direct ties to the Missouri Synod, and early pastors were trained at the Missouri Synod's Concordia Seminary. The major controversy in the 1880s involved interpretation of Lutheran doctrine on predestination. Part of the Crow River group sided with the conservative German Missouri Synod, and the rest refused to accept this orthodox position. For additional information on German-Lutheran churches, see Carl S. Meyer, "Lutheran Immigrant Churches Face the Problems of the Frontier," *Church History* 29 (Dec. 1960):447–48. For a similar discussion on German Catholics, see Jay P. Dolan, *The Immigrant Church: New York's Irish and German Catholics* (Baltimore: Johns Hopkins University Press, 1975).

8. The early decades of Trinity Lutheran Church were marked by debts and financial problems. Besides discussions about finances, *Protokoll*, Book 1, often includes admonishments against certain members who had abdicated their financial responsibilities for church, school, pastor, and teacher.

9. It is clear from *Protokoll* that pastors felt overburdened in trying to manage their church and school duties. They typically would ask to leave Block once they received a call from a congregation who had a teacher already hired. After losing yet another pastor in 1890, the congregation finally decided to hire a teacher.

10. *Protokoll*, Book 1, 18–22 and 47–48. Clergy functioned as district representatives, so a hierarchy of decision making was the specific method of handling a dispute.

11. The educational contrast between lay persons and clergy was profound. First-generation Block residents may have received some elementary education, and later generations were expected to complete eighth grade. Carl Mundinger describes nineteenth-century Concordia Seminary's curriculum for future pastors, stating that the seminary was a nine-year program modeled after the German Gymnasium, with subjects taught by a theology faculty in a German university. Curricula included Greek, Latin, Hebrew, German, English, French, geography, logic, history, arithmetic, and catechetics (*Governance in the Missouri Synod*, 197–98). He further states that "no one on the frontier had an education that could approach that of his pastor."

12. Alan Graebner, "The Acculturation of an Immigrant Lutheran Church — The Lutheran Church–Missouri Synod, 1917–1929," (Ph.D diss., Columbia University, 1965), 273–74.

13. Robert A. Slayton, *Back of the Yards: The Making of a Local Democracy* (Chicago: University of Illinois Press, 1986), 122.

14. Frederick Luebke, *Immigrants and Politics: The Germans in Nebraska, 1880–1900* (Lincoln: University of Nebraska Press, 1969), 35, and Kathleen Neils Conzen, "Historical Approaches to the Study of Rural Ethnic Communities," in *Ethnicity on the Great Plains*, ed. Frederick Luebke (Lincoln: University of Nebraska Press, 1980), 4–5. For earlier but effective arguments on the importance of the pastor's influence on the assimilation process, see Peter

Speek, *A Stake in the Land* (New York: Harper, 1921), 130–31, and Heinrich H. Mauer, "The Lutheran Community and American Society: A Study in Religion as a Condition of Social Accommodation," *American Journal of Sociology* 34 (Sept. 1928):289.

15. Graebner, "Acculturation", 272–73.

16. Author interview with Esther Prothe Maisch, June 25, 1986.

17. Author interview with Lydia Schultz, Feb. 13, 1982. The young man discussed was Lydia's husband, Louis. Lydia said that Lou and the pastor never really "made peace." Interestingly, Louis and Lydia left the congregation at Block in 1921 and became charter members of the daughter church in the nearby town of Paola.

18. Author interview with Nora Ohlmeier Prothe, June 24, 1986.

19. Graebner, *Uncertain Saints*, 4–5. Once again it is interesting to compare the Catholic experience in German and other immigrant parishes; Jay Dolan's work on Catholic immigrant parishes describes a similar scenario. Although American culture encourages the laity to "freedom and independence," Dolan argues that European-educated priests struggled with this "equalitarian" concept and believed that increased lay activity usurped their authority and control (Dolan, *American Catholic Experience*, 221–24).

20. Luebke, *Germans in the New World*, 80. Lutheran doctrine is very clear concerning the distinct separation of church and state. Martin Luther repeatedly repudiated "good works" as a means of salvation and redemption. In essence, charity could be viewed as "good works" and considered the duty of the state and not the church, which needed to focus on spiritual salvation. For examples of synodical attitudes on this subject, see *Lutheran Witness* 18 (1900):134 and *Der Lutheraner* 65 (1909):231. See also Graebner, *Uncertain Saints*, 4–5.

21. Frederick Dean Lueking's *A Century of Caring: "The Welfare Ministry among the Missouri Synod Lutherans, 1868–1968* (St. Louis: Concordia Publishing House, 1968), 3, describes the slow movement toward philanthropy in the late nineteenth century. By the 1890s, the synod did sponsor some urban orphanages and hospitals staffed by "untrained laity" and male clergy. Although C. F. W. Walther stressed that congregations help the poor, widows, orphans, and the aged, nationally the synod focused on the importance of "proclaiming and preserving the Divine Word, Law and Gospel" above any other cause.

22. In the 1880s and 1890s, seven incidents in *Protokoll* refer to charitable giving. All but two involve giving money to financially strapped congregations, local members, or the synod's educational institutions. An undisclosed sum of money was sent to "our needy brothers in the West," and another undisclosed amount was sent to a "heathen mission."

23. *Protokoll*, May 1932, Book 2, 119–20. This is significant since only one other item was on the agenda and this was a "special," not a regularly scheduled, meeting. The sisters apparently accepted the offer and were buried in a special row that includes two other nonmembers of the church. This cemetery was sacred ground kept for those who died in the Lutheran faith in good standing at Trinity Lutheran Church. Anyone who requested burial and was not a member of Trinity Lutheran needed special permission from the voters' assembly.

24. These descriptions of officers' duties are taken from the Trinity Lutheran Constitution, Article 7 — Terms and Duties of Officers (TLC Archives).

25. St. Peter's Church kept a recordbook, membership lists, and *Protokoll* from 1878 to 1882. These two books had been lost or forgotten until 1985 when Lydia Prothe Schultz found them in the stored possessions of her father-in-law,

Michael Schultz, who had died in 1954. Although failing to create a church "across the river," Schultz became a charter member of the first town church in the county. The First Lutheran Church of Paola formed in 1921, and Schultz, his wife Louisa, son Louis, and daughter-in-law Lydia helped establish this daughter church as an alternative to Trinity Lutheran at Block.

26. *Protokoll*, Book 1, 124–25. The 1,000-pound bell was bought from Stuck-stede in St. Louis, Missouri. The congregation spent $450.00 to add additional support to the bell tower and paid $166.86 for the bell itself, which could be heard for miles; it continues to be a great source of pride and a symbol of the past for many residents of Block.

27. Slayton, *Back of the Yards*, 114. He described the church as a place that offered stability, maintained social order, promulgated rules of morality, taught children, and served as a social center for family rituals (119–20).

28. This practice of paying boys and men for some services does not carry over to paying for services provided by women in the congregation.

29. *Protokoll*, Book 1, 3, 8.

30. The *Klingelbeutel* was a tradition in their German churches. The small bell served to attract people's attention and let them know a collection was being gathered.

31. *Protokoll*, Book 1, 27–35. The early minutes were unsigned, but Ursula Huelsbergen, the translator, is convinced that the pastor probably wrote them. The writing is erudite and replete with theological terms that demonstrate a high degree of formal education. Some of the topics discussed appear in the minutes in an essay form and it is quite possible that these topics were the pastor's ideas and that the laymen discussed them or asked questions after his presentation was over.

32. *Protokoll*, Book 1, 45.

33. Gjerde, "Conflict and Community," 692.

34. *Protokoll*, Book 1, 99.

35. Seating position was critical in the church, and the voters' assembly spent time discussing if each change was warranted. Age, gender, infirmity, and marital status determined a person's place. I cannot explain how these decisions were made, but it was obviously important to the voters that these group distinctions be defined clearly. Ironically, only when the new church was constructed in 1959 did men and women sit on the same side of the aisle. Typically, nothing was announced or formally changed, but from the first church service in the new building people simply sat as families instead of grouping themselves according to past distinctions.

36. H. C. Senne was the first pastor to have a long stay in the Block community. His seventeen years there were critical to the community's cultural and conservative tendencies; he ruled with an iron hand. For his "mini-lectures and pronouncements," see *Protokoll*, 1890–1907, Book 1. His successor, F. D. Droegemueller, continued Senne's conservative practices and staying power (1907–1926). Droegemueller would have stayed longer but ill health forced him into retirement.

37. This method of discipline was continued well into the twentieth century. Although fewer individuals seemed to be disciplined in the twentieth century, the process described was the typical form for addressing the controversy.

38. Only in 1904, nine years after the beginning of the controversy and the initial vandalism, was the issue discussed in *Protokoll*. The April 1904 minutes began, "Pastor discussed the topic that everybody knew but hadn't discussed

before the congregation." The congregation not only contacted the sheriff but also the county attorney because "it was clear something had to be done . . . to find out what to do" and to "protect our pastor" (*Protokoll*, Book 1, 160–61).

39. *Protokoll* refers to "Mrs. Block"; at the time there were two Mrs. Blocks, mother-in-law and daughter-in-law. Although the minutes do not make the distinction, I believe the older Mrs. Block (Gesche Mahnken Block) was most likely the woman in question. She and her husband sold the land to the church, and the community was named after them. She was also a practicing midwife and seemed to have considerable respect and prestige in the community. She would have been fifty-four years old at the time. Louis Timken, her proxy, was her daughter's husband and also a church officer.

40. *Protokoll*, Book 1, 49–50.

41. Graebner, *Uncertain Saints*, 115–16.

42. In 1921 the number of persons from Block living in the neighboring town of Paola had reached the point that a daughter church, First Lutheran, was organized. All of the charter members had grown up in Block but for economic or personal reasons had decided to live "in town." Besides St. Peter's Church "across the river," one other attempt was made to rival the church at Block; in 1881 the people living north and east of Block attempted to organize a church in the Highland community, but Zion German Evangelical Church remained small throughout its eighty-five-year history. This church was not affiliated with the Missouri Synod, and some members from Block joined the Highland church if they became dissatisfied with Trinity Lutheran.

43. Catherine M. Prelinger, "The Nineteenth-Century Deaconessate in Germany," in *German Women in the 18th and 19th Century: A Social and Literary History*, ed. Ruth-Ellen Joeres and Mary Jo Maynes (Bloomington: Indiana University Press, 1986), 215–29. This chapter describes the history of the deaconess movement in Germany and also provides a theoretical analysis of its development.

44. The two best sources on the synod's welfare ministry and women's contributions to it are Lueking, *A Century of Caring*, and Ruth Fritz Meyer, *Women on a Mission* (St. Louis: Concordia Publishing House, 1967).

45. See Nancy F. Cott, *The Bonds of Womanhood: "Woman's Sphere" in New England, 1780–1835* (New Haven, Conn.: Yale University Press, 1977), 126–59, and Carroll Smith-Rosenberg's "Beauty, the Beast, and the Militant Woman," in *A Heritage of Her Own*, ed. Nancy F. Cott and Elizabeth H. Pleck (New York: Simon and Schuster, 1979), 197–221.

46. For a more comprehensive and comparative analysis of the activities of lay women and women religious, see Janet Wilson James, ed., *Women in American Religion* (Philadelphia: University of Pennsylvania Press, 1980), and the three-volume work by Rosemary Radford Ruether and Rosemary Skinner Keller, eds., *Women and Religion in America* (New York: Harper and Row, 1986).

47. Women's domestic production was clearly valuable although it was undervalued and often unnoticed. Quilts, food production, and other homemade goods brought profit even in rural communities.

48. Constitution of the Trinity Lutheran Ladies Aid of Block, Kansas (TLC Archives), 1.

49. Although no official membership roster is available, this May 1935 meeting did record the members' names. The minutes also list newly accepted members as well as guests for each meeting, which reveals some information about

the composition of the membership and the rate of growth and change from its inception through 1945.

50. The "hired girl" experience played a crucial role in the education of Block's adolescents and young adults, particularly if the young woman worked in Kansas City.

51. The translator, who worked with both sets of minutes, did not see a gender difference in the written language skills of the recording secretaries. As the secretaries changed for each group, both the men's and the women's groups showed equal variability; some secretaries had excellent skills in written German, and others did not. However, the translator did see skills growing poorer in written German as each group came closer to making the complete change to English. The women began writing in English in 1934 and the men in 1936, but both groups waited until they had finished a recording book. Also, each group voted on making the total switch to English.

52. Ladies Aid Minutes (English translation), April 14, 1926 (TLC Archives), 24.

53. For a good source that focuses on comparing male and female personal writings, see John Mack Faragher, *Women and Men on the Overland Trail* (New Haven, Conn.: Yale University Press, 1979), 128–33. For further understanding of women's writings, see Lillian Schlissel, *Women's Diaries of the Westward Journey* (New York: Schocken Books, 1982); Elizabeth Hampsten, *Read This Only to Yourself: The Private Writings of Midwestern Women, 1880–1910* (Bloomington: Indiana University Press, 1982); and the important work done by the Personal Narratives Group, *Interpreting Women's Lives: Feminist Theory and Personal Narratives* (Bloomington: Indiana University Press, 1989). Other than some correspondence, I have no knowledge of any personal writings left by first-, second-, or third-generation women of Block. Midwest historian Linda Pickle laments the lack of personal writings left by German women in Kansas and Nebraska. "Most often one is forced to glean bits of information from the writings of German men, from public documents and other printed sources" ("Rural German-Speaking Women in Early Nebraska and Kansas," *Great Plains Quarterly* 9 [Fall 1989]:239).

54. Specifically, I am referring to domestic and nurturing activities typically assigned to and performed individually by women. These activities often became formalized when women joined together in groups such as reform societies, clubs, and other charitable organizations operated through churches or secular societies.

55. Author interview with Nora Ohlmeier Prothe, June 24, 1986.

56. Hospitals and orphanages in Kansas, Nebraska, and Colorado received most of the women's work. Also, a black congregation in Alabama, a missionary hospital in India, and a German relief fund received monetary donations from the group.

57. Ellen Condliffe Lagemann, "Looking at Gender in Women's History," in *Historical Inquiry in Education: A Research Agenda*, ed. John Hardin Best (Washington, D.C.: American Educational Research Association, 1983), 251–64.

58. Pickle, "Rural German-Speaking Women," 247.

59. Clarence H. Peters, "Developments of the Youth Programs of the Lutheran Churches in America" (Th.D. diss., St. Louis: Concordia Seminary, 1951), 26.

60. *Lutheran Witness*, "Why Girls Are Ruined," May 1, 1917, 133.

61. Constitution of the Trinity Lutheran Walther League (TLC Archives), 192.

62. Lutheran churches historically have filled services with singing. Martin Luther is given credit for this phenomenon because of his understanding and enthusiasm for music of all kinds; he wanted the congregation to participate actively in worship. The *Lutheran Cyclopedia* quotes Luther as stating that "next to theology there is no art which is the equal of music, for she alone, after theology, can do what otherwise only theology can accomplish" (723).

63. "Block Items" in *Western Spirit*, March 14, 1930.

64. Maxine Schwartz Seller, ed., *Immigrant Women* (Philadelphia: Temple University Press, 1981), 68.

CHAPTER 3. SCHOOL

1. Walter H. Beck, *Lutheran Elementary Schools in the United States* (St. Louis: Concordia Publishing House, 1939), 101. Beck and August C. Stellhorn, *Schools of the Lutheran Church–Missouri Synod* (St. Louis: Concordia Publishing House, 1963), provide the two most complete works concerning synod schools; Stellhorn studies elementary through postsecondary education. For the most recent work that examines Missouri Synod national school policy and its implementation in Wisconsin, see John P. Boubel, "A History of Lutheran Church–Missouri Synod Schools in Wisconsin: National Policies and Local Implementation" (Ph.D. diss., Marquette University, 1989).

2. E. Clifford Nelson, *The Rise of World Lutheranism: An American Perspective* (Philadelphia: Fortress Press, 1982), 295.

3. Stellhorn, *Schools of the Lutheran Church*, 172.

4. Jay Dolan, *The American Catholic Experience: A History from Colonial Times to the Present* (Garden City, N.Y.: Image Books, 1987), 242. Although immigrants from a variety of European countries supported the parochial school, Dolan states that the Germans were some of its strongest supporters. The Catholic Church sponsored the largest number of parochial schools in the United States, but the nineteenth-century Lutheran Church–Missouri Synod created the largest number of schools of all the Protestant denominations. For a discussion of Chicago Catholic immigrants and their schools, see Robert A. Slayton, *Back of the Yards: The Making of a Local Democracy* (Chicago: University of Chicago Press, 1986), 45–55.

5. Slayton, *Back of the Yards*, 46–49; Frederick Luebke, "The Immigrant Condition as a Factor Contributing to the Conservatism of the Lutheran Church–Missouri Synod," *Concordia Historical Institute Quarterly* 38 (April 1965):22–23. For a more in-depth discussion of the importance of moral values in public and private schools, see Barbara Finkelstein, "Casting Networks of Good Influence," in *American Childhood: A Research Guide and Historical Handbook*, ed. Joseph Hawes and N. Ray Hiner (Westport, Conn.: Greenwood Press, 1985), 111–52; Joel Spring, *American School 1642–1990*, 2d ed. (New York: Longman, 1990), 50–62; Lloyd P. Jorgenson, *The State and the Non-Public School, 1825–1925* (Columbia: University of Missouri Press, 1987); and Joseph Neuman, "Private Schools vs. Public Schools," in *America's Teachers*, ed. Joseph Neuman, (New York: Longman, 1989), 276–94.

6. Many sources discuss the problem of ethnic children who assimilate more

quickly than their parents and the resulting difficulties. I would suggest Selma Berrol, "Ethnicity and Children," in *American Childhood*; Leonard Dinnerstein, Roger L. Nichols, and David M. Reimers, *Natives and Strangers: Blacks, Indians, and Immigrants in America*, 2d ed. (New York: Oxford University Press, 1990), 173–75, Spring, *American School*, 162–72; and Lawrence A. Cremin, *American Education: The National Experience, 1783–1876* (New York: Harper and Row, 1980), 375–78.

7. *Protokoll*, April 1896 (quarterly meeting), Book 1, 119.

8. Although specific data are available on the use of the German language in worship services, the parochial school data on language usage are more difficult to obtain. Before the pressures of World War I, most schools taught religion and some reading and writing in the German language; in fact, most Missouri Synod parochial schools were called "German schools" by local communities. Each congregation experienced pressure during World War I and responded to it differently. Some schools stopped using German, some did not use it for a few years but returned to it, and others continued to use it throughout the war. The 1924 *Statistical Yearbook of the Lutheran Church–Missouri Synod* (St. Louis: Concordia Publishing House, 1884–) noted that 60 percent of the Kansas district used the German language predominantly in church services. For a discussion of nineteenth-century bicultural (German) schools in Midwest urban areas, see Audrey L. Olson, "St. Louis Germans, 1850–1920: The Nature of an Immigrant Community and Its Relation to the Assimilation Process" (Ph.D. diss., University of Kansas, 1970), 94–97.

9. Robert M. Toepper, "Rationale for Preservation of the German Language in the Missouri Synod of the Nineteenth Century," *Concordia Historical Institute Quarterly* 41 (Feb. 1968):165. See also Luebke, "Immigrant Condition," 22–23. For a comparison with urban Germans, see Kathleen Neils Conzen, *Immigrant Milwaukee, 1836–1860* (Cambridge, Mass.: Harvard University Press, 1976), 154–224.

10. Since the church had no basement, the schoolhouse was used for Walther League meetings, youth rallies, box suppers, band practice, debates, spelling bees, Red Cross meetings during World War I, telephone meetings, and many other religious and secular activities. This practice was typical of most rural schools, parochial or public, in the nineteenth-century Midwest. For a complete discussion of the importance of the school to a rural community, see Wayne Fuller, *The Old Country School: The Story of Rural Education in the Middle West* (Chicago: University of Chicago Press, 1982); David B. Tyack, "The Tribe and the Common School: Community Control in Rural Education," *American Quarterly* 24 (1972):3–19; and Mary W. M. Hargreaves, "Rural Education on the Northern Plains Frontier," *Journal of the West* 18 (Oct. 1979):25–32.

11. *Statistical Yearbook of the Lutheran Church–Missouri Synod*, 1900, 1916, 1930, 1945.

12. *Protokoll*, July 1872, 6 (quarterly meeting), Trinity Lutheran Church (TLC) Archives, Block, Kansas.

13. Ibid., 98.

14. As childrearing practices changed for white Americans in the nineteenth century and women took a primary role in fostering a child's education and well-being, Missouri Synod doctrine advocated a father's responsibility for his children's education similar to the role that Puritan fathers had been encouraged to fill. See John Demos, *A Little Commonwealth: Family Life in Plymouth Colony* (New York: Oxford University Press, 1970), 100–106 and 131–44, and Edmund

S. Morgan, *The Puritan Family: Religion and Domestic Relations in Seventeenth-Century New England* (New York: Harper and Row, 1966), 65–108. For more recent research on colonial childhood and childrearing patterns, see N. Ray Hiner, "Cotton Mather and His Children: The Evolution of a Parent Educator, 1686–1728," in *Regulated Children, Liberated Children: Education in Psychohistorical Perspective,* ed. Barbara Finkelstein (New York: Psychohistory Press, 1979), 24–43.

15. Nineteenth-century Protestant clergy modified but continued this educational legacy of placing fathers at the center of responsibility for the child's moral education. For a fascinating discussion of evangelical childrearing, see William G. McLoughlin, "Evangelical Childrearing in the Age of Jackson: Francis Wayland's Views on When and How to Subdue the Willfulness of Children," in *Growing Up in America,* ed. N. Ray Hiner and Joseph P. Hawes (Urbana: University of Illinois Press, 1985), 87–107.

16. 1 Cor. 14:35 (King James Version). This passage defined women's silent role in the Missouri synod church, effectively barring them from voting, speaking, or becoming a pastor or teacher.

17. *Protokoll,* Book 2, 15–16. Because of the large German-Lutheran influx around Block Village, the public schools in the area were "nearly empty." The public school enrollment in this area of the county was small because the vast majority of children, who were German Lutherans, went to the (very crowded) parochial school. In 1911 the two-room Block school housed seventy-seven students in eight grades.

18. Federal and state census data show inconsistencies in literacy rates for first-generation adults in Block and are not always dependable. For example, the 1865 Kansas State Census ("Miami County," microfilm #6, Topeka) and the 1870 Federal Census ("Population, Miami County, Kans.," microfilm #12, Washington, D.C.: GPO) show Dietrich and Gesche Block as literate. However, 1870 is the year the Blocks sold land to the church, and the deed records an "X" for both Dietrich and Gesche; neither wrote their signatures. Scholars of German education described elementary education before 1870 as inconsistent, particularly for women, and people from the rural regions had even less opportunity for schooling. See Gerald Strauss, "The Social Function of Schools in the Lutheran Reformation in Germany," *History of Education Quarterly* 28 (Summer 1988):191–206; Marjorie Lamberti, *State, Society, and the Elementary School in Imperial Germany* (New York: Oxford University Press, 1989); and George and Lottelore Bernstein, "Attitudes toward Women's Education in Germany, 1870–1914," *International Journal of Women's Studies* 2 (1979):473–88.

19. Author interview with Elsie Prothe Dageforde, Oct. 21, 1986.

20. Author interview with Irene Minden Prothe, July 18, 1986. Parents whose children attended public schools used a similar strategy for ensuring school attendance. See Hargreaves, "Rural Education," 30, and Elliott West, *Growing Up in the Country: Childhood on the Far West Frontier* (Albuquerque: University of New Mexico Press, 1989), 186–89.

21. Author interview with Minnie Cahman Debrick, Sept. 23, 1986.

22. This description is a composite provided by interviewees and a 1922 visiting county superintendent, Emma Mills; her comments and description were published in *Western Spirit,* Jan. 27, 1922. Since the school was not under county supervision, she was probably invited by the teacher, H. F. Klinkermann, to alleviate some political pressure brought about by past and current legislation attacking parochial schools as "un-American." The two-room school was built

in 1916 with a basement furnace; before, the school had been a one-room build-ing and the church annex had served the primary grades when student numbers exceeded expectations after the turn of the century.

23. Allan H. Jahsmann, *What's Lutheran in Education? Explorations into Principles and Practices* (St. Louis: Concordia Publishing House, 1960), x.

24. Beck, *Lutheran Elementary Schools,* 114, and Stellhorn, *Schools of the Lutheran Church,* 125. The importance of Concordia Publishing House to the synod cannot be overemphasized. Many church groups understood the neces-sity of creating their own educational materials, and several Protestant denom-inations used a church-sponsored publishing house to educate the laity. Jay Dolan adamantly states that Catholic literature was an important component in the main reading material in Catholic homes *(American Catholic Experience,* 246–47). Contemporary Christian fundamentalist groups use their own publish-ing companies to ensure Christian-oriented textbooks for their schools.

25. Beck, *Lutheran Elementary Schools,* 396.

26. *Protokoll,* Oct. 10, 1937, Book 2, 145.

27. Music and singing were excellent for instilling German values and cul-ture, and interviewees reported that they always sang in German. The inter-viewees may have forgotten much of the German language, but typically they remembered songs in German. Music and singing were an important part of every religious and cultural activity in Block.

28. The term "hidden curriculum" is a label used by contemporary educators in describing informal or incidental activities not considered part of the formal curriculum, and it usually includes values, beliefs, and behavior that the culture reinforces in response to gender, age, class, or racial differences.

29. Laura Koelsch Ohlmeier told how young girls after confirmation would be asked by teacher Wolters to clean the school on a Saturday and added that he often provided watermelon as a reward for their voluntary work. She also de-scribed how the confirmation class of the 1930s (girls and boys) would clean their instruction room in the spring. After the cleaning, new members of the group were supposed to climb across the crossbeams in the old church and touch the bell as a rite of initiation; some children resisted this dare, but most girls and boys accepted the challenge and made the climb (conversation, Sept. 4, 1986).

30. Interviewees described a "tomball" as a sponge or string ball larger and softer than a baseball; a large oversized bat was used to hit it. A fielder could record an out by catching the ball after one bounce or by throwing the ball ahead of the runner to a base.

31. Childrens' games in Block were typical of rural children's games in the Midwest and West. Elliott West, *Growing Up in the Country,* 101–17, provides a fascinating discussion and categorization of children's play and compares the play of midwestern and western children with that of their peers in more settled parts of the country.

32. Oral interview with Minnie Cahman Debrick, Sept. 23, 1986.

33. I am referring to shame as the act of degrading, ostracizing, or humiliating a child in the presence of his or her peers; it requires the presence of a community or group that has similar attitudes and beliefs. Guilt refers to instilling in the child more internalized feelings as a control mechanism. Both are used as a means of social control, but guilt relies more on children's internalizing their belief systems and self-control. As a group or community becomes more heter-ogeneous, shame becomes less effective since important values and beliefs may no longer be shared by the group. There is an abundance of literature discussing

childhood disciplinary methods; see especially Bernard Wishy, *The Child and the Republic* (Philadelphia: University of Pennsylvania Press, 1968), and Finkelstein, *Regulated Children, Liberated Children.*

34. Author interview with Marie Dageforde Monthey, Aug. 16, 1986.

35. Author interview with Elmer Prothe, April 23, 1987.

36. Author interview with Minnie Cahman Debrick, Sept. 23, 1986.

37. For a discussion of differences in male and female teachers behavior, see Deborah Fitts, "Una and the Lion: The Feminization of District School-Teaching and Its Effects on the Roles of Students and Teachers in Nineteenth-Century Massachusetts," in *Regulated Children, Liberated Children,* 140–57.

38. Stellhorn, *Schools of the Lutheran Church,* 73.

39. Thomas Morain, "The Departure of Males from the Teaching Profession in Nineteenth-Century Iowa," *Civil War History* 26 (1980):161–70. See also Spring, *American Schools,* 115–34.

40. Stellhorn, *Schools of the Lutheran Church,* 210. A call is sanctified and directed by God through his human representatives in the congregation.

41. In 1864 extensive work in Bible study and the Lutheran confessions was combined with history, arithmetic, geography, and drawing. Incredibly, the teacher-trainee had to be proficient in violin, piano, organ, and vocal music and also had to know some music theory (Stellhorn, *Schools of the Lutheran Church,* 136).

42. Beck, *Lutheran Elementary Schools,* 380.

43. Ibid., 116–17 .

44. In 1934 Trinity Lutheran at Block hosted a Kansas district teachers' conference that included sixty teachers and teaching pastors. A small article appeared in the October 26 *Western Spirit* on the conference, which included guest speakers, "theoretical papers," and "practical demonstrations" on all types of curriculum — religious and secular.

45. *Protokoll,* Book 1, 98.

46. My thanks to Myrtle Neu Thoden, who sent me the official list of teachers and the dates they taught in Block (correspondence, Oct. 11, 1985). Although the *Protokoll* (Books 1 and 2) mentions most of these individuals by name, the minutes do not always include first names or the names of teaching assistants.

47. In 1880 a Kansas public-school teacher received an average salary of $27.56 per month; in 1890 Block's first teacher received $25.00 per month. Two years later, the congregation built a teachers' residence and continued to provide housing and fuel (Federal Census, 1880, microfilm #17 and #18, 1:916–17, and *Protokoll,* Book 1, 107.

48. Interestingly, the organ was viewed as an instrument that a female could play. Although all the teachers were male, interviewees said that they took lessons from the teacher, as many of their friends did. The girls would play the church organ for weddings, funerals, Sunday worship services, or for the pleasure of their families; however, most other instruments were seen as masculine. The band at Block in 1916 was all male, with trumpets, trombones, a baritone, and a bass drum. Men also played stringed instruments (fiddle and guitar) for dances or for entertainment.

49. *Western Spirit,* June 29, 1894.

50. J. C. W. Lindemann quote is taken from Carl S. Meyer, ed., *Moving Frontiers: Readings in the History of the Lutheran Church–Missouri Synod* (St. Louis: Concordia Publishing House, 1964), 374.

51. Much of the synod's theory on the subordination of women is based on St. Paul's letter to the Corinthians (1 Cor. 13:34–35); see also 1 Tim. 2:11–12.

52. *Protokoll*, Book 1, 158–59. This salary was approximately one-third of the male teacher's salary; he also had free housing and fuel.

53. Myrtle Neu Thoden correspondence, Oct. 11, 1985.

54. In 1919 at Concordia College in Seward, Nebraska, women were allowed to make up 20 percent of the total enrollment; in 1938 at the teaching college at River Forest, enrollment of women was held to 30 percent. For further data see Stellhorn, *Schools of the Lutheran Church*, 424–26. See also George J. Gude, "Women Teachers in the Missouri Synod," *Concordia Historical Institute Quarterly* 44 (Nov. 1971):163–70.

55. John Eiselmeier, "The Feminization of the Teaching Profession," *Lutheran School Journal* 40 (Jan. 1925):17–20.

56. A 1938 survey describes the problem. Of the women teaching in synod schools, 40 percent had degrees from state colleges, 20 percent had only an elementary education, 4.5 percent held degrees from sectarian colleges, and 35.5 percent held degrees from Missouri Synod institutions (Gude, "Women Teachers in the Missouri Synod," 167).

57. Alan Graebner, "Attitudes in the Lutheran Church–Missouri Synod toward Sexual Morality, 1900–1960" (Master's Thesis, Columbia University, 1961), 80–81.

58. Clarence Peters, "Developments of the Youth Programs of the Lutheran Churches in America" (Th.D. diss., Concordia Theological Seminary, 1951), 26.

59. For interesting discussions on the synod's view of revivals, see Heinrich H. Mauer, "The Consciousness of Kind of a Fundamentalist Group," *American Journal of Sociology* 31 (Jan. 1926):494, and Ralph Dornfeld Owen, "The Old Lutherans Come," *Concordia Historical Institute Quarterly* 20 (1948): 3–56.

60. Author interview with Marie Dageforde Monthey, Aug. 16, 1986.

61. Author interview with Minnie Cahman Debrick, Sept. 23, 1986.

62. Slayton, *Back of the Yards*, 47. For additional information on Catholic confirmation practices and school, see Dolan, *American Catholic Experience*, 255–57.

63. For the first four decades of the twentieth century few children from Block attended the high school in Paola. Some car pooled before the bus service began in 1936; however, if children wanted to stay on the farm, the difficulties of transportation and economic exigencies contributed to keeping most of them out of high school until the 1940s.

64. In the nineteenth century, most girls hired out to family members or friends, but as economic needs in the twentieth century changed, girls were working as live-in maids in Paola and later in Kansas City.

65. *Protokoll*, April 1896 (quarterly meeting), Book 1, 119.

CHAPTER 4. FAMILY

1. Charles H. Mindel and Robert W. Habenstein, "The Ethnic Family: Protean and Adaptive," in *Ethnic Families in America: Patterns and Variations*, ed. Mindel and Habenstein (New York: Elsevier, 1976), 418–19. See also Richard J. Evans and W. R. Lee, *The German Family: Essays on the Social History of the Family in Nineteenth- and Twentieth-Century Germany* (Totowa, N.J.: Barnes and No-

ble, 1981). For a discussion of German and other ethnic families, see Leonard Dinnerstein, Roger L. Nichols, and David M. Reimers, *Natives and Strangers: Blacks, Indians, and Immigrants in America*, 2d ed. (New York: Oxford University Press, 1990), 90–97 and 110–14.

2. Kathleen Neils Conzen, "Historical Approaches to the Study of Rural Ethnic Communities," in *Ethnicity on the Great Plains*, ed. Frederick Luebke (Lincoln: University of Nebraska Press, 1980), 10. See also Kathleen Neils Conzen, "Peasant Pioneers: Generational Succession among German Farmers in Frontier Minnesota," in *The Countryside in the Age of Capitalist Transformation*, ed. Stephen Hahn and Jonathan Prude (Chapel Hill: University of North Carolina Press, 1985), 259–92.

3. Heinrich H. Mauer, "Studies in the Sociology of Religion: The Sociology of Protestantism," *American Journal of Sociology* 30 (Nov. 1924):269–70.

4. Lydia said that her mother was warned not to let her daughter sleep with her grandmother because folk wisdom deemed that a child's energy would be sapped by sleeping with an older person. This example illustrates that the house was indeed crowded, but it also demonstrates the lack of privacy because non-family members obviously knew other families' sleeping arrangements.

5. For descriptions of German family life and the importance of duty and order, see Evans and Lee, *German Family*; John C. Fout, ed., *German Women in the Nineteenth Century: A Social History* (New York: Holmes and Meier, 1984); and Hinda Winawer-Steiner and Norbert A. Wetzel, "German Families," in *Ethnicity and Family Therapy*, ed. Monica McGoldrick, John K. Pearce, and Joseph Geordano (New York: Guilford Press, 1982). The writings of Martin Luther and early church fathers unfailingly supported and espoused the importance of order and duty in the family setting. For a more contemporary discussion of parental duty and authority over children, see Allan H. Jahsmann, *What's Lutheran in Education? Explorations into Principles and Practices* (St. Louis: Concordia Publishing House, 1960).

6. Elliott West, *Growing Up in the Country: Childhood on the Far West Frontier* (Albuquerque: University of New Mexico Press, 1989), 158–61. I would argue that West's informants may have been reluctant to discuss disciplinary practices because by contemporary standards they would have seemed harsh and abusive. These informants may not have wanted their parents to appear unduly or inappropriately severe in their administration of corporal punishment. The informants from Block certainly seemed to feel that some corporal punishment was necessary and appropriate, but most commented on how differently spanking was viewed in their era from the way it is viewed today.

7. Author interview with Frieda Timkin Baumgardt, Nov. 12, 1988.

8. Author interview with Marie Dageforde Monthey, Aug. 16, 1986.

9. West, *Growing Up in the Country*, 160.

10. Karin Hausen, "Family and Role-Division: The Polarisation of Sexual Stereotypes in the Nineteenth Century — an Aspect of the Dissociation of Work and Family Life," in *German Family*, 52.

11. Author interview with Elmer Prothe, April 23, 1987.

12. Elliott West describes this all too common nineteenth-century frontier scenario that forced many young children into adult responsibilities in *Growing Up in the Country*, 95.

13. Author interview with Clarence Clausen, March 15, 1986.

14. Author interview with Elsie Prothe Dageforde, Oct. 21, 1986.

15. Author interview with Minnie Cahman Debrick, Sept. 23, 1986.

16. Author interview with Marie Dageforde Monthey, Aug. 16, 1986.

17. For a detailed look at children's work responsibilities, see West, *Growing Up in the Country*, 73–100. I agree with West that gender was an important variable, but need always took precedence over gender in a rural setting.

18. For a detailed examination of the hired-girl experience of adolescents from Block, see Carol K. Coburn, "Learning to Serve: Education and Change in the Lives of Rural Domestics in the Early Twentieth Century," *Journal of Social History* 25 (Fall 1991):571–84.

19. For an excellent discussion of *Geschlechtscharakter* ("complementary nature of the sexes"), see Hausen, "Family and Role-Division," 51–83. Basically the term means that mental and physical attributes are related specifically to biological sexuality. The ideology of "complementary roles" accepts this perceived innate difference between men and women and espouses the necessity of heterosexual marriage as the ideal partnership since male and female "characteristics" can then merge and become whole, one complementing the other.

20. John Mack Faragher, "History from the Inside-Out: Writing the History of Women in Rural America," *American Quarterly* 33 (Winter 1981):541. To quote Faragher on the meaning of status: "The question of status is not primarily a question of what people do, but rather of the recognition they are granted for what they do and the authority that recognition confers." I certainly believe that the residents of Block understood the value of women's work, but since culturally males were viewed as superior, whatever work they did would automatically carry more status.

21. Juliane Jacobi-Dittrich, "Growing Up Female in the Nineteenth Century," in *German Women in the Nineteenth Century*, 199.

22. Linda Pickle, "Stereotypes and Realities: Nineteenth-Century German Women in Missouri," *Missouri Historical Review* 79 (April 1985):294. Pickle particularly singles out the synod's prescriptive literature and the constant efforts to maintain this female stereotype. *Der Lutheraner* and *Lutheran Witness* magazines are replete with articles on the importance of marriage and motherhood and the dangers of rejecting "God's plan" for the sexes.

23. Faragher, "History from the Inside-Out," 540. See also Faragher's *Sugar Creek: Life on the Illinois Prairie* (New Haven, Conn.: Yale University Press, 1986); Glenda Riley, "Farm Women's Roles in the Agricultural Development of South Dakota," *South Dakota History* 13 (Spring/Summer 1983):83–121; Glenda Riley, *The Female Frontier: A Comparative View of Women on the Prairie and the Plains* (Lawrence: University Press of Kansas, 1988); Wava G. Haney and Jane B. Knowles, *Women and Farming: Changing Roles and Structures* (Boulder, Colo.: Westview Press, 1988); and Joan M. Jensen, *Promise to the Land: Essays on Rural Women* (Albuquerque: University of New Mexico Press, 1991). Jensen's book also addresses the contributions of Native American and African American women.

24. Author interview with Marie Dageforde Monthey, Aug. 16, 1986.

25. Electricity did not come to Block until 1948, and the acquisition of indoor plumbing varied greatly from family to family. For an interesting and thorough review of household technology and its development, see Susan Strasser, *Never Done: A History of American Housework* (New York: Pantheon Books, 1982).

26. Riley, "Farm Women's Roles," 98, and Pickle, "Stereotypes and Reality," 294. See also Jacobi-Dittrich, "Growing Up Female," 197–217. Interviewees continued to discuss female friends and relatives, using the same descriptive terms.

a

27. Author interview with Ida Minden Peckman, Aug. 18, 1986.

28. Pickle, "Stereotypes and Reality," 294.

29. For additional discussion on the "fluidity" of rural women's roles, see Jensen, *Promise to the Land*; Glenda Riley, "Women's Responses to the Challenges of Plains Living," *Great Plains Quarterly* 9 (Summer 1989):174–84; Cornelia Butler Flora and Jan L. Flora, "Structure of Agriculture and Women's Culture on the Great Plains," *Great Plains Quarterly* 8 (Fall 1988):195–205; and also in the same *GPQ* issue, see Carol K. Coburn, "Ethnicity, Religion and Gender: The Women of Block, Kansas, 1868–1940," 222–32.

30. Over one-half of the third-generation interviewees came from families of seven children or more. Of the sixteen women from Block forced to register as aliens during World War I, eight had given birth to seven children or more; twelve to six or more; and three to ten children or more.

31. Carol K. Coburn, "Learning to Serve." For a larger examination of fertility patterns on the frontier, see Lee L. Bean, Geraldine P. Mineau, and Douglas L. Anderson, *Fertility Patterns on the American Frontier: Adaptation and Innovation* (Berkeley: University of California Press, 1990).

32. Author interview with Lydia Prothe Schultz, Jan. 26, 1985.

33. A. W. Meyer, *Lutheran Witness* 24 (1905):157; Richard Jesse, *Lutheran Witness* 44 (1925):337; quoted in *Lutheran Witness* 20 (1901):55. These quotes and others are found in Alan Graebner, "Birth Control and the Lutherans: The Missouri Synod as a Case Study," in *Women and American Religion*, ed. Janet Wilson James (Philadelphia: University of Pennsylvania Press, 1980), 229–52.

34. Graebner, "Birth Control and the Lutherans," 236. This article provides an interesting look at attitudes and the prescriptive literature of clergy and compares this review with actual birth records of synod congregations. Graebner thinks the most important cause for change in clerical attitudes was the behavior of the laity, who continued to have fewer children in the twentieth century.

35. Author interview with Lydia Prothe Schultz, Nov. 25, 1984. Lydia heard this comment as she sat with her sister Lena after childbirth; apparently Lena's husband took her seriously as they had no more children.

36. Although three granddaughters, Frieda Timken Baumgardt, Lydia Prothe Schultz, and Nora Ohlmeier Prothe, provided the most information on Grandma Block, other interviewees remembered her or remembered stories told about her.

37. *Western Spirit*, Jan. 5, 1912. Doctors traveled seven miles from Paola or seven miles from New Lancaster to come to Block.

38. Conversation with Louise Timken Mammen on June 5, 1987.

39. Timothy J. Kloberdanz, "The Daughters of Shiphrah: Folk Healers and Midwives of the Great Plains," *Great Plains Quarterly* 9 (Winter 1989):3–12; see also Kloberdanz, "Cross Makers: German-Russian Folk Specialists of the Great Plains" (Ph.D. diss., Indiana University, 1986). For a broader perspective on women healers and midwifery, see Barbara Ehrenreich and Deirdre English, *For Her Own Good* (Garden City, N.Y.: Anchor Books, 1979).

40. Author interview with Frieda Timken Baumgardt, Nov. 12, 1988. Interestingly, Grandma Block had two granddaughters who became involved in healing: Mary Tinken Koelsch was said to be a "healer" and helped people by touching them with her hands, and Elizabeth Block Thomas became a Red Cross nurse and served in France during World War I. Since both women grew into adulthood during Grandma Block's lifetime, it is interesting to speculate about her influence; both women healed the sick but used very different methods.

41. There are many excellent sources on midwifery and historical views of women's health issues. See Richard W. Wertz and Dorothy C. Wertz, *Lying-In: A History of Childbirth in America* (New York: Free Press, 1977), and Judith Barrett Litoff, *American Midwives: 1860 to the Present* (Westport, Conn.: Greenwood Press, 1978). For a review of midwifery and women's health issues, see Judith Walzer Leavitt, ed., *Women and Health in America* (Madison: University of Wisconsin Press, 1984), and Judith Walzer Leavitt, *Brought to Bed: Childbirth in America, 1750–1950* (New York: Oxford University Press, 1986).

42. These statistics are taken from death records kept by Trinity Lutheran Church from 1868 to the present. In each case the cause of death is listed as "stillborn." Some children died within hours of birth, but they are not counted in these figures.

43. I wish to express my thanks to Mary Zimmerman, associate professor, Health Services Administration, at the University of Kansas. She helped me interpret the data and suggested various approaches to clarify the statistics.

44. Jensen, *Promise to the Land*, 259. Other scholars have strongly agreed with this premise. See Riley, *Female Frontier*, 73–74, and Paula Petrik, *No Step Backward: Women and Family on the Rocky Mountain Mining Frontier, Helena, Montana, 1865–1900* (Helena: Montana Historical Society Press, 1987), xvii. For additional discussions on women's activities and support networks, see Micaela di Leonardo, "The Myth of the Urban Village: Women, Work, and Family among Italian-Americans in Twentieth-Century California," in *The Women's West*, ed. Susan Armitage and Elizabeth Jameson (Norman: University of Oklahoma Press, 1987): 277–90; Sylvia Yanagisako, *Transforming the Past: Tradition and Kinship among Japanese Americans* (Stanford: Stanford University Press, 1985); and Linda S. Pickle, "Rural German-Speaking Women in Early Nebraska and Kansas: Ethnicity as a Factor in Frontier Adaptation, *Great Plains Quarterly* 9 (Fall 1989):239–51.

45. Flora and Flora, "Structure of Agriculture," 204. The Floras argue that women's networks mitigated men's absolute control over resources. They acknowledge the importance of informal networks, and they specifically label Catholic and Lutheran churches as important sites for women's formal networks.

46. Mindel and Habenstein, "Ethnic Family," 415–16.

47. Author interview with Marie Dageforde Monthey, Aug. 16, 1986.

48. Author interview with Clarence Clausen, March 13, 1986.

49. Author interview with Marie Dageforde Monthey, Aug. 16, 1986.

50. Author interview with Lydia Prothe Schultz, Feb. 13, 1982. Lydia is Henry's daughter; she told and retold this story many times to me. Although she cannot remember the name of the medicine, she assures me it "cured him." Home remedies were prevalent in Block well into the twentieth century. Doctors were accepted but not used unless really needed, and hospitals were considered frightening places where people went to die.

51. Author interview with Nora Ohlmeier Prothe, June 24, 1986.

52. Nine drought years are officially recorded in the "Progress Report" (Topeka: Kansas State Planning Board, 1934). The years listed are 1860, 1874, 1901, 1911, 1913, 1917, 1918, 1930, and 1934. The devastating drought of 1936 put the count at ten. For this and other information on Kansas agriculture and population, see Carroll D. Clark and Roy L. Roberts, eds., *People of Kansas: A Demographic and Sociological Study* (Topeka: Kansas State Planning Board, 1936), 11.

53. Mrs. John Sponable, "The History of Block Community," *Miami County Republican,* Aug. 17, 1951.

54. "The Christian Home," *Lutheran Witness,* Sept. 1922, 290.

55. For a discussion of this subject, see Aurel Ende, "Battering and Neglect: Children in Germany, 1860–1978," *Journal of Psychohistory* 7 (1979–1980):250–69; Evans and Lee, *German Family;* and Fout, *German Women in the Nineteenth Century.*

56. Mindel and Habenstein, "Ethnic Family," 419.

57. Some adults chose to remain single, and those who remained in Block typically lived with parents or another family member. Although I have no specific statistics, it appears as though more men remained single than women. Single women sometimes chose to work in another community as hired help.

58. Author interview with Ida Minden Peckman, Aug. 18, 1986.

59. West, *Growing Up in the Country,* 164–66.

60. Lydia laughingly recalled this anecdote and added that "they ate every bit of it even as they complained loudly." Ironically, after this early lesson, Lydia perfected her pie-baking skills into a money-making enterprise. She spent the latter part of her adult life earning a living by making twenty pies a day to support herself after her husband's death. The *Miami County Republican* (Jan. 21, 1987) recorded her death and in her obituary stated that "she was known for her pie baking." She would have been pleased.

61. Mindel and Habenstein, "Ethnic Family," 415; Hausen, "Family and Role-Division," 105.

62. Between 1868 and 1920, approximately fifteen children were baptized each year; after 1920 baptisms averaged around nine per year, although during World War II the figure was much lower.

63. The doctrine of original sin specifies that each newborn comes into the world a sinner and must be redeemed, first through infant baptism and then later through confirmation and acceptance of Christ as Savior. In fact, emergency baptism is allowed in the Missouri Synod whereby a lay person can baptize a child if a pastor is unavailable and the child is not expected to live. Children in confirmation class are taught how to perform this emergency baptism. In 1889 newborn Heinrich Herman Wendte was baptized by his father; the baby lived, and the baptism was formally acknowledged by the pastor in church two months later.

64. *Dr. Martin Luther's Small Catechism* (St. Louis: Concordia Publishing House, 1943), 174.

65. Baptismal records, 11, Trinity Lutheran Church (TLC) Archives, Block, Kansas. Although giving five first names was highly unusual, this example demonstrates the importance of family connections in the naming process. In nineteenth-century Block, the custom of using the names of dead children was practiced by many families; if a family lost a child, the next same-sex child born would receive the first name of the deceased child.

66. Edwin L. Lueker, ed., *Lutheran Cyclopedia* (St. Louis: Concordia Publishing House, 1954), 655.

67. It was not until the 1920s that dancing and card playing became more acceptable in Block. Before the arrival of Pastor O. C. J. Keller, the pastors were rigid in their rhetoric against dancing and card playing. Dancing was considered a preliminary to "whoring behavior," and card playing was always associated with gambling. *Protokoll* entries in the 1870s sternly admonish members caught dancing and provide explicit definitions of engagement, adultery, and divorce.

68. Author interview with Esther Prothe Maisch, June 25, 1986.

69. Marriage records, TLC Recordbook. These figures are the average marital ages compiled from 1885 to 1945. Since during some years no marriages took place and in others there were seven or eight, I decided that looking at individual years was not representative and chose to examine decades to calculate an average marital age for men and women. There were marriages before 1885, but ministers did not begin recording ages until that year.

70. For an excellent description of the synod's stand on engagement and other moral issues, see Alan Graebner, "Attitudes in the Lutheran Church — Missouri Synod toward Sexual Morality: 1900–1960 (Master's thesis, Columbia University, 1961).

71. Author interview with Marie Dageforde Monthey, Aug. 16, 1986.

72. Author interview with Nora Ohlmeier Prothe, June 24, 1986. For a detailed account of the *Hochzeitsbitter*, see William G. Bek, "Survival of Old Marriage Customs among the Low Germans of West Missouri," *Journal of American Folklore* 21 (1908):60–66.

73. *Western Spirit*, Oct. 23, 1891. Although the author is not known, it was probably B. J. Sheridan, editor of a Paola newspaper. Sheridan grew up in Osage Township and had known many of the residents of Block for years. His friendship woth "the Germans" gave the Block community extensive coverage in the Paola paper, and he covered many activities in Block himself.

74. Stanley Nadel, *Little Germany: Ethnicity, Religion, and Class in New York City, 1845–80* (Urbana: University of Illinois Press, 1990), 48.

75. Death records, TLC Recordbook. This record provides date of death, exact age, survivors, and the cause of death. Also, all statistics are grouped using figures for the entire decade as follows: 1868–1879, 1880–1889, 1890–1899, 1900–1909, 1910–1919, 1920–1929, 1930–1939. Since yearly numbers were too small to be significant, I decided that decade averages would be more representative.

76. The decade of the 1890s is an exception to this, as then the average age of females at death was only four years less than that of males.

77. Author interview with Nora Ohlmeier Prothe, June 24, 1986.

78. *Protokoll*, 1921, Book 2, 60–61, TLC Archives, Block, Kansas.

79. Author interview with Alma Clausen Debrick, March 15, 1986.

80. No one living in Block can explain why the cemetery is in chronological order. "It's always been that way, so why change now?" I have been told this custom is definitely not a carryover from Germany, but I have little other information.

81. For an interesting discussion of conflict within the patriarchal family, see Heidi I. Hartmann, "The Family as the Locus of Gender, Class, and Political Struggle: The Example of Housework," *Signs* 6 (Spring 1981):366–94, and Heidi Hartmann, "Capitalism, Patriarchy, and Job Segregation by Sex," *Signs* 1 (Spring 1976):137–69. For the potential conflicts that could arise during the depression, see Lois Rita Helmbold, "Beyond the Family Economy: Black and White Working-Class Women during the Great Depression," *Feminist Studies* 13 (Fall 1987):629–55.

CHAPTER 5. THE OUTSIDE WORLD

1. Heinrich H. Mauer, "The Lutheran Community and American Society: A Study in Religion as a Condition of Social Accommodation," *American Journal of Sociology* 34 (Sept. 1928): 285.

2. Frederick C. Luebke, "The Immigrant Condition as a Factor Contributing to the Conservatism of the Lutheran Church–Missouri Synod," *Concordia Historical Institute Quarterly* 38 (April 1965):27. For a compilation of essays that focuses on the German Lutherans, particularly on the Missouri Synod, see Luebke, *Germans in the New World: Essays in the History of Immigration* (Urbana: University of Illinois Press, 1990).

3. Author interview with Mildred Block, Nov. 22, 1985. Although I have quoted only Mildred Block I was repeatedly told a similar story by other interviewees.

4. Charles H. Mindel and Robert W. Habenstein, "The Ethnic Family: Protean and Adaptive," in *Ethnic Families in America: Patterns and Variations*, ed. Mindel and Habenstein (New York: Elsevier, 1976), 417. Other examples that reinforce this contention concerning family economic adaptability include Kathleen Neils Conzen, *Immigrant Milwaukee, 1836–1860* (Cambridge, Mass.: Harvard University Press, 1976), and Virginia Yans-McLaughlin, *Family and Community: Italian Immigrants in Buffalo, 1880–1930* (Ithaca, N.Y.: Cornell University Press, 1978). More recent contributions but equally excellent scholarship include Micaela di Leonardo, *The Varieties of Ethnic Experience: Kinship, Class, and Gender among California Italian-Americans* (Ithaca, N.Y.: Cornell University Press, 1984), and Sylvia Yanagisako, *Transforming the Past: Tradition and Kinship among Japanese Americans* (Stanford: Stanford University Press, 1985).

5. Church records clearly demonstrate that when carpenters or any labor for the church was hired, members were always chosen if they had the necessary skills. When the church or individuals needed skills or materials unavailable within the Block community, the individual or business chosen to do the work invariably had a German surname. In discussing the business development of the Block community, J. Neale Carman writes, "Only a Lutheran could succeed commercially" ("Foreign Language Units of Kansas," [Manuscript, University of Kansas Archives], 2:1292).

6. This description of the two men and their stores is a compilation of information from interviews and newspaper accounts.

7. Interview with Marie Dageforde Monthey, Aug. 16, 1986. Marie also described a "butcher ring": One family would butcher and then share with other families in the group; then another family in the "ring" butchered and once again shared with the others until each family had shared their butchered meat with the others.

8. Alan Graebner, "Attitudes in the Lutheran Church — Missouri Synod toward Sexual Morality: 1900–1960" (Master's thesis, Columbia University, 1961), 13. For discussions on each issue, see Carl S. Meyer, ed., *Moving Frontiers: Readings in the History of the Lutheran Church — Missouri Synod* (St. Louis: Concordia Publishing House, 1964), 344–49; see also Luebke, *Germans in the New World*, xiv and 8–11.

9. For an excellent analysis of women's contributions to buttermaking see Joan M. Jensen, "Buttermaking and Economic Development in Mid-Atlantic America from 1750–1850," *Signs* 13 (Summer 1988):813–29. For a larger in-depth analysis, see Joan M. Jensen, *Loosening the Bonds: Mid-Atlantic Farm Women* (New Haven, Conn.: Yale University Press, 1986).

10. Author interview with Lydia Prothe Schultz, Feb. 13, 1982.

11. Kansas State Census "Miami County," (1875). Microfilm, reel #13, Topeka: Kans. Board of Agriculture.

12. Author interview with Esther Prothe Maisch, June 25, 1986.

13. For a particular focus on work roles of midwestern farm women, see John Mack Faragher, "History from the Inside-Out: Writing the History of Women in Rural America," *American Quarterly* 33 (Winter 1981):537–57; Deborah Fink, *Open Country, Iowa: Rural Women, Tradition, and Change* (Albany, N.Y.: SUNY Press, 1986); Glenda Riley, "Farm Women's Roles in the Agricultural Development of South Dakota," *South Dakota History* 13 (Spring/Summer 1983):83–121; Wava G. Haney and Jane B. Knowles, eds., *Women and Farming: Changing Roles, Changing Structures* (Boulder, Colo.: Westview Press, 1988); Rachel Ann Rosenfeld, *Farm Women: Work, Farm, and Family in the United States* (Chapel Hill: University of North Carolina Press, 1985); and Joan M. Jensen, *Promise to the Land: Essays on Rural Women* (Albuquerque: University of New Mexico Press, 1991).

14. The subject of how women felt about their work has been greatly ignored, but recent oral history projects have attempted to fill in the large gaps about this topic. Rural women, particularly midwestern women, often did not leave written diaries, nor did they articulate their feelings about their work; they were either too busy or simply felt that they had nothing important to say or write. For a discussion of midwestern women's writing and introspection, see Elizabeth Hampsten, *Read This Only to Yourself: The Private Writings of Midwestern Women, 1880–1910* (Bloomington: Indiana University Press, 1982); Jensen, *Promise to the Land*; and Lillian Schlissel, Vicki L. Ruiz, and Janice Monk, eds., *Western Women: Their Land, Their Lives* (Albuquerque: University of New Mexico Press, 1988).

15. There is some interesting anthropological research concerning women and markets. See Jane Collier, Michelle Z. Rosaldo, and Sylvia Yanagisako, "Is There a Family? New Anthropological Views," in *Rethinking the Family: Some Feminist Questions*, ed. Barrie Thorne, with Marilyn Yalom (New York: Longman, 1982). See also Deborah Fink, "Sidelines and Moral Capital: Women on Nebraska Farms in the 1930s," in *Women and Farming*, and Carolyn E. Sachs, *The Invisible Farmers: Women in Agricultural Production* (Totowa, N. J.: Rowman and Allanheld, 1983).

16. Mrs. John Sponable, "The History of the Block Community," *Miami County Republican*, Aug. 17, 1951. Mrs. Sponable's article draws heavily from the reminiscence of Michael Schultz, who grew up in Block in the 1870s.

17. Kansas State Census "Miami County," (1865), Microfilm, reel #6, Topeka: Kansas Board of Agriculture. The state census provides a cumulative list of agricultural products for each household in each township of the county, and thus shows the value and amount of women's domestic products. All agricultural products are listed together, however, so that male heads of households are given exclusive credit for all production.

18. For an insightful examination of contemporary problems in assessing women's work and value, see Katherine Jensen, "Mother Calls Herself a Housewife but She Buys Bulls," in *The Technological Woman: Interfacing with Tomorrow*, ed. Jan Zimmerman (New York: Praeger, 1983), 136–43, and Rosenfeld, *Farm Women*; see also Haney and Knowles, *Women and Farming*.

19. Nancy Grey Osterud, "The Valuation of Women's Work: Gender and the Market in a Dairy Farming Community during the Late Nineteenth Century," *Frontiers* 10 (1988):18–24. For an in-depth study, see Nancy Grey Osterud, *Bonds of Community and the Lives of Farm Women in Nineteenth-Century New York* (Ithaca, N. Y.: Cornell University Press, 1991).

20. Cornelia Butler Flora and Jan L. Flora, "Structure of Agriculture and Women's Culture in the Great Plains," *Great Plains Quarterly* 8 (Fall 1988):195–205. See also Carolyn E. Sachs, "The Participation of Women and Girls in Market and Non-Market Activities on Pennsylvania Farms," in *Women and Farming*, 123–34.

21. In 1900 the Peiker-Wishropp grocery store printed a large front-page advertisement in a Paola paper offering "to take all produce our county customers can offer" (*Western Spirit*, Aug. 24, 1900).

22. Author interview with Minnie Cahman Debrick, Sept. 23, 1986.

23. Women in Block, like other twentieth-century farm women, took jobs in town for wages during times of financial need. Usually these jobs were temporary, and the women returned to the farm when their families were financially stable again.

24. Jensen, *Loosening the Bonds*, 91.

25. Author interview with Irene Minden Prothe, July 18, 1986.

26. Author interview with Marie Dageforde Monthey, Aug. 28, 1986.

27. Author interview with Lydia Prothe Schultz, Feb. 13, 1982.

28. See Virginia Scharff, *Taking the Wheel: Women and the Coming of the Motor Age* (New York: Free Society Press, 1991), and Virginia Scharff, "Putting Wheels on Women's Sphere," in *Technology and Women's Voices: Keeping in Touch*, ed. Cheris Kramarae (New York: Routledge, Chapman Paul, 1988), 135–46. Scharff focuses specifically on the automobile and how it has historically affected women's lives. See also Jensen, "Mother Calls Herself a Housewife," 139.

29. For a discussion of generational succession among German farmers, see Kathleen Neils Conzen, "Peasant Pioneers: Generational Succession among German Farmers in Frontier Minnesota," in *The Countryside in the Age of Capitalist Transformation*, ed. Steven Hahn and Jonathan Prude (Chapel Hill: University of North Carolina Press, 1985), 259–92. Although time and place are very different, there are some similarities to colonial America and the effects that land division had on colonial patriarchy and male inheritance. The lack of inheritable land forced some people from the community or into other occupations. For examples of this, see John Demos, *The Little Commonwealth: Family Life in Plymouth Colony* (New York: Oxford University Press, 1970), and Philip Greven, *Four Generations: Population, Land, and Family in Colonial Andover, Massachusetts* (Ithaca, N. Y.: Cornell University Press, 1972).

30. Schultz's German Lutheranism actually helped him acquire the coveted mechanic's job on the railroad. The local union had become embroiled in a strike with the Missouri Pacific Railroad, and since the synod forbade men to join labor unions because of secular (particularly socialist) associations, Schultz willingly crossed the picket lines and was hired immediately.

31. For a brief history of First Lutheran Church in Paola, see *History of Churches: Miami County Kansas*, ed. Sister M. Charles McGrath (Paola, Kans.: Paola Association for Church Action, 1976), 67–70. There were some specific differences between the mother and daughter churches. Only English was spoken in First Lutheran, and the town church attempted to interact with outsiders economically, politically, and socially. Lutheran theology could not be compromised, however, and the church community in Paola retained its exclusivity in doctrinal practices.

32. Once again colonial literature provides a similar example of a mother-daughter church situation that pits town dwellers against farmers. In Salem,

Massachusetts, the town church was established first, unlike the Block-Paola situation. As the community grew, a strong rural contingency began to demand a church and governing body of their own in Salem Village; they felt their needs were not being addressed by the urban group. Competition and rivalry abounded and with much more serious consequences (see Paul Boyer and Stephan Nissenbaum, *Salem Possessed* [Cambridge, Mass.: Harvard University Press, 1974]).

33. Although First Lutheran remained less conservative than Trinity Lutheran, the late 1940s and 1950s saw a return to more conservative practices. Some older couples in Block who turned over farm operations to sons moved into town and began attending the Paola church. Their presence, in addition to a conservative minister, provided a powerful conservative element to the town church.

34. Author interview with Elmer Prothe, June 15, 1987.

35. Although this movement began in the 1920s, the depression pushed many men of Block into traveling or relocating to find work. *Western Spirit* recorded such visits and returns in a special section called "Block Items," which appeared weekly. Trips to see family and friends working elsewhere became commonplace in the 1930s.

36. Doris Weatherford, *Foreign and Female: Immigrant Women in America, 1840–1930* (New York: Schocken Books, 1986), 148, and Laurence A. Glasco, "The Life Cycles and Household Structure of American Ethnic Groups: Irish, Germans, and Native-born Whites in Buffalo, New York, 1855," in *A Heritage of Her Own*, ed. Nancy F. Cott and Elizabeth H. Pleck (New York: Simon and Schuster, 1979), 288; see also Joanne J. Meyerwitz, *Women Adrift: Independent Wage Earners in Chicago, 1880–1930* (Chicago: University of Chicago Press, 1988), and Lauren Ann Kattner, "Growing Up Female in New Braunfels: Social and Cultural Adaptations in a German-Texas Town," *Journal of Ethnic History* (Spring 1990):49–72.

37. For the best sources on domestic service, see David Katzman, *Seven Days a Week: Women and Domestic Service in Industrializing America* (Urbana: University of Illinois Press, 1981); Daniel E. Sutherland, *Americans and Their Servants: Domestic Service in the United States from 1800 to 1920* (Baton Rouge: Louisiana State University Press, 1981); Faye E. Dudden, *Serving Women: Household Service in Nineteenth-Century America* (Middletown, Conn.: Wesleyan University Press, 1983); Judith Rollins, *Between Women: Domestics and Their Employers* (Philadelphia: Temple University Press, 1985); Linda Martin, *The Servant Problem: Domestic Workers in North America* (Jefferson, N.C.: McFarland, 1985); and Alan A. Brookes and Catharine A. Wilson, " 'Working Away' from the Farm: The Young Women of North Huron, 1920–1930," *Ontario History* 77 (Dec. 1985):281–300. See also the soon to be completed work of Silke Wehner, "Auswanderung deutscher Dienstmädchen in die Vereinigten Staaten, 1850–1914" (Ph.D. diss., University of Muenster, 1992).

38. For an in-depth analysis of this experience of females in Block, see Carol K. Coburn, "Learning to Serve: Education and Change in the Lives of Rural Domestics in the Early Twentieth Century," *Journal of Social History* 25 (Fall 1991):571–84.

39. Juliane Jacobi-Dittrich, "Growing Up Female in the Nineteenth Century," in *German Women in the Nineteenth Century: A Social History*, ed. John Fout (New York: Holmes and Meier, 1984), 199; Linda Pickle, "Stereotypes and Realities: Nineteenth-Century German Women in Missouri," *Missouri Historical Review* (April 1985):294; Alan Graebner, *Uncertain Saints: The Laity in the*

Lutheran Church–Missouri Synod, 1900–1970 (Westport, Conn.: Greenwood Press, 1975).

40. An example of the synod's change of position on domestic work involves the use of contraceptives and birth control. Early synod prescriptive literature recommended domestic service for young women. In the early twentieth century, however, when the fertility rate declined for Missouri Synod women, the synod blamed "hired girls," who had the most access to "outsiders" (Alan Graebner, "Birth Control and the Lutherans: The Missouri Synod as a Case Study," in *Women and American Religion*, ed. Janet Wilson James [Philadelphia: University of Pennsylvania Press, 1980], 232). The widely read lay magazine *Lutheran Witness* published an article in the May 22, 1923, issue that labeled birth control as "infanticide."

41. In order to obtain the most accurate data, I have labeled a girl as a "hired girl" only if all the interviewees identified her as such; therefore, my estimates are conservative. The 1913 confirmation class was the earliest group the interviewees could remember accurately. The 1937 confirmation group seems to be the last class that included girls who worked as domestics.

42. Author interview with Nora Ohlmeier Prothe, June 24, 1986. This firstborn hiring-out practice for German girls was also noticed by Laurence Glasco, "Life Cycles," 288.

43. Author interview with Lydia Prothe Schultz, Feb. 13, 1986.

44. Author interview with Irene Minden Prothe, July 18, 1986.

45. Virginia Yans-McLaughlin, *Family and Community*. Other scholars have challenged McLaughlin's emphasis on ethnicity over other imperatives that affect life choices for women (see Micaela di Leonardo, "The Myth of the Urban Village: Women, Work, and Family among Italian-Americans in Twentieth-Century California," in *The Women's West*, ed. Susan Armitage and Elizabeth Jameson [Norman: University of Oklahoma Press, 1987], 277–90).

46. Interview with Ida Minden Peckman, Aug. 18, 1986.

47. Interview with Lydia Prothe Schultz, Feb. 3, 1986. See Sylvia Lea Sallquist, "The Image of the Hired Girl in Literature: The Great Plains, 1860 to World War I," *Great Plains Quarterly* 4 (Summer 1984):166–77. Although Sallquist focuses most of her analysis on fiction, she wrote that the hired girls' memoirs mention "education as a motive for being a hired girl" as well as the "opportunity to be in town."

48. The Neuers and the Wilsons were two of the wealthy families served by the hired girls from Block. These two families owned and operated the lucrative Wilson Meat Packing Company in Kansas City.

49. Author interview with Irene Minden Prothe, July 18, 1986.

50. Author interview with Frieda Timken Baumgardt, Nov. 12, 1988.

51. Author interview with Irene Minden Prothe, July 18, 1986.

52. Meyer, *Moving Frontiers*, 352, and Heinrich H. Mauer, "The Fellowship Law of a Fundamentalist Group. The Missouri Synod," *American Journal of Sociology* 31 (July 1925):56.

53. Mauer, "Fellowship Law," 42.

54. Graebner, *Uncertain Saints*, 26–27. See also Luebke, "Immigrant Condition," 26.

55. Frederick Luebke, "German Immigrants and American Politics: Problems of Leadership, Parties, and Issues," in *Germans in the New World*, 79–92. Luebke goes on to state that the Germans were the most politically divided of any ethnic group in the United States. Carl Wittke, *We Who Built America*, rev.

ed. (Cleveland, Ohio: Western Reserve University Press, 1964), writes that the conservative Lutherans tended to remain with the Democratic party since they (the Lutherans) approved of slavery on biblical authority (245).

56. Audrey Olson, "St. Louis Germans, 1850–1920: The Nature of an Immigrant Community and Its Relation to the Assimilation Process" (Ph.D. diss., University of Kansas, 1970), 121–24.

57. *Western Spirit*, June 29, 1877.

58. *Western Spirit*, Nov. 12, 1880. This and all other election information quoted in this section were taken from election results printed in the Paola paper. The votes on each issue or person are recorded by township. Although East Valley Township contained some non-Germans, the Block community represents the vast majority of voters in the township.

59. *Western Spirit*, May 27, 1927. B. J. Sheridan, editor, wrote a series of essays on the early political days of the county; this story is taken from his reminiscence.

60. *Western Spirit*, Sept. 16, 1904.

61. The following description of B. J. Sheridan is a compilation of information gleaned from studying *Western Spirit* from 1870 to 1945. Many of the interviewees mentioned Sheridan, and their impressions have also helped create the portrait.

62. Author interview with Clarence Clausen and Alma Clausen Debrick, March 15, 1986.

63. *Western Spirit*, July 30, 1880.

64. Information on the AHTA was gleaned from newspaper notices in *Western Spirit*, May 28, 1886; Nov. 15, 1901; Aug. 17, 1906; and Feb. 13, 1914.

65. Meyer, *Moving Frontiers*, 383–85 and 408–10.

66. *Protokoll*, Jan. 1, 1901, Book 1, 135, and Jan. 15 (special meeting), 1901, 135–36, Trinity Lutheran Church (TLC) Archives, Block, Kansas. There is no indication that the pastor or the synod disapproved of the AHTA's tactics or purpose; the objection was to the secret nature of the society and its required oath.

67. *Protokoll*, Jan. 1, 1902, Book 1, 137–38.

68. Author interview with Marie Dageforde Monthey, Aug. 16, 1986.

69. *Protokoll*, July 9, 1888, Book 1, 89, and *Western Spirit*, Aug. 20, 1886. Although the newspaper does not make it clear that the mission meeting was attended by members from the church at Block, the gathering was held in Henry Block's grove where all future mission festivals were held.

70. All information on the origin of the mission festival is taken from Paul F. Koehneke, "Joint Mission Festivals in the Lutheran Church–Missouri Synod until 1868," *Concordia Historical Institute Quarterly* 24 (April 1951):24–34.

71. Author interview with Nora Ohlmeier Prothe, June 24, 1986. The festival setting was moved in the 1920s to a site one-half mile south of the church grounds.

72. *Western Spirit*, Aug. 25, 1893. Although the author of the article is unknown, one hopes that he or she understood German since all early festivals were in the German language only.

73. In *Protokoll*, from 1900 into the 1940s, both ministers' names are usually listed along with the language of his sermon.

74. For examples of these announcements, see *Western Spirit*, Aug. 3, 1923; July 29, 1927; Aug. 1, 1930; and Aug. 2, 1935.

75. *Protokoll*, July 3, 1904, Book 1, 151.

76. *Western Spirit*, Aug. 7, 1914.

77. *Western Spirit*, Aug. 2, 1918. This picnic appears to have been an obvious ploy to exhibit American patriotism; the program was full of American patriotic songs, drills, and recitations. The proceeds of the picnic were donated to the Red Cross, something never done before or after 1918.

78. *Western Spirit*, June 19, 1925, and June 10, 1932.

79. *Western Spirit*, July 19, 1935.

80. Author interview with Clarence Clausen, March 15, 1986.

81. *Western Spirit*, Aug. 15, 1913, and May 8, 1914.

82. Block residents played some baseball in the 1920s, but the local paper did not cover the games until interest was renewed in the 1930s.

83. The 1920s, 1930s, and 1940s, "Block Items," a section of the local paper, shows the extent to which residents of Block traveled to see family and friends. It also describes anniversary celebrations, young people's employment, and lists of out-of-town guests and activities.

84. The role of the ethnic community in easing the process of assimilation by slowing it down has been discussed in other rural and ethnic research. See the summary section in Kathleen Neils Conzen, *Immigrant Milwaukee*; Frederick C. Luebke, *Immigrants and Politics: The Germans in Nebraska, 1880–1900* (Lincoln: University of Nebraska Press, 1969), 35; and Russell Gerlach, *Immigrants in the Ozarks* (Columbia: University of Missouri Press, 1976), 174–75.

CHAPTER 6. AT WAR WITH GERMANY

1. *Western Spirit*, April 19, 1918.

2. Alan Graebner, "The Acculturation of an Immigrant Lutheran Church: The Lutheran Church–Missouri Synod, 1917–1929" (Ph.D. diss., Columbia University, 1965), 1; Frederick Nohl, "The Lutheran Church–Missouri Synod Reacts to the Anti-Germanism during World War I," *Concordia Historical Institute Quarterly* 35 (July 1962):62; Frederick C. Luebke, *Bonds of Loyalty: German Americans and World War I* (DeKalb: Northern Illinois University Press, 1974), 232–38; Frederick Luebke, "Legal Restrictions on Foreign Languages in the Great Plains States, 1917–23," in *Germans in the New World: Essays in the History of Immigration*, ed. Frederick Luebke (Urbana: University of Illinois Press, 1990), 31–50.

3. Luebke, *Bonds of Loyalty*, 15; E. Clifford Nelson, *The Rise of World Lutheranism: An American Perspective* (Philadelphia: Fortress Press, 1982), 397; Frederick Luebke, "Superpatriotism in World War I: The Experience of a Lutheran Pastor," *Concordia Historical Institute Quarterly* 41 (Feb. 1968):3–11.

4. Religion and some reading and writing were always taught in the German language; singing was also usually in German.

5. *Western Spirit* printed a number of pro-German articles before American involvement in World War I. For examples, see *Western Spirit*, July 7, 1916; Dec. 22, 1916; and March 30, 1917. After U.S. entry in April 1917, both papers began a series of anti-German essays and editorials, some local and some reprinted from other newspapers. For examples, see *Western Spirit*, May 18, 1917, and Jan. 25, 1918, and *Miami County Republican*, Oct. 19, 1917, and Oct. 26, 1917.

6. Author interview with Elsie Prothe Dageforde, Oct. 21, 1986.

7. Neil M. Johnson, "The Patriotism and Anti-Prussianism of the Lutheran

Church—Missouri Synod, 1914–1918," *Concordia Historical Institute Quarterly* 39 (Oct. 1966):101–5.

8. Luebke, "Legal Restrictions," 36–40. See also Graebner, "Acculturation," 81.

9. Author interview with Marie Peckman Wendte, Feb. 22, 1988.

10. *Western Spirit*, Feb. 1, 1918, explained "alien enemy" registration and on June 21, 1918, described the registration of "enemy females."

11. Ladies Aid Minutes (English translation), March 6, 1918, 11, Trinity Lutheran Church (TLC) Archives, Block, Kansas.

12. *Protokoll*, April 1, 1918, Book 2, 47, TLC. This was an important meeting since for the first time the pastor read a dictate from the synod office and also a letter from the government. "War time" refers to contemporary daylight savings time, which moved the clock forward one hour. The school and church service were moved to ten o'clock from nine o'clock.

13. Ibid., May 12, 1918, 48.

14. Ibid., July 7, 1918, 49–50.

15. *Western Spirit*, Aug. 2, 1918.

16. *Protokoll*, Oct. 6, 1918, Book 2, 50–51. It is impossible to determine if the "patriotic committee" was from the national synod or the Kansas district offices, as each group had a public relations board to render advice and help congregations minimize problems. The Army/Navy Board was the national synod's committee organized to provide Missouri Synod chaplains for the military. For a description of the problems and pressures of the Missouri Synod in creating its own independent board, see Alan Graebner, "World War I and the Lutheran Union: Documents from the Army and Navy Board, 1917–1918," *Concordia Historical Institute Quarterly* 41 (May 1968):51–64.

17. The synod's rigid definition of the separation of church and state remained an important issue for Missouri Synod officials, who continuously refused to use the pulpit for purposes of drumming up support for the war and the sale of liberty bonds. For more detailed descriptions, see Luebke, *Bonds of Loyalty*, 232–39; Graebner, "Acculturation," 54–56; and Ralph L. Moellering, "Some Lutheran Reactions to War and Pacifism, 1917 to 1941," *Concordia Historical Institute Quarterly* 41 (Aug. 1968):121–31.

18. Graebner, "Acculturation," 129.

19. Ibid., 54–56. Although Graebner generalizes in his comments on resistance even to synod dictates on change, the Block community certainly moved slowly in accommodating and responding to pressure from the synod. Officially, the synod ended its "official silence" in December 1917, but the voters' assembly did not act officially to make changes until April 1918.

20. Luebke discusses and analyzes this type of personal response to the war in *Bonds of Loyalty*, 232–38.

21. Correspondence of Lydia Prothe Schultz in the possession of her granddaughter, Carol Coburn. Translated from the German by Ursula Huelsbergen, Lawrence, Kansas, 1987.

22. Most of the individuals who continued to correspond with relatives before World War I stated that correspondence was impossible during the war, and this often signaled the end of family connections with relatives in the old country. All of the second- and some of the third-generation interviewees recalled that their parents subscribed to German-American newspapers as well as to local county papers; both mothers and fathers seemed to be newspaper readers and often read to their children. The most likely German-American paper to be read

in Block was *Staats-Zeitung* from Kansas City. Luebke states that by 1919, 47 percent of all German-American newspapers had stopped publishing (*Bonds of Loyalty*, 271).

23. Graebner, "Acculturation," 90. In discussing army life for German-American youth, Graebner adds, "Probably no melting pot functioned with such brutal efficiency as army life."

24. Sarah D. Shields, "The Treatment of Conscientious Objectors during World War I: Mennonites at Camp Funston," *Kansas History* 4 (Winter 1981):255–69. According to Shields and other scholars, the Mennonites were sent to Leavenworth to be imprisoned. If they refused to work they were forced to stand chained to the bars for nine hours a day, abused and beaten by guards. These men were all released by mid-1919.

25. *Western Spirit*, Feb. 1, 1918, 1.

26. Ibid., June 21, 1918, 1.

27. Author interview with Esther Prothe Maisch, June 25, 1986.

28. Rosena Debrick Schultz's registration form and those of all the men and women required to register can be found in "Registration Affidavit of Alien Enemy," 1918 (Marshall-Miami County), Box 17, Federal Archives–Kansas City Regional Branch, Kansas City, Missouri. These documents are a rare find since most states destroyed them some time after the war.

29. Author interview with Nora Ohlmeier Prothe, June 24, 1986.

30. "Registration Affidavit of Alien Enemy," Miami County, Box 17.

31. All information concerning Elizabeth Block was obtained from two articles in *Western Spirit*, June 28, 1918, and March 8, 1935. She was considered unique in the Block community because she was one of the few if not the only single woman to leave the community before World War I. Her pursuit of a career and her special out-of-state training also made her a curiosity, but she was highly respected because of the profession she chose. She went to Chicago after the war and returned to Block only for family visits.

32. Interview with Elsie Prothe Dageforde, Oct. 21, 1986.

33. *Miami County Republican*, Oct. 26, 1918.

34. *Western Spirit*, April 5, 1918.

35. Ibid., March 15, 1918.

36. The April and June listings were published in *Western Spirit*, April 19, 1918, and June 7, 1918. The May listing included sixty-five of seventy new Red Cross members from the Block community (*Miami County Republican*, May 24, 1918).

37. The threat of violence was quite real, and many German communities in Kansas and throughout the Midwest suffered from the anti-German backlash of 1918. Churches and schoolhouses were burned and vandalized; individual German Americans were verbally and physically abused. For excellent descriptions and analyses of the situation, see John A. Hawgood, *The Tragedy of German America* (New York: Putnam, 1940); Luebke, *Bonds of Loyalty*, 238–50; and Nelson, *Rise of World Lutheranism*, 397–98. Nelson states that the central Midwest suffered the most, and the more immigrants a community had, the more despised it was.

38. Graebner, "Acculturation," 85; Luebke, *Bonds of Loyalty*, Preface.

39. August C. Stellhorn, *Schools of the Lutheran Church–Missouri Synod* (St. Louis: Concordia Publishing House, 1963), 236–45; see also Luebke, "Legal Restrictions on Foreign Language," 31–34.

40. Walter H. Beck, *Lutheran Elementary Schools in the United States* (St.

Louis: Concordia Publishing House, 1939), 326. As recorded in the Kansas State Statutes (352), the state passed such a law on March 3, 1919. The state law also required that patriotism and citizenship be taught and stipulated that each school could be visited by the State Board of Education.

41. The particular Supreme Court cases that resolved the issue are *Meyer* v. *Nebraska* (1923) and *Pierce* v. *Society of Sisters* (1925). The former struck down English-only language laws for public and private schools, and the latter affirmed the right of private and public schools to educate children.

42. Graebner, "Acculturation," 110.

43. *Protokoll*, Jan. 1923, Book 2, 66–67.

44. Ibid., Jan. 1925, 76–77.

45. Ibid., Jan.–July 1929, 101–6.

46. Ibid., Jan. 1931, 112–13.

47. Ibid., April–July 1931, 114–17.

48. Ibid., Oct. 1932, 121–22.

49. Ibid., Jan. 1936, 140, and Oct. 1937, 145.

50. Many of the interviewees described this problem, and most were upset that some women were forced to do this for so long. One of the interviewees, Josephine Overbeck Prothe, and her two sisters married Lutherans from Block and found themselves in such a situation.

51. J. Neale Carman, "Foreign Language Units of Kansas" (Manuscript, University of Kansas Archives), 2:1294.

52. *Western Spirit*, July 19, 1935.

53. *Protokoll*, May 1940, Book 3, 15, and April 1941, 21.

54. Ibid., April 1942, 28, and Oct. 1942, 31.

55. Ladies Aid Minutes (English translation), Aug. 1942, 38.

56. *Protokoll*, Oct. 1942, Book 3, 31. German services were finally discontinued in 1950.

57. Ibid., April–Oct. 1944, 41–43.

58. Ladies Aid Minutes (English translation), Jan. 1944, 43.

59. *Western Spirit*, Sept. 4, 1942.

60. Carman, "Foreign Language Units," 2:1291.

61. Author interview with Alma Clausen Debrick, March 15, 1986.

62. *Western Spirit*, April 20, 1945.

CONCLUSION

1. Jon Gjerde, "Conflict and Community: A Case Study of the Immigrant Church in the United States," *Journal of Social History* (Summer 1986):681–97.

2. For other examples of immigrant-church controversies and struggles to learn democratic processes, see Stanley Nadel, *Little Germany: Ethnicity, Religion, and Class in New York City, 1845–80* (Urbana: University of Illinois Press, 1990), 91–103; Jay P. Dolan, *The American Catholic Experience: A History from Colonial Times to the Present* (Garden City, N.Y.: Image Books, 1987), 158–94; Robert Slayton, *Back of the Yards: The Making of a Local Democracy* (Chicago: University of Chicago Press, 1986), 118–22; and Gjerde, "Conflict and Community."

3. Although it is not unusual that institutions, particularly churches, are slow to change, it is important to remember that the extreme conservatism and

exclusivity practiced by the church at Block were part of an attempt to resist powerful external pressures brought about by World War I. Few institutions have been subjected to such virulent, inflammatory attacks by the national and local media. Even with these types of pressures, the church resisted and sought every opportunity to avoid Americanization.

4. According to the interviewees, the environment of the school at Block in the late 1920s and the 1930s became less "hostile." Although corporal punishment was still used, its severity and frequency seemed to decrease. More "accountability" was required by parents, but the church was also subject to some state requirements that included on-site visits by the county superintendent.

5. Frederick C. Luebke, *Immigrants and Politics: The Germans in Nebraska, 1880–1900* (Lincoln: University of Nebraska Press, 1969), 35.

6. Gerda Lerner, *The Creation of Patriarchy* (New York: Oxford University Press, 1986), 217.

7. Claire Farrer, "Women and Folklore: Images and Genres," *Journal of American Folklore* 88 (Jan./March 1975):ix.

8. See Joan Jensen, *Loosening the Bonds: Mid-Atlantic Farm Women* (New Haven, Conn.: Yale University Press, 1986), 91.

9. Kathleen Neils Conzen, "Peasant Pioneers: Generational Succession among German Farmers in Frontier Minnesota," in *The Countryside in the Age of Capitalistic Transformation*, ed. Steven Hahn and Jonathan Prude (Chapel Hill: University of North Carolina Press, 1985), 259–92; Robert C. Ostergre, "Land and Family in Rural Immigrant Communities, *Annals of the Association of American Geographers* 71 (1981):400–411; Jon Gjerde, *From Peasants to Farmers: The Migration from Balestrand, Norway, to the Upper Middle West* (New York: Cambridge University Press, 1985).

10. Conzen, "Peasant Pioneers," 285.

11. I use these cities as examples because each has had a definitive study completed on its nineteenth-century German population — Audrey Olson, "St. Louis Germans, 1850–1920: The Nature of an Immigrant Community and Its Relation to the Assimilation Process" (Ph.D. diss., University of Kansas, 1970); Kathleen Neils Conzen, *Immigrant Milwaukee, 1836–1860* (Cambridge, Mass.: Harvard University Press, 1976); and Nadel, *Little Germany*. St. Louis provides a particularly appropriate comparison because it is the home of Missouri Synod Lutheranism, and the publishing house and seminary are located there.

12. Gerda Lerner, *The Majority Finds Its Past: Placing Women in History* (New York: Oxford University Press, 1979), 148.

13. Lerner, *Creation of Patriarchy*, 38.

14. Joan Scott, "Gender: A Useful Category of Historical Analysis," *American Historical Review* 5 (Dec. 1986):1063, 1067.

15. A number of scholars have examined the changes in gender behavior in women's church organizations. For an excellent example, see Carroll Smith-Rosenberg, *Disorderly Conduct: Visions of Gender in Victorian America* (New York: Oxford University Press, 1986).

16. Many scholars have documented the importance of women's support networks; see Nancy A. Hewitt, "Beyond the Search for Sisterhood: American Women's History in the 1980s," in *Unequal Sisters: A Multicultural Reader in U.S. Women's History* (New York: Routledge, 1990), 11; Joan M. Jensen, *Promise to the Land: Essays on Rural Women* (Albuquerque: University of New Mexico Press, 1991), 259; Glenda Riley, "Women's Responses to the Challenges of Plains

Living," *Great Plains Quarterly* 9 (Summer 1989):180; and Lerner, *Creation of Patriarchy,* 217.

17. Jensen, *Promise to the Land,* 259.

18. Joan Jensen, "Buttermaking and Economic Development in Mid-Atlantic America from 1750–1850," *Signs* 13 (1988):826. See also Cornelia Butler Flora and Jan L. Flora, "Structure of Agriculture and Women's Culture on the Great Plains," *Great Plains Quarterly* 8 (Fall 1988):195–205.

19. Micaela di Leonardo, "The Myth of the Urban Village: Women, Work, and Family among Italian-Americans in Twentieth-Century California," in *The Women's West,* ed. Susan Armitage and Elizabeth Jameson (Norman: University of Oklahoma Press, 1987), 279.

20. Carol K. Coburn, "Learning to Serve: Education and Change in the Lives of Rural Domestics in the Early Twentieth Century, *Journal of Social History* 25 (Fall 1991):571–84.

21. For excellent examples, see Jensen, *Promise to the Land;* Personal Narratives Group, *Interpreting Women's Lives: Feminist Theory and Personal Narratives* (Bloomington: Indiana University Press, 1989); and Lillian Schlissel, Byrd Gibbens, and Elizabeth Hampsten, *Far from Home: Families on the Westward Journey* (New York: Schocken Press, 1990). *Oral History Review* devoted its Spring 1989 issue to women's oral history.

22. Mary Leach, "Toward Writing Feminist Scholarship into History of Education," *Educational Theory* 40 (Fall 1990):453–61.

23. Notable exceptions are Wayne Fuller, *The Old Country School: The Story of Rural Education in the Middle West* (Chicago: University of Chicago Press, 1982), and David B. Tyack, "The Tribe and the Common School: Community Control in Rural Education," *American Quarterly* 24 (1972):3–19.

24. Some examples include Dolan, *American Catholic Experience;* Eileen Mary Brewer, *Nuns and the Education of American Catholic Women, 1820–1920* (Chicago: Loyola University Press, 1987); Timothy Walch, "The Diverse Origins of American Catholic Education: Chicago, Milwaukee and the Nation" (Ph.D. diss., Northwestern University, 1975); Fayette Breaux, "For God and Country: Catholic Schooling in the 1920s" (Ph.D. diss., Columbia University, 1984); and Michael F. Perko, S.J., ed., *Enlightening the Next Generation: Catholics and Their Schools, 1830–1980* (New York: Garland Press, 1988).

25. An excellent source that examines a wide range of variables for future research in educational history is John Best, ed., *Historical Inquiry into Education: A Research Agenda* (Washington, D.C.: American Educational Research Assoc., 1983).

26. Martin E. Marty, "Forward," in Eileen Mary Brewer, *Nuns and the Education of Catholic Women 1860–1920* (Chicago: Loyola University Press, 1987), xi–xii.

NOTE ON SOURCES

1. I have ended my study in 1945 because the major battles of assimilation and Americanization seem to have ended by the end of World War II. Also, to ensure the privacy of the people who currently remain in the community, I felt I should not continue the study.

2. I have great confidence in their meticulous and time-consuming endeavor.

This couple spent two years completing their verbatim translations of the recordbook. Their primary concern was in translating the correct "cause of death" in the death records. Periodically, they consulted a German medical dictionary to ensure a correct translation in labeling various diseases or ailments.

3. For additional discussion on the importance of this type of methodology to immigrant history, see Virginia Yans-McLaughlin, "Metaphors of Self in History: Subjective, Oral Narrative, and Immigrant Studies," in *Immigration Reconsidered: History, Sociology, and Politics* (New York: Oxford University Press, 1990), 254–90; and Kerry William Bate, "Family History: Some Answers, Many Questions," *Oral History Review* 16 (Spring 1988):127–30.

4. Joan M. Jensen and Mary Johnson, "What's in a Butter Churn? Objects and Women's Oral History," *Frontiers: A Journal of Women's Studies* 7 (1983):103–8. Two anthologies provide a comprehensive view of the many uses of material-culture analysis; see Thomas J. Schlereth, ed., *Material Culture Studies in America* (Nashville, Tenn.: American Association for State and Local History, 1982), and Ian M. G. Quimby, ed., *Material Culture and the Study of American Life* (New York: W. W. Norton, 1978). See also Thomas J. Schlereth, *Cultural History and Material Culture: Everyday Life, Landscapes, Museums* (Ann Arbor: UMI Research Press, 1990).

BIBLIOGRAPHY

MAPS AND ATLASES

Baughman, Robert W. *Kansas in Maps*. Topeka: Kansas State Historical Society, 1961.

Brock and Company. *Standard Atlas of Miami County, Kansas*. Chicago, 1927.

Carman, J. Neale. *Foreign Language Units of Kansas: Historical Atlas and Statistics*. Vol. 1. Lawrence: University Press of Kansas, 1962.

————. "Foreign Language Units of Kansas." Vols. 2 and 3. Lawrence: University of Kansas Archives. Manuscript.

Edwards Brothers. *An Historical Atlas of Miami County, Kansas*. Philadelphia, 1878.

Everts, L. N., and Company. *The Original State Atlas of Kansas*. Philadelphia, 1887.

Gallup Map and Supply Company. *Miami County, Kansas*. Kansas City, Mo., n.d. [ca. 1930].

Investors Loan and Abstract Company. *Miami County, Kansas*. Paola, Kans., 1934.

Kloss, Heinz. *Atlas of German American Settlements*. Marburg, Germany: N. G. Elwert, 1974.

Ogle, George A. *Standard Atlas of Miami County, Kansas*. Chicago, 1901.

Robinson, E. W. *Sectional Map of Miami County, Kansas*. Paola, Kans., 1868.

Socolofsky, Homer E., and Huber Self, eds. *Historical Atlas of Kansas*. Norman: University of Oklahoma Press, 1972.

PRIMARY SOURCES

Official Documents

Kansas State Census. Topeka. "Miami County." 1865, Microfilm #6; 1875, Microfilm #13; and 1885, Microfilm #88. Topeka; Kansas Board of Agriculture.

National Archives, Kansas City Branch. "Registration Affidavit of Alien Enemy," State of Kansas, Marshall-Miami Counties. Box 17. Kansas City, Mo., 1918.

National Headquarters of the Lutheran Church–Missouri Synod. *Statistical Yearbook*. St. Louis: Concordia Publishing House, 1900, 1902–5, 1907–8, 1912, 1916, 1920, 1924–26, 1929–45.

Trinity Lutheran Church Archives. Church Recordbook, "Baptisms." Block, Kans., 1868–1945.

————. Church Recordbook, "Confirmation:." Block, Kans., 1868–1945.

_____. Church Recordbook, "Deaths." Block, Kans., 1868–1945.

_____. Church Recordbook, "Marriages." Block, Kans., 1869–1945.

_____. "Constitution." Block, Kans., 1870.

_____. Contract for Deed of Church Property. Block, Kans., 1870.

_____. Dedication Booklet. Block, Kans., 1959.

_____. Ladies Aid Meeting Minutes. Block, Kans., 1912–1945.

_____. One Hundred Year Anniversary Booklet. Block, Kans., 1968.

_____. *Protokoll* ("minutes" from the voters' assembly). 3 vols. Block, Kans., 1870–1945.

_____. Walther League Meeting Minutes (including constitution). Block, Kans., 1924–1937.

U. S. Bureau of Census. Population. Miami County, Kansas, 1860, Microfilm #6; 1870, Microfilm #12; 1880, Microfilm #17 and 18. Washington, D.C.: Government Printing Office.

U. S. Treasury Department. *Arrivals of Alien Passengers and Immigrants in the United States from 1820–1892.* Washington, D.C.: Government Printing Office, 1893.

Interviews and Manuscripts

Baumgardt, Frieda Timken. Taped interview with author. Drexel, Mo., Nov. 12, 1988.

Block, Mildred. Taped interview with author. Fontana, Kans., Nov. 22, 1985.

Clausen, Clarence. Taped interview with author. Block, Kans., March 15, 1986.

Dageforde, Elsie Prothe. Taped interview with author. Paola, Kans., Oct. 21, 1986.

Debrick, Alma Clausen. Taped interview with author. Block, Kans., March 15, 1986.

Debrick, Minnie Cahman. Taped interview with author. Paola, Kans., Sept. 23, 1986.

_____. "The Cahman Family Tree." N.d.

Maisch, Esther Prothe. Taped interview with author. Block, Kans., June 25, 1986.

Monthey, Marie Dageforde. Taped interview with author. Block, Kans., Aug. 16, 1986.

Peckman, Ida Minden. Taped interview with author. Block, Kans., Aug. 18, 1986.

Prothe, Elmer, and Josephine Overbeck Prothe. Taped interview with author. Paola, Kans., June 15, 1987.

Prothe, Irene Minden. Taped interview with author. July 18, 1986.

_____. Papers. 1931–1950.

Prothe, Nora Ohlmeier. Taped interview with author. Block, Kans., June 24, 1986.

Schultz, Lydia Prothe. Taped interviews with author. Feb. 13, 1982, and Jan. 26, 1985.

_____. Correspondence from Gertrude Krause, April 12, 1917.

_____. Papers. St. Peter's Lutheran Church records and correspondence, 1878–1882.

Thoden, Myrtle Neu. Taped interview with author. Block, Kans., July 2, 1986.

_____. Papers. George Reifel reminiscence. Block, Kans., 1951.

Wendte, Marie Peckman. Taped interview with author. Block, Kans., Feb. 22, 1988.

SECONDARY SOURCES

Books

Anderson, Charles H. *White Protestant Americans: From National Origins to Religious Group.* Englewood Cliffs, N.J.: Prentice-Hall, 1970.

Anderson, Lorraine. *Sisters of the Earth: Women's Prose and Poetry about Nature.* New York: Vintage Books, 1991.

Andreas, A. T. *History of the State of Kansas.* Chicago: A. T. Andreas, 1883.

Archdeacon, Thomas J. *Becoming American: An Ethnic History.* New York: Free Press, 1983.

Aries, Philippe. *Centuries of Childhood: A Social History of Family Life.* Trans. by Robert Baldick. New York: Random House, 1962.

Armitage, Susan, and Elizabeth Jameson, eds. *The Women's West.* Norman: University of Oklahoma Press, 1987.

Arndt, Karl J. R., and Mary E. Olson, eds. *German-American Newspapers and Periodicals 1732–1955: History and Bibliography.* New York: K. G. Sauer, 1976.

Bailyn, Bernard. *Education in the Forming of American Society.* Chapel Hill: University of North Carolina Press, 1960.

Bean, Lee L., Geraldine P. Mineau, and Douglas L. Anderson. *Fertility Patterns on the American Frontier: Adaptation and Innovation.* Berkeley: University of California Press, 1990.

Beck, Walter H. *Lutheran Elementary Schools in the United States.* St. Louis: Concordia Publishing House, 1939.

Benjamin, Gilbert G. *The Germans in Texas: A Study in Immigration, 1874–1941.* Austin: Jenkins Press, 1974.

Best, John, ed. *Historical Inquiry into Education: A Research Agenda.* Washington D.C.: American Educational Research Association, 1983.

Blicksilver, Edith. *The Ethnic Woman: Problems, Protests, and Lifestyles.* Dubuque: Kendall/Hunt, 1978.

Bogen, F. W. *The German in America: Advice and Instruction for German Emigrants in the United States of America.* Boston: B. H. Greene, 1851.

Boyer, Paul, and Stephan Nissenbaum. *Salem Possessed.* Cambridge, Mass.: Harvard University Press, 1974.

Bremner, Robert H., ed. *Children and Youth in America: A Documentary History, 1600–1973.* 3 vols. Cambridge, Mass.: Harvard University Press, 1974.

Brewer, Eileen Mary. *Nuns and the Education of American Catholic Women, 1820–1920.* Chicago: Loyola University Press, 1987.

Bright, John D., ed. *Kansas: The First Century.* Vol. 1. New York: Lewis Historical Publishing Company, 1956.

Brunner, Edmund, ed. *Immigrant Farmers and Their Children.* Garden City, N.J.: Doubleday, 1929.

Bundenthal, Theodore. *An Outline of A History of the Kansas District of the Evangelical Lutheran Synod of Missouri, Ohio, and Other States.* St. Louis: Concordia Publishing House, 1913.

Chafe, William H. *Women and Equality.* New York: Oxford University Press, 1977.

Clark, Carroll D., and Roy L. Roberts, eds. *People of Kansas: A Demographic and Sociological Study.* Topeka: Kansas State Planning Board, 1936.

Cohen, Sol. *Education in the United States.* 5 vols. Westport, Conn.: Greenwood Press, 1974.

Conzen, Kathleen Neils. *Immigrant Milwaukee, 1836–1860.* Cambridge, Mass.: Harvard University Press, 1976.

Cott, Nancy F. *The Bonds of Womanhood: "Woman's Sphere" in New England, 1780–1835.* New Haven, Conn.: Yale University Press, 1977.

Cott, Nancy F., and Elizabeth H. Pleck, eds. *A Heritage of Her Own: Toward a New Social History of American Women.* New York: Simon and Schuster, 1979.

Cowan, Ruth Schwartz. *More Work for Mother: The Ironies of Household Technology from the Open Hearth to the Microwave.* New York: Basic Books, 1983.

Cremin, Lawrence A. *American Education: The National Experience, 1783–1876.* New York: Harper and Row, 1980.

Curti, Merle. *The Making of an American Community: A Case Study of Democracy in a Frontier Community.* Stanford: Stanford University Press, 1969.

Degler, Carl N. *At Odds: Women and the Family in America from the Revolution to the Present.* New York: Oxford University Press, 1980.

DeMause, Lloyd. *The History of Childhood.* New York: Psychohistory Press, 1974.

Demos, John. *The Little Commonwealth: Family Life in Plymouth Colony.* New York: Oxford University Press, 1970.

Detjen, David W. *The Germans in Missouri, 1900–1918.* Columbia: University of Missouri Press, 1985.

di Leonardo, Micaela. *The Varieties of Ethnic Experience: Kinship, Class, and Gender among California Italian-Americans.* Ithaca, N.Y.: Cornell University Press, 1984.

Diner, Hasia. *Erin's Daughters in America.* Baltimore: Johns Hopkins University Press, 1983.

Dinnerstein, Leonard, Roger L. Nichols, and David M. Reimers. *Natives and Strangers: Ethnic Groups and the Building of America.* 2d ed. New York: Oxford University Press, 1979.

————. *Natives and Strangers: Blacks, Indians, and Immigrants in America.* 2d ed. New York: Oxford University Press, 1990.

Dinnerstein, Leonard, and David M. Reimers. *Ethnic Americans.* 2d. ed. New York: Harper and Row, 1982.

Dolan, Jay P. *The Immigrant Church: New York's Irish and German Catholics.* Baltimore: Johns Hopkins University Press, 1975.

————. *The American Catholic Experience: A History from Colonial Times to the Present.* Garden City, N.Y.: Image Books, 1987.

————. *The American Catholic Parish, 1850 to the Present.* New York: Paulist Press, 1987.

Doyle, Don H. *Social Order of a Frontier Community: Jacksonville, Illinois, 1825–1870.* Urbana: University of Illinois Press, 1978.

DuBois, Ellen Carol, and Vicki L. Ruiz, eds. *Unequal Sisters: A Multicultural Reader in U.S. Women's History.* New York: Routledge, 1990.

Dudden, Faye E. *Serving Women: Household Service in Nineteenth Century America.* Middletown, Conn.: Wesleyan University Press, 1983.

Ehrenreich, Barbara, and Deirdre English. *For Her Own Good.* Garden City, N.Y.: Anchor Books, 1979.

Evans, Richard J., and W. R. Lee, eds. *The German Family: Essays on the Social History of the Family in Nineteenth- and Twentieth-Century Germany.* Totowa, N.J.: Barnes and Noble, 1986.

Fairbanks, Carol. *Prairie Women: Images in American and Canadian Fiction.* New Haven, Conn.: Yale University Press, 1986.

Faragher, John Mack. *Men and Women on the Overland Trail.* New Haven, Conn.: Yale University Press, 1979.

———. *Sugar Creek: Life on the Illinois Prairie.* New Haven, Conn.: Yale University Press, 1986.

Fink, Deborah. *Open Country Iowa: Rural Women, Tradition, and Change.* Albany, N.Y.: SUNY Press, 1986.

Finkelstein, Barbara., ed. *Regulated Children, Liberated Children: Education in Psychohistorical Perspective.* New York: Psychohistory Press, 1979.

Forster, Walter O. *Zion on the Mississippi: The Settlement of the Saxon Lutherans in Missouri, 1839–1841.* St. Louis: Concordia Publishing House, 1953.

Fout, John C., ed. *German Women in the Nineteenth Century: A Social History.* New York: Holmes and Meier, 1984.

Fuller, Wayne. *The Old Country School: The Story of Rural Education in the Middle West.* Chicago: University of Chicago Press, 1982.

Furer, Howard B., ed. *The Germans in America, 1607–1970.* Dobbs Ferry, N.Y.: Oceana Publications, 1973.

Garkovich, Lorraine. *Population and Community in Rural America.* Westport, Conn.: Greenwood Press, 1989.

Gerlach, Russell. *Immigrants in the Ozarks.* Columbia: University of Missouri Press, 1976.

Gjerde, Jon. *From Peasants to Farmers: The Migration from Balestrand, Norway, to the Upper Middle West.* New York: Cambridge University Press, 1985.

Gordon, Milton. *Assimilation in American Life: The Role of Race, Religion, and National Origins.* New York: Oxford University Press, 1964.

Graebner, Alan. *Uncertain Saints: The Laity in the Lutheran Church–Missouri Synod, 1900–1970.* Westport, Conn.: Greenwood Press, 1975.

Greven, Philip. *Four Generations: Population, Land, and Family in Colonial Andover, Massachusetts.* Ithaca, N.Y.: Cornell University Press, 1972.

Guillet, Edwin C. *The Great Migration: The Atlantic Crossing by Sailing-Ship since 1770.* New York: Nelson, 1937.

Gulliford, Andrew. *America's Country Schools.* Washington D.C.: Preservation Press, 1984.

Hampsten, Elizabeth. *Read This Only to Yourself: The Private Writings of Midwestern Women, 1880–1910.* Bloomington: Indiana University Press, 1982.

Haney, Wava G., and Jane B. Knowles. *Women and Farming: Changing Roles, Changing Structures.* Boulder, Colo.: Westview Press, 1988.

Hansen, Marcus Lee, ed. *The Immigrant in American History.* New York: Harper and Row, 1961.

Hawes, Joseph, and N. Ray Hiner, eds. *American Childhood: A Research Guide and Historical Handbook.* Westport, Conn.: Greenwood Press, 1985.

Hawgood, John A. *The Tragedy of German America.* New York: Putnam, 1940.

Hibbard, Benjamin Horace. *A History of the Public Land Policies.* Madison: University of Wisconsin Press, 1965.

Higgins, George. *Miami County: The King of Counties*. Paola, Kans., 1877.

Hine, Robert V. *Community on the American Frontier*. Norman: University of Oklahoma Press, 1980.

Hiner, N. Ray, and Joseph M. Hawes. *Growing Up in America: Children in Historical Perspective*. Urbana: University of Illinois Press, 1985.

Huebener, Theodore. *The German in America*. Philadelphia: Chilton Book Company, 1962.

Jahsmann, Allan H. *What's Lutheran in Education? Explorations into Principles and Practices*. St. Louis: Concordia Publishing House, 1960.

James, Janet Wilson, ed. *Women in American Religion*. Philadelphia: University of Pennsylvania Press, 1980.

Jeffrey, Julie Roy. *Frontier Women: The Trans-Mississippi West, 1840–1880*. New York: Hill & Wang, 1979.

Jensen, Joan M. *Loosening the Bonds: Mid-Atlantic Farm Women*. New Haven, Conn.: Yale University Press, 1986.

———. *Promise to the Land: Essays on Rural Women*. Albuquerque: University of New Mexico Press, 1991.

Joeres, Ruth-Ellen, and Mary Jo Maynes, eds. *German Women in the 18th and 19th Century: A Social and Literary History*. Bloomington: Indiana University Press, 1986.

Jordan, Terry G. *German Seed in Texas Soil: Immigrant Families in Nineteenth Century Texas*. Austin: University of Texas Press, 1975.

Jorgenson, Lloyd P. *The State and the Non-Public School 1825–1925*. Columbia: University of Missouri Press, 1987.

Joyce, Rosemary O. *A Woman's Place: The Life History of a Rural Ohio Grandmother*. Columbus: Ohio State University Press, 1983.

Kaestle, Carl F. *Pillars of the Republic: Common Schools and American Society, 1780–1860*. New York: Hill and Wang, 1983.

Kamphoefner, Walter D. *The Westfalians: From Germany to Missouri*. Princeton, N.J.: Princeton University Press, 1987.

Katz, Michael B. *Class, Bureaucracy and Schools*. New York: Holt, Rinehart and Winston, 1975.

Katzman, David M. *Seven Days a Week: Women and Domestic Service in Industrializing America*. Urbana: University of Illinois Press, 1981.

Kerber, Linda K., and Jane DeHart Mathews., eds. *Women's America: Refocusing the Past*. New York: Oxford University Press, 1982.

Kirk, Gordon W. *The Promise of American Life: Social Mobility in a Nineteenth-Century Immigrant Community, Holland, Michigan, 1847–1894*. Philadelphia: American Philosophical Society, 1978.

Kleppner, Paul. *The Cross of Culture: A Social Analysis of Midwestern Politics, 1850–1900*. New York: Free Press, 1970.

Kolodny, Annette. *The Land before Her: Fantasy and Experience of the American Frontiers, 1830–1860*. Chapel Hill: University of North Carolina Press, 1984.

Lagemann, Ellen Condliffe. *A Generation of Women: Education in the Lives of Progressive Reformers*. Cambridge, Mass.: Harvard University Press, 1979.

Lamberti, Marjorie. *State, Society, and the Elementary School in Imperial Germany*. New York: Oxford University Press, 1989.

Leavitt, Judith. *Brought to Bed: Childbirth in America, 1750–1950*. New York: Oxford University Press, 1986.

Leavitt, Judith, ed. *Women and Health in America*. Madison: University of Wisconsin Press, 1984.

Lerner, Gerda. *The Majority Finds Its Past: Placing Women in History*. New York: Oxford University Press, 1979.

———. *The Creation of Patriarchy*. New York: Oxford University Press, 1986.

Lerner, Gerda, ed. *The Female Experience: An American Documentary*. Indianapolis: Bobbs-Merrill, 1977.

Litoff, Judith Barrett. *American Midwives: 1860 to the Present*. Westport, Conn.: Greenwood Press, 1978.

Lockridge, Kenneth. *A New England Town: The First Hundred Years*. 2d. ed. New York: Norton, 1985.

Luebke, Frederick C. *Immigrants and Politics: The Germans in Nebraska, 1880–1900*. Lincoln: University of Nebraska Press, 1969.

———. *Bonds of Loyalty: German Americans and World War I*. DeKalb: Northern Illinois University Press, 1974.

———. *Germans in the New World: Essays in the History of Immigration*. Urbana: University of Illinois Press, 1990.

Luebke, Frederick C., ed. *Ethnicity on the Great Plains*. Lincoln: University of Nebraska Press, 1980.

Lueker, Erwin L., ed. *Lutheran Cyclopedia*. St. Louis: Concordia Publishing House, 1954.

Lueking, F. Dean. *A Century of Caring: The Welfare Ministry among the Missouri Synod Lutherans, 1868–1968*. St. Louis: Concordia Publishing House, 1968.

Mann, Ralph. *After the Gold Rush: Society in Grass Valley and Nevada City, California, 1849–1870*. Stanford: Stanford University Press, 1982.

Martin, Linda. *The Servant Problem: Domestic Workers in North America*. Jefferson, N.C.: McFarland, 1985.

McClellan, B. Edward, and William J. Reese., eds. *The Social History of Education*. Urbana: University of Illinois Press, 1988.

McGrath, Sister M. Charles., ed. *History of Churches: Miami County Kansas*. Paola, Kans.: Paola Association for Church Action, 1976.

Meyer, Carl S., ed. *Moving Frontiers: Readings in the History of the Lutheran Church–Missouri Synod*. St. Louis: Concordia Publishing House, 1964.

Meyer, Ruth Fritz. *Women on a Mission*. St. Louis: Concordia Publishing House, 1967.

Meyerwitz, Joanne J. *Women Adrift: Independent Wage Earners in Chicago, 1880–1930*. Chicago: University of Chicago Press, 1988.

Miller, Kerby A. *Emigrants and Exiles: Ireland and the Irish Exodus to North America*. New York: Oxford University Press, 1985.

Mindel, Charles H., and Robert W. Habenstein, eds. *Ethnic Families in America: Patterns and Variations*. New York: Elsevier, 1976.

Moquin, Wayne, ed. *Makers of America-Hyphenated Americans, 1914–1924*. Vol. 7. Chicago: Encyclopedia Brittanica Educational Company, 1971.

Morgan, Edmund S. *The Puritan Family: Religion and Domestic Relations in Seventeenth-Century New England*. New York: Harper and Row, 1966.

Moynihan, Ruth B., and Susan Armitage, eds. *So Much to be Done: Women Settlers on the Mining and Ranching Frontier*. Lincoln: University of Nebraska Press, 1990.

Mundinger, Carl S. *Government in the Missouri Synod*. St. Louis: Concordia Publishing House, 1947.

Myers, Sandra. *Westering Women and the Frontier Experience, 1800–1915.* Las Cruces: New Mexico State University Press, 1982.

Nadel, Stanley. *Little Germany: Ethnicity, Religion, and Class in New York City, 1845–80.* Urbana: University of Illinois Press, 1990.

Nelson, E. Clifford. *The Rise of World Lutheranism: An American Perspective.* Philadelphia: Fortress Press, 1982.

Nelson, E. Clifford., ed. *The Lutherans in North America.* Philadelphia: Fortress Press, 1975.

Nelson, Lowry. *Rural Sociology.* New York: American Book Company, 1948.

Norton, Mary Beth, ed. *Major Problems in American Women's History.* Lexington, Mass.: D.C. Heath, 1989.

O'Connor, Richard. *The German-Americans: An Informal History.* Boston: Little, Brown, 1968.

Osterud, Nancy Grey. *Bonds of Community and the Lives of Farm Women in Nineteenth-Century New York.* Ithaca, N.Y.: Cornell University Press, 1991.

Perkinson, Henry J. *The Imperfect Panacea: American Faith in Education, 1865–1990.* 3d ed. New York: McGraw Hill, 1991.

Perko, Michael F., S.J., ed. *Enlightening the Next Generation: Catholics and Their Schools, 1830–1980.* New York: Garland Press, 1988.

Personal Narratives Group. *Interpreting Women's Lives: Feminist Theory and Personal Narratives.* Bloomington: Indiana University Press, 1989.

Petrik, Paula. *No Step Backward: Women and Family on the Rocky Mountain Mining Frontier, Helena, Montana, 1865–1900.* Helena: Montana Historical Society Press, 1987.

Quimby, Ian M. G., ed. *Material Culture and the Study of American Life.* New York: W. W. Norton, 1978.

Riley, Glenda. *Frontierswoman: The Iowa Experience.* Ames: Iowa State University Press, 1981.

————. *The Female Frontier: A Comparative View of Women on the Prairie and the Plains.* Lawrence: University Press of Kansas, 1988.

Robb, Theodore K., and Robert I. Rotberg, eds. *The Family in History: Interdisciplinary Essays.* New York: Harper Torchbooks, 1973.

Rollins, Judith. *Between Women: Domestics and Their Employers.* Philadelphia: Temple University Press, 1985.

Rosenfeld, Rachel Ann. *Farm Women: Work, Farm, and Family in the United States.* Chapel Hill: University of North Carolina Press, 1985.

Ross, Nancy Wilson. *Westward the Women.* New York: Noonday Press, 1990.

Ruether, Rosemary Radford, and Rosemary Skinner Keller, eds. *Women and Religion in America.* 3 vols. New York: Harper and Row, 1986.

Ryan, Mary P. *Womanhood in America: From Colonial Times to the Present.* 2d ed. New York: New Viewpoints, 1979.

————. *Cradle of the Middle Class.* Cambridge, Mass.: Harvard University Press, 1981.

Sachs, Carolyn E. *The Invisible Farmers: Women in Agricultural Production.* Totowa, N.J.: Rowman and Allanheld, 1983.

Scharff, Virginia. *Taking the Wheel.* New York: Free Society Press, 1991.

Schlereth, Thomas J., ed. *Material Culture Studies in America.* Nashville, Tenn.: American Association for State and Local History, 1982.

————. *Cultural History and Material Culture: Everyday Life, Landscapes, Museums.* Ann Arbor: UMI Research Press, 1990.

Schlissel, Lillian. *Women's Diaries of the Westward Journey.* New York: Schocken Books, 1982.

Schlissel, Lillian, Byrd Gibbens, and Elizabeth Hampsten. *Far from Home: Families of the Westward Journey.* New York: Schocken Books, 1990.

Schlissel, Lillian, Vicki L. Ruiz, and Janet Monk, eds. *Western Women: Their Land, Their Lives.* Albuquerque: University of New Mexico Press, 1988.

Scholten, Catherine M. *Childbearing in American Society, 1650–1850.* New York: New York University Press, 1985.

Seller, Maxine Schwartz, ed. *Immigrant Women.* Philadelphia: Temple University Press, 1981.

Slayton, Robert A. *Back of the Yards: The Making of a Local Democracy.* Chicago: University of Chicago Press, 1986.

Smith, Judith E. *Family Connections: A History of Italian and Jewish Immigrants' Lives in Providence, R.I. 1900–1940.* Albany, N.Y.: SUNY Press, 1985.

Smith-Rosenberg, Carroll. *Disorderly Conduct: Visions of Gender in Victorian America.* New York: Oxford Univesity Press, 1986.

Speek, Peter A. *A Stake in the Land.* New York: Harper and Brothers, 1921.

Spring, Joel. *The American School, 1642–1990.* 2d ed. New York: Longman, 1990.

Stellhorn, August C. *Schools of the Lutheran Church–Missouri Synod.* St. Louis: Concordia Publishing House, 1963.

Strasser, Susan. *Never Done: A History of American Housework.* New York: Pantheon Books, 1982.

Suelflow, August R. *The Heart of Missouri: A History of the Western District of the Lutheran Church–Missouri Synod, 1854–1954.* St. Louis: Concordia Publishing House, 1954.

Sutherland, Daniel E. *Americans and Their Servants: Domestic Service in the United States from 1800 to 1920.* Baton Rouge: Louisiana State University Press, 1981.

Taylor, Philip A. M. *The Distant Magnet: European Immigration to the U.S.A.* New York: Harper and Row, 1971.

Thernstrom, Stephan, ed. *Harvard Encyclopedia of American Ethnic Groups.* Cambridge, Mass.: Harvard University Press, 1980.

Thomas, Sherry. *We Didn't Have Much but We Sure Had Plenty: Stories of Rural Women.* Garden City, N.J.: Doubleday, Anchor Press, 1981.

Tyack, David B. *The One Best System.* Cambridge, Mass.: Harvard University Press, 1974.

Walker, Mack. *Germany and the Emigration 1816–1885.* Cambridge, Mass.: Harvard University Press, 1964.

Weatherford, Doris. *Foreign and Female: Immigrant Women in America, 1840–1930.* New York: Schocken Books, 1986.

Werling, J. W. *History of the Kansas District, 1888–1938.* Newton, Kans.: Herald Publishing Company, 1938.

Wertheimers, Barbara Mayer. *We Were There: The Story of Working Women in America.* New York: Pantheon Books, 1977.

Wertz, Richard W., and Dorothy C. Wertz. *Lying-In: A History of Childbirth in America.* New York: Free Press, 1977.

West, Elliot. *Growing Up in the Country: Childhood on the Far West Frontier.* Albuquerque: University of New Mexico Press, 1989.

Wishy, Bernard. *The Child and the Republic.* Philadelphia: University of Pennsylvania Press, 1968.

Wittke, Carl. *The German-Language Press in America.* Louisville: University of Kentucky Press, 1957.

———. *We Who Built America.* Rev. ed. Cleveland, Ohio: Western Reserve University Press, 1964.

Yanagisako, Sylvia Junko. *Transforming the Past: Tradition and Kinship among Japanese Americans.* Stanford: Stanford University Press, 1985.

Yans-McLaughlin, Virginia. *Family and Community: Italian Immigrants in Buffalo, 1880–1930.* Ithaca, N.Y.: Cornell University Press, 1978.

Yans-McLaughlin, Virginia, ed. *Immigration Reconsidered: History, Sociology, and Politics.* New York: Oxford University Press, 1990.

Zelinsky, Wilbur. *The Cultural Geography of the United States.* Englewood Cliffs, N.J.: Prentice-Hall, 1973.

Articles, Chapters, Dissertations

Armitage, Susan H. "Household Work and Childrearing on the Frontier: The Oral History Record." *Sociology and Social Research* 63 (April 1979):467–74.

Bate, Kerry William. "Family History: Some Answers, Many Questions." *Oral History Review* 16 (Spring 1988):127–30.

Beasley, Maurine Hoffman. "Life as a Hired Girl in South Dakota, 1907–1908: A Woman Reflects." *South Dakota History* 12 (Summer/Fall 1982):147–62.

Bek, William G. "Survival of Old Marriage Customs among the Low Germans of West Missouri." *Journal of American Folklore* 21 (1908):60–67.

Bernstein, George, and Lottelore Bernstein. "Attitudes toward Women's Education in Germany, 1870–1914." *International Journal of Women's Studies* 2 (1979):473–88.

Berrol, Selma. "Ethnicity and Children." In *American Childhood: A Research Guide and Historical Handbook,* ed. Joseph Hawes and N. Ray Hiner. Westport, Conn.: Greenwood Press, 1985.

Bieder, Robert E. "Kinship as a Factor in Migration." *Journal of Marriage and Family* 35 (1973):429–39.

Bird, Roy. "The Rural Intellectuals: Kansas Country Schools." *Heritage of the Great Plains* 22 (Winter 1989):12–19.

Borhek, J. T. "Ethnic Group Cohesion." *American Journal of Sociology* 76 (July 1970):33–46.

Boubel, John P. "A History of Lutheran Church–Missouri Synod Schools in Wisconsin: National Policies and Local Implementation." Ph.D. diss., Marquette University, 1989.

Boylan, Ann. "Growing Up Female." In *American Childhood: A Research Guide and Historical Handbook,* ed. Joseph Hawes and N. Ray Hiner. Westport, Conn.: Greenwood Press, 1985.

Breaux, Fayette. "For God and Country: Catholic Schooling in the 1920s." Ph.D. diss., Columbia University, 1984.

Carman, J. Neale. "Germans in Kansas." *American-German Review* (1961):4–8.

Coburn, Carol K. "Ethnicity, Religion, and Gender: The Women of Block, Kansas 1868–1940." *Great Plains Quarterly* 8 (Fall 1988):222–32.

———. "Learning to Serve: Education and Change in the Lives of Rural Domestics in the Early Twentieth Century." *Journal of Social History* 25 (Fall 1991):571–84.

Collier, Jane, Michelle Z. Rosaldo, and Sylvia Yanagisako. "Is There a Family? New Anthropological Views." In *Rethinking the Family: Some Feminist Questions*, ed. Barrie Thorne and Marilyn Yalom. New York: Longman, 1982.

Conzen, Kathleen Neils. "Germans." In *Harvard Encyclopedia of American Ethnic Groups*, ed. Stephan Thernstrom. Cambridge, Mass.: Harvard University Press, 1980.

———. "Historical Approaches to the Study of Rural Ethnic Communities." In *Ethnicity on the Great Plains*, ed. Frederick C. Luebke. Lincoln: University of Nebraska Press, 1980.

———. "Peasant Pioneers: Generational Succession among German Farmers in Frontier Minnesota." In *The Countryside in the Age of Capitalist Transformation*, ed. Steven Hahn and Jonathan Prude. Chapel Hill: University of North Carolina Press, 1985.

Dietz, Paul T. "The Transition from German to English in the Missouri Synod from 1910 to 1947." *Concordia Historical Institute Quarterly* 22 (Oct. 1949):97–127.

di Leonardo, Micaela. "The Myth of the Urban Village: Women, Work, and Family among Italian-Americans in Twentieth-Century California." In *The Women's West*, ed. Susan Armitage and Elizabeth Jameson. Norman: University of Oklahoma Press, 1987.

Eiselmeier, John. "The Feminization of the Teaching Profession." *Lutheran School Journal* 40 (Jan. 1925):17–25.

Ende, Aurel. "Battering and Neglect: Children in Germany, 1860–1978." *Journal of Psychohistory* 7 (1979–80):249–79.

Fairbanks, Carol. "Lives of Girls and Women on the Canadian and American Prairies." *International Journal of Women's Studies* 2 (Sept./Oct. 1979):452–72.

Faragher, John Mack. "History from the Inside-Out: Writing the History of Women in Rural America." *American Quarterly* 33 (Winter 1981):537–57.

Farrer, Claire R. "Women and Folklore: Images and Genres." *Journal of American Folklore* 88 (Jan./March 1975):v–xv.

Fink, Deborah. "Sidelines and Moral Capital: Women on Nebraska Farms in the 1930s." In *Women and Farming: Changing Roles, Changing Structures*, ed. Wava Haney and Jane Knowles. Boulder, Colo.: Westview Press, 1988.

Finkelstein, Barbara. "Casting Networks of Good Influence." In *American Childhood: A Research Guide and Historical Handbook*, ed. Joseph Hawes and N. Ray Hiner. Westport, Conn.: Greenwood Press, 1985.

Fitts, Deborah. "Una and the Lion: The Feminization of District School-Teaching and Its Effects on the Roles of Students and Teachers in Nineteenth-Century Massachusetts." In *Regulated Children, Liberated Children: Education in Psychohistorical Perspective*, ed. Barbara Finkelstein. New York: Psychohistory Press, 1979.

Flora, Cornelia Butler, and Jan L. Flora. "Structure of Agriculture and Women's Culture in the Great Plains." *Great Plains Quarterly* 8 (Fall 1988):195–205.

Freedman, Estelle. "Separatism as Strategy: Female Institution Building and American Feminism, 1870–1930." *Feminist Studies* 5 (Fall 1979):512–29.

Gjerde, Jon. "Conflict and Community: A Case Study of the Immigrant Church in the United States." *Journal of Social History* (Summer 1986):681–97.

Glasco, Laurence A. "The Life Cycles and Household Structure of American Ethnic Groups: Irish, Germans, and Native-born Whites in Buffalo, New

York, 1855." In *A Heritage of Her Own*, ed. Nancy F. Cott and Elizabeth H. Pleck. New York: Simon and Schuster, 1979.

Gluck, Sherna. "What's So Special about Women? Women's Oral History." *Frontiers* 2 (1979):3–11.

Graebner, Alan. "Attitudes in the Lutheran Church–Missouri Synod toward Sexual Morality: 1900–1960. Master's Thesis, Columbia University, 1961.

———. "The Acculturation of an Immigrant Lutheran Church: The Lutheran Church–Missouri Synod, 1917–1929." Ph.D. diss., Columbia University, 1965.

———. "World War I and the Lutheran Union: Documents from the Army and Navy Board, 1917–1918." *Concordia Historical Institute Quarterly* 41 (May 1968):51–64.

———. "Birth Control and the Lutherans: The Missouri Synod as a Case Study." In *Women and American Religion*, ed. Janet Wilson James. Philadelphia: University of Pennsylvania Press, 1980.

Gude, George J. "Women Teachers in the Missouri Synod." *Concordia Historical Institute Quarterly* 44 (Nov. 1971):163–70.

Hahn, Gertrude, and Naomi Hahn. "Frieda M. Damm, Red Cross Nurse – 1917–1919." *Concordia Historical Institute Quarterly* 57 (Summer 1984):53–59.

Hargreaves, Mary W. M. "Homesteading and Homemaking on the Plains: A Review." *Agricultural History* 47 (1973):156–63.

———"Women in the Agricultural Settlements of the Northern Plains." *Agricultural History* 50 (1976):179–89.

———. "Rural Education on the Northern Plains Frontier." *Journal of the West* 18 (Oct. 1979):25–32.

Hartmann, Heidi I. "The Family as the Locus of Gender, Class, and Political Struggle: The Example of Housework." *Signs* 6 (Spring 1981):366–94.

Hausen, Karin. "Family and Role-Division: The Polarisation of Sexual Stereotypes in the Nineteenth Century – an Aspect of the Dissociation of Work and Family Life." In *The German Family*, ed. Richard J. Evans and W. R. Lee. Totowa, N.J.: Barnes and Noble, 1981.

Helmbold, Lois Rita. "Beyond the Family Economy: Black and White Working-Class Women during the Great Depression." *Feminist Studies* 13 (Fall 1987):629–55.

Hewitt, Nancy A. "Beyond the Search for Sisterhood: American Women's History in the 1980s." In *Unequal Sisters: A Multicultural Reader in U.S. Women's History*. New York: Routledge, 1990.

Jacobi-Dittrich, Juliane. "Growing Up Female in the Nineteenth Century." In *German Women in the Nineteenth Century: A Social History*, ed. John C. Fout. New York: Holmes and Meier, 1984.

Jameson, Elizabeth. "Women as Workers, Women as Civilizers: True Womanhood in the American West." *Frontiers* 8 (1984):1–8.

Jensen, Joan M. "Buttermaking and Economic Development in Mid-Atlantic America from 1750–1850." *Signs* 13 (Summer 1988):813–29.

Jensen, Joan M., and Mary Johnson. "What's in a Butter Churn? Objects and Women's Oral History." *Frontiers* 7 (1983):103–8.

Jensen, Joan M., and Darlis A. Miller. "The Gentle Tamers Revisited: New Approaches to the History of Women in the American West." *Pacific Historical Review* 49 (May 1980):173–213.

Jensen, Katherine. "Mother Calls Herself a Housewife but She Buys Bulls." In

The Technological Woman: Interfacing with Tomorrow, ed. Jan Zimmerman. New York: Praeger, 1983.

Johnson, Neil M. "The Patriotism and Anti-Prussianism of the Lutheran Church–Missouri Synod, 1914–1918." *Concordia Historical Institute Quarterly* 39 (Oct. 1966):99–118.

Kattner, Lauren Ann. "Growing Up Female in New Braunfels: Social and Cultural Adaptations in a German-Texas Town." *Journal of Ethnic History* (Spring 1990):49–72.

Kloberdanz, Timothy J. "Cross Makers: German-Russian Folk Specialists of the Great Plains." Ph.D. diss., Indiana University, 1986.

———. "The Daughters of Shiphrah: Folk Healers and Midwives of the Great Plains." *Great Plains Quarterly* 9 (Winter 1989):3–12.

Koch, John B. "Friedrich Bente on World War I in *Lehre und Wehre*." *Concordia Historical Institute Quarterly* 42 (Aug. 1968):133–35.

Koehneke, Paul F. "Joint Mission Festivals in the Lutheran Church–Missouri Synod until 1868." *Concordia Historical Institute Quarterly* 24 (April 1951):24–34.

Lagemann, Ellen Condliffe. "Looking at Gender in Women's History." In *Historical Inquiry into Education: A Research Agenda*, ed. John Hardin Best. Washington, D.C.: American Educational Research Association, 1983.

Leach, Mary. "Toward Writing Feminist Scholarship into History of Education." *Educational Theory* 40 (Fall 1990):453–61.

Litoff, Judith Barrett. "Forgotten Women: American Midwives at the Turn of the Twentieth Century." *Historian* 40 (1978):235–51.

Luebke, Frederick C. "The Immigrant Condition as a Factor Contributing to the Conservatism of the Lutheran Church – Missouri Synod." *Concordia Historical Institute Quarterly* 38 (April 1965):19–28.

———. "Superpatriotism in World War I: The Experience of a Lutheran Pastor." *Concordia Historical Institute Quarterly* 41 (Feb. 1968): 3–11.

———. "Ethnic Group Settlement on the Great Plains." *Western Historical Quarterly* 8 (Oct. 1977):405–30.

Lueker, Erwin L. "The Stance of Missouri in 1917." *Concordia Historical Institute Quarterly* 40 (Oct. 1967):118–26.

McLoughlin, William G. "Evangelical Childrearing in the Age of Jackson: Francis Wayland's Views on When and How to Subdue the Willfulness of Children." In *Growing Up in America*, ed. N. Ray Hiner and Joseph P. Hawes. Urbana: University of Illinois Press, 1985.

Mauer, Heinrich H. "Studies in the Sociology of Religion: The Sociology of Protestantism." *American Journal of Sociology* 30 (Nov. 1924):257–86.

———. "The Problems of Group Consensus: Founding the Missouri Synod." *American Journal of Sociology* 30 (May 1925):665–82.

———. "The Fellowship Law of a Fundamentalist Group. The Missouri Synod." *American Journal of Sociology* 31 (July 1925):39–57.

———. "The Consciousness of Kind of a Fundamentalist Group." *American Journal of Sociology* 31 (Jan. 1926):485–506.

———. "The Political Attitude of the Lutheran Parish in America: A Study in Religious Sectionalism." *American Journal of Sociology* 33 (Jan. 1928):568–85.

———. "The Lutheran Community and American Society: A Study in Religion as a Condition of Social Accommodation." *American Journal of Sociology* 34 (Sept. 1928):282–95.

Meyer, Carl S. "Lutheran Immigrant Churches Face the Problems of the Frontier." *Church History* 29 (Dec. 1960):440–62.

Miami County Republican. 1868–1876, 1916–1919, Paola, Kansas.

Moellering, Ralph L. "Some Lutheran Reactions to War and Pacifism, 1917 to 1941." *Concordia Historical Institute Quarterly* 41 (Aug. 1968):121–31.

Neuman, Joseph. "Private Schools vs. Public Schools." In *America's Teachers.* New York: Longman, 1989.

Nohl, Frederick. "The Lutheran Church–Missouri Synod Reacts to the U.S. Anti-Germanism during World War I." *Concordia Historical Institute Quarterly* 35 (July 1962):49–66.

Olson, Audrey. "St. Louis Germans, 1850–1920: The Nature of an Immigrant Community and Its Relation to the Assimilation Process." Ph.D. diss., University of Kansas, 1970.

Ostergre, Robert C. "Land and Family in Rural Immigrant Communities." *Annals of the Association of American Geographers* 71 (1981):400–411.

Osterud, Nancy Grey. "The Valuation of Women's Work: Gender and the Market in a Dairy Farming Community during the Late Nineteenth Century." *Frontiers* 10 (1988):18–24.

Owen, Ralph Dornfeld. "The Old Lutherans Come." *Concordia Historical Institute Quarterly* 20 (1948):3–56.

Peters, Clarence H. "Developments of the Youth Programs of the Lutheran Churches in America." Th.D. diss., Concordia Theological Seminary, 1951.

Pickle, Linda. "Stereotypes and Realities: Nineteenth-Century German Women in Missouri." *Missouri Historical Review* 79 (April 1985):293–301.

———. "Rural German-Speaking Women in Early Nebraska and Kansas." *Great Plains Quarterly* 9 (Fall 1989):239–51.

Prelinger, Catherine M. "The Nineteenth-Century Deaconessate in Germany: The Efficacy of a Family Model." In *German Women in the 18th and 19th Century: A Social and Literary History,* ed. Ruth-Ellen Joeres and Mary Jo Maynes. Bloomington: Indiana University Press, 1986.

Rabinowitz, Howard N. "Race, Ethnicity, and Cultural Pluralism in American History." In *Ordinary People and Everyday Lives,* ed. James B. Gardner and George Rollie Adams. Nashville, Tenn.: American Association for State and Local History, 1983.

Riley, Glenda. "Images of the Frontierswoman: Iowa as a Case Study." *Western Historical Quarterly* 8 (April 1977):189–202.

———. "Farm Women's Roles in the Agricultural Development of South Dakota." *South Dakota History* 13 (Spring/Summer 1983):83–121.

———. "Women on the Great Plains: Recent Developments Research." *Great Plains Quarterly* 5 (Spring 1985):81–92.

———. "Women's Responses to the Challenges of Plains Living." *Great Plains Quarterly* 9 (Summer 1989):174–84.

Sachs, Carolyn E. "The Participation of Women and Girls in Market and Non-Market Activities on Pennsylvania Farms." In *Women and Farming,* ed. Wava G. Haney and Jane B. Knowles. Boulder, Colo.: Westview Press, 1988.

Sallquist, Sylvia Lea. "The Image of the Hired Girl in Literature: The Great Plains, 1860 to World War I." *Great Plains Quarterly* 4 (Summer 1984):166–77.

Scharff, Virginia. "Putting Wheels on Women's Sphere." In *Technology and Women's Voices: Keeping in Touch,* ed. Cheris Kramarae. New York: Routledge, Chapman Paul, 1988.

Scott, Joan W. "Gender: A Useful Category of Historical Analysis." *American Historical Review* 5 (Dec. 1986):1053–75.

Seller, Maxine. "The Education of the Immigrant Woman, 1900–1935." *Journal of Urban History* 4 (1978):307–30.

Shields, Sarah D. "The Treatment of Conscientious Objectors during World War I: Mennonites at Camp Funston." *Kansas History* 4 (Winter 1981):255–69.

Smith-Rosenberg, Carroll. "The Female World of Love and Ritual: Relations between Women in Nineteenth-Century America." *Signs* 1 (1975):1–29.

———. "Beauty, the Beast, and the Militant Woman." In *A Heritage of Her Own*, ed. Nancy F. Cott and Elizabeth H. Pleck. New York: Simon and Schuster, 1979.

Socolofsky, Homer E. "How We Took the Land." In *Kansas: The First Century*, Vol. 1. Edited by John D. Bright. New York: Lewis Historical Publishing Company, 1956.

Stansell, Christine. "Women on the Great Plains, 1865–1890." *Women's Studies* 4 (1976):87–98.

Strauss, Gerald. "The Social Function of Schools in the Lutheran Reformation in Germany." In *History of Education Quarterly* 28 (Summer 1988):191–206.

Stucky, Harley J. "The German Element in Kansas." In *Kansas: The First Century*. Vol. 1. Edited by John D. Bright. New York: Lewis Historical Publishing Company, 1956.

Swierenga, Robert. "Ethnicity and American Agriculture." *Ohio History* 89 (1980):323–44.

Tilly, Charles. "Transplanted Networks." In *Immigration Reconsidered: History, Sociology, and Politics*, ed. Virginia Yans-McLaughlin. New York: Oxford University Press, 1990.

Toepper, Robert M. "Rationale for Preservation of the German Language in the Missouri Synod of the Nineteenth Century." *Concordia Historical Institute Quarterly* 41 (Feb. 1968):156–67.

Turk, Eleanor L. "The German Newspapers of Kansas." *Kansas History* 6 (1983):46–64.

Tyack, David B. "The Tribe and the Common School: Community Control in Rural Education." *American Quarterly* 24 (1972):3–19.

Vecoli, Rudolph J. "Contadini in Chicago: A Critique of the Uprooted." *Journal of American History* 51 (1964):404–17.

Walch, Timothy. "The Diverse Origins of American Catholic Education: Chicago, Milwaukee and the Nation." Ph.D. diss., Northwestern University, 1975.

Wehner, Silke. "Auswanderung deutscher Dienstmädchen in die Vereinigten Staaten, 1850–1914." Ph.D. diss. University of Muenster, 1992.

Western Spirit. Paola, Kansas, 1868–1945.

Winawer-Steiner, Hinda, and Norbert A. Wetzel. "German Families." In *Ethnicity and Family Therapy*, ed. Monica McGoldrick, John K. Pearce, and Joseph Geordano. New York: Guilford Press, 1982.

Yans-McLaughlin, Virginia. "Metaphors of Self in History: Subjective, Oral Narrative, and Immigrant Studies." In *Immigration Reconsidered: History, Sociology, and Politics*, ed. V. Yans-McLaughlin. New York: Oxford University Press, 1990.

INDEX

Abuse, of children and spouses, 100
Adolescents: as farm labor, 98, 120–21;
    Walther League effect on, 55–58, 153
Age: average marriage, 106, 189n.69; and
    entry/exit patterns in church net-
    works, 152; of hired girls, 122–23;
    and Sunday afternoon activities, 103;
    and trips to outside world, 117–18
Agriculture. See Farming
AHTA (Anti-Horse Thief Protective Asso-
    ciation), 129–30, 195n.66
Alien enemy registration, in Block, 138–
    39, 143–44, 145, 197n.10
Alpert, Fritz, 22
Altar, ornateness of, 41–42
Americanization, 6, 48, 151; Catholic fear
    of, 61; of clergy, 36; effect of World
    War I on, 56, 113, 142–43, 157, 198
    n.23, 199 n.3; of festivals during
    World War I, 132, 196n.77. See also
    Assimilation
American Legion, 135
American Lutheran Church (ALC),
    166n.10
Anti-German behavior, during World War
    I, 136–39, 145
Anti-Horse Thief Protective Association
    (AHTA), 129–30, 195n.66
Apology, public, for wayward behavior,
    46–48, 153, 175n.37
Assimilation, 6, 40, 91; baseball as form
    of, 133–34, 156; in community
    through religious/ethnic bonding, 2–
    3, 6, 25–30, 135, 154, 157; of hired
    girls, 121–22. See also
    Americanization
Automobiles, 24, 118, 155

Back of the Yards (Slayton), 35, 175n.27
Baptisms, 32, 42; as major family event,
    36, 103–6

Baseball, 68, 133–34, 156, 196n.82
Baumgardt, Frieda Timken, 83, 93
Beckman family, 16, 18
Behavior, 154; pastor as arbiter of, 35–36,
    45–47, 153; public apology for, 46–48,
    153, 175n.37; public as opposed to pri-
    vate, 4, 155
Bennett Law (Wis., 1890), on foreign lan-
    guage use in schools, 146
Bergman, Christina, 115
Bergman, Henry, 20
Bergman family, 16
Birth. See Childbirth
Birth control, 91, 186n.30, 194n.40
Block, Dick, Jr., 22, 99
Block, Dietrich, Sr., 20, 128
Block, Elizabeth, 143–44, 198n.31
Block, Gesche Mahnken ("Grandma"), 20,
    48, 176n.39; as local midwife, 92–93
Block, Gesche Schnakenberg, 11
Block, Mildred, 85, 112
Block community, 1–2; business district,
    19–23, 170n.37; homogeneity, 6–7, 8,
    150, 157, 166n.9; immigrant infusions,
    10–11, 14–15; religious isolation, 28, 112;
    rural isolation, 5, 7, 122, 134, 154, 157
"Block Grays" (baseball team), 133
Block Mutual Telephone Company, 25
Bogen, F. W., 11–12
Boys: school activities of, 68; school pun-
    ishments of, 69–70; work in farm fami-
    lies, 86–87, 98
Bridges, lack of in early Miami County, 13,
    23, 40–41, 65, 170n.40
Buenger (district synod president), 34
Bull Creek, 15, 24
Business relations: among German Lu-
    therans, 113–14, 190n.5

Cahman, Eidena Johnson, 11
Card playing, 36, 188n.67

Catechismal instruction, 76
Catholic church, 50, 77, 127; cooperation on language proposals, 30, 172n.64; German pluralistic ethnic identity, 9, 167n.11; parochial school system, 61, 73, 161, 178n.4; urban parishes, 35, 174n.19
Cemetery, 1, 31, 148; burial of nonsynod members, 39, 109–10, 174n.23; grave arrangement in, 108, 109–10
Chain migration, 14, 169n.21
Charity, 38–39, 50, 174nn.21,22,23
Childbirth, 94; mother's health affected by, 91, 122, 186n.34; stillbirths, 93, 187n.42; use of midwives, 92–93; womanhood defined by, 90–91, 186n.30
Children, 32, 109, 117–18, 172n.4; abuse of in family system, 100; cemetery plots for, 108, 110; confirmation of, 36, 71, 76–79, 105; use as farm labor, 85–87. See also Boys; Girls
Christenlehre ("religious instruction"), 76–77, 147–48
Clausen, Clarence, 10, 86–87, 97
Clausen, Doris Wilkens, 77
Clausen, Herman, 22, 77–78, 86–87, 128
Clergy, Catholic, role in urban parishes, 35, 174n.19
Clergy, Missouri Synod, 29, 141; adjustment to women teachers, 75; birth control view, 91, 186n.34; influence in congregations, 27, 35–36, 58–59, 171n.53; marriage of as Lutheran doctrine, 49–50; relations with laity, 34–36. See also Pastors
Communication, effect on rural isolation, 112, 134
Concordia College, women at, 183n.54
Concordia Publishing House, 27; publications of, 66–67, 181n.24
Concordia Seminary, 34, 173nn.7,11
Confession, frequency of, 46
Confirmation, 36, 71, 76–79, 105
Con men, preying on immigrants, 11–12
Constitution, church, 32, 172n.5; translation into English, 147
Contraception, 91, 186n.30, 194 n.40
Control: within the family, 155; by first-generation male church members, 40–41; through community educational network, 30
Conzen, Kathleen Neils, 35, 81, 156
Correspondence, between Block and Germany, 10, 24, 197n.22
Courtships, 106
Creation of Patriarchy, The (Lerner), 155
Crow River, Minn., 34, 173n.7

Culture, German, 3, 61; German language newspapers, 18, 141–42, 169n.33, 197n.22; as interdependent part of Missouri Synod Lutheranism, 6, 28, 152–53
Curriculum: Lutheran teachers' colleges, 72, 182n.41; parochial schools, 66–68

Dageforde, Elsie Prothe, 87, 97, 137, 145
Dageforde, William, 43
Dancing, 36, 188n.67
Daylight savings time ("war time"), 139, 197n.12
Deaconessate, German, function of, 50
Deacons (elders), 40
Death, 87; funeral customs, 108–9; of newborn infants, 84–85, 108–9; role of men during, 100–101
Debrick, Alma Clausen, 109
Debrick, Ed, 65–66
Debrick, Minnie Cahman, 14, 85, 87, 116; on school days, 65–66, 68, 70–71, 77
Debrick-Schultz cane mill, 22
Democratic party, and Missouri Synod Lutherans, 127–28, 194n.55
Depression. See Great Depression
Diploma, grammar school, 77
Diploma of Vocation, 72
Discipline: congregational, 45–48, 175n.37; at home, 83–85, 100, 184n.6; in parochial schools, 68–71, 83, 154, 200n.4
Doctors, 92, 93, 187n.50
Dolan, Jay: on Catholic church, 61, 174n.19, 178n.4, 181n.24
Domestic activities: in church building, 54; in school building, 68, 181n.29
Domestic production, women's, 37, 50, 53; for outside markets, 115–17, 155; as vital income contribution, 44, 88–89, 159
Domestic service. See Hired girls
Drinking, views on of clergy, 36
Droegemueller, F. D. (pastor), 50–51, 52, 175n.36
Duden, Gottfried, Report on a Journey to the Western States of North America, 10, 168n.6
Duties: blurring in farm work, 85–90, 97; in church maintenance chores, 54; gender-derived in school chores, 68, 181n.29
Duty, as espoused by German Lutheranism, 83, 85, 110–11, 155, 184n.5

East Prussian dialect, 13–14, 25, 40. See also German language usage
East Valley Township, 2; politicking in, 127–28, 195n.58
Education, 160; of an ethnic-rural commu-

nity, 3, 4, 30, 160–61; of clergy compared to laity, 26–27, 34–35, 173n.11; system created by Missouri Synod, 27, 28, 60–80, 161. *See also* School, parochial; School, public
Edwards Law (Ill., 1889), on foreign language use in schools, 146
Eiselmeier, John, 74
Elders (deacons), 40
Embalming, 109
Emigration, 9–15
Emmanuel Lutheran Church, Kansas City, 124–25
Employment, paid, 88, 98; for church property maintenance, 43–44, 175n.28. *See also* Hired girls; Hired men
English language usage, 32, 68, 131; at First Lutheran Church in Paola, 120, 192n.31; in minutes of Ladies Aid Society, 53, 177n.51
English-only laws, 30, 146, 172n.64, 199n.41
Ethnicity, bonding with religion, 2–3, 6, 25–30, 135, 157
Evangelical Lutheran Church of America (ELCA), 166n.10
Evangelische-Lutheran Schulblatt, Das (school journal), 72, 73

Family: as core of religious education, 28; German-Lutheran, 81–111; networks as work units, 101–3, 154–55; size, 90–91, 186n.30
Farm Bureau, 135
Farm Bureau Auxiliary, 55
Farmer's Union, 156
Farming, 16, 82, 96, 113; labor of adolescent boys, 98; labor of children and women, 85–90, 115–16; and men's tasks, 96–97; work in other German-Lutheran communities, 120–21
Farrer, Clair, 155
Fathers: role in child's education, 64, 179n.14, 180n.15; role in Missouri Synod belief system, 29, 100
Females. *See* Women
Fertility patterns, changes in, 91–92
Fieldwork, done by women and girls, 89–90
Finances, church, 32–33, 34, 44, 173n.8
First Lutheran Church, Paola, 120, 148, 174n.25, 176n.42, 192nn.31,32, 193n.33
Fischer, H. (teacher), 62, 72–73
Folk medicine, 93
Food production, by women, 88–89, 159
"Four Corners." *See* Block community

Frank, August, 92
Frauenvereine. See Ladies Aid Society
Freemasons, synod's views on, 129
Funerals, 103, 108–9

Games: baseball, 68, 133–34, 156, 196n.82; card playing, 36, 188n.67; gender-oriented, 68, 181n.31; Sunday afternoon, 103; "tomball," 68, 181n.30
Gender differences, 2–3, 4, 29, 53–54; blurring in farm work, 85–90, 97; changes in Block's patriarchal system, 157–58; in school activities, 68–69, 181n.29; in Sunday afternoon activities, 103; and trips to outside world, 117–18. *See also* Boys; Girls; Men; Women
Gerken, Elsie, 79
Gerken, Martin, 143–44
Gerken family, 16, 18
German language usage, 10, 32; after World War I, 146–48; and East Prussian dialect, 13–14, 25, 40; and Hannoverian dialect, 7, 13, 25, 40; as interdependent part of Lutheranism, 6, 25, 28, 30, 112, 152–53, 172n.64; and low German, 13, 35; maintenance through school system, 61–62, 68, 179n.8; and standard (high) German, 13, 35; during World War II, 149–51; as World War I issue, 137, 139, 140, 196n.4
"Germanness": of early mission festivals/ school picnics, 131–32, 196n.77; seen as threat during World War I, 136, 140–41
Germans in the New World (Luebke), 174n.20
Germany, outmigration, 10, 167n.1
Geschlechtscharakter, 88, 185n.19
Gilderhaus sisters, 39, 174n.23
Girls: organ lessons for, 73, 182n.48; physical punishment of in school, 70–71; tasks assigned to in school, 68, 181n.29; Walther League participation of, 57; women teachers as role models for, 75; work in farm families of, 86–89. *See also* Hired girls
Gjerde, Jon, 34, 46, 152, 173n.7
Godparents (sponsors), 104–5
Good Friday, as first communion day, 77
Good works, Luther on, 28, 174n.20
Graebner, Alan, 35, 48, 76, 127, 186n.34; on Missouri Synod Lutheranism, 26, 27–28, 140, 197n.19
Graebner, Martin, 138
Graebner, Theodore, 139
Grandma Block. *See* Block, Gesche Mahnken
Grandparents, 98, 101–2

Graves, 39, 108, 110, 174n.23
Great Depression, 18, 53, 159, 170n.35
Growing Up in the Country (West), 83, 184n.6
Guy, Joe, 18

Hands, healing by, 93, 186n.40
Hannoverian dialect, 7, 13, 25, 40. *See also* German language usage
Hannover Province, Germany, 6–7, 12
Hausen, Karen, 85
Health: home remedies, 97–98, 187n.50; women as healers, 93, 186n.40. *See also* Childbirth
Hensen, C. F., 139
Henson (Pendleton), Kans., 24
Hidden curriculum, 68, 181n.28
High German, 13, 35. *See also* German language usage
High school, 56, 77, 154, 183n.63
Hired girls, 77, 88, 151, 158, 177n.50, 183n.64; exposure to outside world, 53, 121–26, 155, 194nn.40,41,47,48; synod's changing views on, 121–22, 159–60, 194n.40; use during illness/childbirth, 94, 97
Hired men, 97, 102, 120–21
Hochzeitsbitter (wedding custom), 106–7, 108
Home remedies, use of, 97–98, 187n.50
Homogeneity, of Block community, 6–7, 8, 150, 157, 166n.8
Hospitals, 174n.21, 187n.50
Houses, farm, 82–83
Hunting, 96

Illness: effect of on child's family duties, 87; role of men during, 100–101; use of hired girl during, 94
Immigrants, 7, 10–14, 63; assimilation of eased by church institutions, 2–3, 6, 25–30, 135, 154, 157
Immigrants, urban: in Catholic parishes, 35, 174n.19; enclave homogeneity of, 8, 157, 167n.12
Income: earned by women's activities, 115, 116; of hired girls, 123–24; of pastors, 37; of teachers, 73
Infant mortality, 84–85, 108–9
Interdependence: of farm families, 81–82; in village communities, 3
Isolation: of Block as a rural community, 5, 7, 29–30, 122, 134, 151, 154, 157; religious, 28, 112

Jacobi-Dittrich, Juliane, 88

Jensen, Joan, 94–95, 116–17, 158–59
Jugendverein (early youth group), 55–56

Kansas City, as workplace for hired girls, 53, 122, 124–25, 158
Kansas Immigration Society, 12
Kansas-Nebraska Act of 1854, 16
Kansas State Census, 1865, women's occupations, 115, 191n.17
Keller, O. C. S. (pastor), 78
Kinship, 39; network patterns in, 54, 88, 101–3, 154–55
Klingelbeutel (alms bag), 44, 175n.30
Klinkermann, H. F. (teacher), 139, 144, 180n.22
Kloberdanz, Timothy, 93
Know-Nothing party, 127
Koelsch, Lena Prothe, 91
Krause, Gertrude, 141

Labor: children as farm family resource, 85–87; outside of Block farm community for males, 118–21; as physical for rural men, 96–97; sexual division of, 85–90; valuation of women's contribution, 115–16; women as temporary wage earners, 116, 150, 192n.23. *See also* Hired girls
Ladies Aid Society, 5, 39, 135, 153, 158; aid to school, 79; gifts to pastor/family, 37; role of, 49–55, 176n.49; wartime contributions, 139, 149, 150
Lagemann, Ellen Condliffe, 55
Laity: activities in Missouri Synod, 37, 39, 174n.19; education of compared to clergy, 26–27, 34–35, 173n.11; relations with clergy, 34–35; and role of male voters' assembly, 39–41; and Walther League, 55–58, 106, 153. *See also* Ladies Aid Society
Land ownership, 2, 12, 16–18, 41; labor opportunities affected by unavailability, 112–13, 118–19
Language, foreign, use of in school as issue, 30, 146, 172n.64, 198n.40, 199n.41. *See also* English language usage; German language usage
LaPorte, Ind., 13, 18
Leach, Mary, 160
Leonarda, Micaela di, 160
Lerner, Gerda, 155, 157
Letters, to relatives in Germany, 10, 24–25, 197n.22
Liberalism, American, synod view of, 26
Liberty bonds, 144–46
Life expectancy, 109

Lindemann, J. C. W., 73
Literacy, value placed on by immigrants, 64–65, 180n.18
Literature: against birth control, 186n.34; of Catholic church, 181n.24; Concordia Publishing House, 27, 66–67, 181n.24; of Kansas Immigration Society, 12
Low German, 13, 35. *See also* German language usage
Luebke, Frederick, 28, 29, 35, 154; on anti-German violence during World War I, 137–38; on German-American political activity, 127, 194n.55; *Germans in the New World*, 174n.20
Luther, Martin, 13, 28, 50, 174n.20, 178n.62, 184n.5
Lutheran Church–Missouri Synod, 6, 25–30; and church-state separation, 126–27, 136, 140, 197n.17; conservatism, 153, 199n.3; cooperation with Catholics on language usage, 30, 172n.64; disciplinary action of, 45–48, 153, 175n.37; father's role in, 29, 100; German usage in services, 61–62, 146–48, 179n.8; isolation of membership, 28, 112; male political behavior patterns, 126–28; networks as essentially male, 152, 158; role in Block, 31–59; school system, 60–80; views on gender differences, 29, 47–48, 175n.35; views on hired girl system, 121–22, 159–60, 194n.40
Lutheran Church–Norwegian Synod, 34, 46, 152, 173n.7
Lutheran Church–Wisconsin Synod, 166 n.10
Lutheran Church of America, 166n.10
Lutheraner, Der (magazine), 26, 27, 60, 171n.53
Lutherans, Scandinavian, 166n.10
Lutheran School Journal, 72, 74
Lutheran Witness (magazine), 27, 55, 137
Lykins, David, 169n.25

Mahnken family, 16
Maisch, Esther Prothe, 35, 115, 143
Maisch, J. M. (pastor), 34
Mammen, Louise Timken, 92
Marais des Cygnes River, 13, 15, 23, 40–41, 65
Marriage: ceremony, 36, 103, 105–8; with non-Germans in 1920s, 148
Marty, Martin, 161–62
Matthias, J. (pastor), 32, 34
Mauer, Heinrich, 81, 112
Medicine. *See* Health
Meetings, presence of pastor at, 51, 57

Melting pot: army as, 142, 198n.23; public high school as, 154
Membership, church, nineteenth-century reports, 31–32, 172nn.2,4
Men, 3, 29, 44, 71, 120–21; business relations of, 113–14; farm tasks of, 96–97; and politics as entrance to the secular world, 126–28, 156; role of as teachers, 71–72; role of in sickness and death, 100–101, 109; rural networks among, 95–96; voters' assembly, 32, 38, 39–41, 44–46, 152
Mennonites, German, treatment of during World War I, 142–43, 198n.24
Meyer v. Nebraska (U.S. Supreme Court), on foreign language usage in schools, 146, 199n.41
Miami County, Kans., 12, 16, 169n.25
Miami County Republican (newspaper), 128, 145
"Middle thing," theological definition of, 46
Midwifery, 92–93
Military service, German, as a reason for immigration, 10, 11
Military service, U.S.: in World War I, 118, 136, 142, 149, 156, 198 n.23; in World War II, 150
Miller, Dietrich, 20
Miller family, 16, 18
Mills, Emma, 180n.22
Minden, Irene, 122, 124
Minden, Joe, 58
Mission festivals, 130–31, 195n.69
Missouri Synod Lutheranism. *See* Lutheran Church–Missouri Synod
Monthey, August, 12
Monthey, Marie Dageforde, 96, 97, 106, 117, 130; childhood discipline memories of, 69, 76, 84; farm work memories of, 87, 89
Moral values, teaching of, 61
Motherhood: as defining adult womanhood, 90; and effects of frequent childbirth, 91, 123, 186n.34; role of in patriarchal system, 155
Music: emphasis on in teachers' colleges, 72, 182n.41; parochial school instruction in, 68, 181n.27; school organ lessons, 73, 182n.48; as Walther League entertainment, 57, 178n.62
Musician, teacher as, 71, 73

Naming process, 148; during baptismal rites, 104–5, 188n.65
Networks, 4, 30, 152, 154, 158; among

Networks, *continued*
  rural men, 95–96; among rural women,
    94–95, 158, 187n.45; and family groups
    as work units, 154–55; and Walther
    League, 55–58, 106, 153. *See also* Ladies
    Aid Society
Neu, Jacob, 20, 24
Newspapers, German: as community
    links, 18, 169n.33; reading of during
    World War I, 141–42, 197n.22
Newspapers, local: coverage of Block
    events, 131–33, 133, 196nn.82,83; World
    War I stances of, 137, 138–39, 196n.5
Non-Lutherans: burial of, 39, 110,
    174n.23; marriage to, 107; Missouri
    Synod's attitude toward, 29; socializing
    with, 135
Norwegian Synod–Lutheran Church, 34,
    46, 152, 173n.7
"No Union without Unity" (slogan), 28,
    171n.59

Officers, church: financial expectations
    of, 44; role in male voters' assembly,
    39–40
Ohlmeier, Dick, 22, 143
Ohlmeier, Dietrich, 11, 12
Ohlmeier, Johann, 11
Ohlmeier, Laura Koelsch, 181n.29
"Old Lutherans," 26, 171n.52
Old World villages, re-creations of, 22–23,
    43, 175n.27
Order, as espoused by German Lutherans,
    83, 184n.5
Organ, 43, 66; lessons for girl students, 73,
    182n.48
Original sin, 104, 188n.63
Orphanages, 174n.21
Osterud, Nancy Grey, 116
Outsiders: Block residents as, 140; busi-
    ness as means to socialize with, 114;
    growing contact with, 155–56; shunning
    of, 6, 112

Pagels, Henry, 150
Palm Sunday, as confirmation day, 77
Paola, Kans., 15; as county's rail center, 24,
    170n.43; German-owned businesses in,
    114; memories of hired girls in, 124; as
    source of work for Block males, 119–20
Parochial school. *See* School, parochial
Parsonage, 31, 37
Pastors, 37, 75–76, 106, 152; as anti-Ger-
    man targets during World War I, 136; as
    early school teachers in Block, 34, 62,
    72, 173 n.9; presence of at meetings, 51;

57; role of in Walther League, 57, 58;
    school discipline by, 69–71; as traveling
    preachers, 27–28
Patent medicines, 97–98, 187n.50
Patriarchy: in an ethnic-rural community,
    4, 38, 95–96, 165n.4; family members'
    acquiescence to, 110–11, 155; in Mis-
    souri Synod belief system, 29, 45
Payment: for help during farm emergen-
    cies, 98; for services rendered to church,
    43–44, 175n.28
Peckman, Ida Minden, 89, 124
Peiker's clothing store, 114
Pendleton (Henson), Kans., 24
Philanthropy, 38–39, 49–50, 174n.21
Pickle, Linda, 89, 185n.22
Picnics, school, 130, 131–32, 139, 196n.77
Pierce v. *Society of Sisters* (U.S. Supreme
    Court), on foreign language usage in
    schools, 146, 199n.41
Plat maps, 2, 16, 18
Politics: as entrance to secular world for
    males, 126–28, 156; separation of church
    and state, 126–27, 136, 140–41, 197n.17
Pope, Ed, 69–70
Posen region, Germany, 13
Post office, Block, 19, 24–25
Power: of Catholic church as threat, 127;
    use of by males, 100
Prescriptive literature, effect on birth con-
    trol, 91, 186n.34
Priests, Catholic, 35, 174n.19
Privacy, lack of in early houses, 82
Private interactions, as opposed to public
    behavior, 4, 155
Prothe, Ada, 58
Prothe, August, 11, 107
Prothe, Elmer, 69–70, 120
Prothe, Fred, 13, 20–22, 41
Prothe, Fritz, 151
Prothe, Henry, 82, 97–98, 187n.50
Prothe, Irene Minden, 65, 117
Prothe, Johann and Magdalena Rehr, 19
Prothe, John, 13, 41
Prothe, Marie Block, 53, 82, 94, 115
Prothe, Martin, 119
Prothe, Nora Ohlmeier, 37, 109, 123, 131
Prothe, William, 98
Pulpit, decription of, 42
Punishment, corporal: use in home, 83–
    84, 100, 184n.6; use in parochial school,
    69–71, 83, 154, 200n.4
Pure doctrine (*reine Lehre*), 6, 26, 28, 60, 140

Railroads, 23–24, 170n.41; hired girls'
    travel experience on, 124, 125

Red Cross, 55, 144–46, 198n.36
Reifel, George, 13, 20–22, 24, 25
Reifel general store, 20–22, 24, 25, 83
Reine Lehre ("pure doctrine"), 6, 26, 28, 60, 140
Reiseprediger ("traveling preacher"), 27–28
Religion: bonding with ethnicity, 2–3, 6, 25–30, 135, 157; environment for German women, 158; isolation of communicants, 28, 112; parochial school, 61–63
Religious instruction (*Christenlehre*), 76–77, 145–48
Religious orders, Catholic, 49, 50
Report on a Journey to the Western States of North America (Duden), 10, 168n.6
Republican party, in East Valley Township, 128
Revivals, Protestant, 76, 131
Roads, county, 23, 24, 170n.40
Rodewald, Anna, 58
Rodewald, Dorothea Pagels, 150
Role model: hired men seen as for children, 102; male teachers as, 75–76; pastor's wife as, 35, 36–37; women teachers as, 75
Roman Catholic church. *See* Catholic church
Rural-ethnic community, nineteenth century, 1–2, 7–8

St. Peter's German Evangelical Church, 41, 174n.25, 176n.42
Salary: of Block's pastors, 37, 43; of hired girls, 123–24; of teachers, 73
Salvation, Luther on, 28, 174n.20
School, parochial, 60–80, 98, 137, 161; elders' role in, 40; first Block church as, 31; introduction of report cards, 147; as norm, 7, 28
School, public: avoidance by Missouri Synod parents, 61, 64, 180n.17; Catholic fear of Protestantism in, 61; high school attendance, 56, 77, 154, 183n.63
Schoolbooks. *See* Textbooks
Schoolhouse: burning of by anti-German groups, 137, 198n.37; as church activity center, 62, 179n.10; physical description, 66, 180n.22
Schroeder, Will, 136, 142
Schultz, Louis, 36, 119, 174n.17, 192n.30
Schultz, Lydia Prothe, 118, 122, 124, 141, 174nn.17,25; crowded childhood household of, 82–83, 184n.4; memories of parents, 85, 91; piebaking skills of, 102, 188n.60
Schultz, Michael, 14, 18, 174n.25

Schultz, Rosena Debrick, 143, 144
Scott, Joan, 157–58
Seating: in church, 38, 46, 175n.35; in schoolrooms, 68
Secret societies, 29, 129, 195n.66
Seller, Maxine, 58–59
Seminary, 54; faculty influence in congregations, 27, 171n.54
Senne, Anna (teacher), 73
Senne, H. C. (pastor), 46–47, 107, 175n.36
Services, free, as supplement to pastor's salary, 37, 43
Services, paid, 43–44, 175n.28
Shame, as school discipline method, 69, 181n.33
Sheridan, B. J. (Barney), 128, 132, 144, 145
Sickness. *See* Illness
Singing: parochial school instruction in, 68, 181n.27; as Walther League entertainment, 57, 178n.62
Single adults, perceived role of, 102, 188n.57
Slayton, Robert: on Catholics, 35, 77; on re-created Old World villages, 23, 43, 175n.27
Small Catechism (Luther), 45, 76
Social activities, 57, 103, 106; baptisms, 36, 103–6; baseball as, 133–34, 156; of hired girls, 124–25; schoolhouse as center for, 62, 179n.10; weddings, 36, 103, 106–8. *See also* Ladies Aid Society
Social skills, acquisition of, 54–55, 57; by hired girls, 52–53, 121–26, 155, 194nn.40,41,47,48
Sons: as farm labor, 98; as second generation church officers, 41
Sponsors (godparents), 104–5
Spouse abuse, 100
Standard (high) German, 13, 35. *See also* German language usage
Standards, community, 35–36
State, separation from church in synod's teachings, 126–27, 136, 140, 197n.17
Status, of male and female types of work, 88, 185n.20
Stephan, Martin (pastor), 26
Stillbirths, 93, 187n.42
Sunday afternoons: baseball games during, 133; traditions of, 102–3
Sunday school, synod's views on, 29
Supreme Court, U.S., on school usage of foreign language, 146, 199n.41

Teacher, 31, 72, 182n.46; early pastors' role as, 34, 62, 72, 173n.9; German deaconessate role as, 50; music ability of,

Teacher, *continued*
   71–73, 182n.41; position in Lutheran society, 71–72, 152; role in Walther
   League, 57, 58; school punishment by,
   69–71, 152, 200n.4; women as in synod
   system, 73–75, 152, 183n.54
Teaching colleges, enrollment of women,
   74, 183 nn.54,56
Telephone service, use of German on
   party lines, 25, 137, 151, 170n.48
*Testimony and Proof Bearing on the Rela-
   tion of the American Lutheran Church
   to the German Emperor* (Graebner), 139
Textbooks, 66–67, 181n.24
Theological questions, male discussion of,
   34, 45–46, 152
Timken, Herman, 92
Timken, Louis, 48, 176n.39
Timken, Martin, 83–84
Tinken family, blacksmith shop of, 21,
   22, 24
Toepper, Robert, 62
"Tomball," as girl's game, 68, 181n.30
Tower, church, 42–43
Township offices, synod members as can-
   didates for, 127–28, 195n.58
Transatlantic crossings, 10, 11
Transportation: automobiles, 24, 118,
   155; effects on rural isolation, 5, 7, 112,
   134; of immigrants westward, 14; rail-
   roads, 23–24, 170n.41; transatlantic
   crossings, 10, 11
Travel: by children to school, 65–66; hired
   girls, 124, 125; locally by women, 117–
   18; to outside jobs, 120–21; visiting out-
   of-state relatives, 135
Traveling preacher (*Reiseprediger*), 27–28
Trinity Lutheran Church, 1–2, 16; constitution of, 32, 147, 172n.5; erection of,
   31–32; maintenance of property, 41, 43–
   44, 54, 175n.28, 190n.5; physical structure of, 41–43; role in Block, 31–59, 153;
   Walther League, 55–58, 106, 153. *See
   also* Ladies Aid Society; Lutheran
   Church–Missouri Synod; School,
   parochial
Trips. *See* Travel
Trustees, role in male voters' assembly,
   39–40

Un-Americanism, German Lutherans accused of, 136–37
Undertakers, use of, 109
Urban immigrants: Catholic parishes as
   stability centers, 35, 174n.19; enclave
   homogeneity, 8, 167n.12

Urban life: as contrast for hired girls, 124;
   influence on German immigrants, 157

Valuation, of women's contributions,
   115–16
Vandalism: of church property, 47,
   175n.38; of synod churches and schools
   during World War I, 137
Violence, against German-Americans,
   137, 146, 198n.37
Visits, social: to out-of-state relatives,
   135; on Sunday afternoons, 103
Volunteerism, American, as alien to
   synod, 38
Voters' assembly (male), 32, 38, 39–41, 44–
   46, 152
Voting, in Walther League, 57

Wages. *See* Payment; Salary
Walker, Mack, 9
Walther, C. F. W., 60–61, 127, 174n.21;
   role in synod, 26, 171n.59
Walther League, 55–58, 106, 153
"War time" (daylight savings time), 139,
   197n.12
War work, effect on World War II Ameri-
   canization, 150
Weddings, 36, 103, 106–8
Wendte, Heinrich August Herman, 133
Wendte, Marie Peckman, 138
West, Elliott, 83, 85, 184n.6
Western Spirit (newspaper), 128, 132;
   World War I stance of, 145, 196n.5,
   197n.10
Wilkens, Fred, 10
Windler, Katie, 107
Windler, Lawrence, 58
Windler family, 16, 18
Windows, stained glass, use of, 42
Wishropp's grocery, 114, 192n.21
Wolters, A. P. (teacher), 78
Women, 39, 50, 143, 150; discipline of in
   the church, 46, 47–48; domestic production of, 37, 44, 50, 176n.47; forays
   into the outside world, 114–15, 155; local travel by, 117–18; in Missouri Synod
   belief system, 29, 64, 153, 172n.62,
   180n.16; networking of in rural areas,
   94–95, 187n.45; pastor's wife as role
   model for, 35, 36–37; role of in burial
   process, 109; role of in child's education,
   64, 180n.16; role of in the German
   home, 88–91; as teachers in synod system, 73–75, 154; third-generation as automobile drivers, 118, 155. *See also*

Women, *continued*
  Childbirth; Ladies Aid Society;
  Motherhood
Worldview: of German farm families, 90;
  of Missouri Synod Lutheranism, 25,
  29, 82
World War I: as beginning of German-
  English language controversy, 32; effect
  on Block's Americanization, 56, 113,
  136–46, 198n.23, 199n.3; and end of correspondence to Germany, 24–25, 197n.22
World War II, effect on Block community,
  148–51

Worship services: introduction of English
  in, 147–48; use of German language in,
  61–62, 149–50, 179n.8

Yans-McLaughlin, Virginia, 123
Yorky, Frank, 20

Zion German Evangelical Church,
  176n.42
Zschoche, W. (pastor), 31, 63–64